lonely planet

JAPANESE

Travel Phrasebook & Dictionary

Credits

Production Editor Graham O'Neill

Language Writers Pietro Iagnocco, Karina Coates, Susie Walker, Mirna Cicioni, Anna Beltrami

Thanks

Sofie Andersen, Marc Backwell, Laura Crawford, Kellie Langdon, Saralinda Turner

Published by Lonely Planet Global Limited
CRN 554153

Digital Depot, Roe Lane off Thomas Street, Dublin
D08 TCV4, Ireland (EU authorised representative)

11th Edition – Sep 2026
ISBN 978 1 80653 132 5

Printed in Malaysia 10 9 8 7 6 5 4 3 2 1

Contact lonelyplanet.com/contact

Look out for the following icons throughout the book:

'Shortcut' Phrase
Easy-to-remember alternative to the full phrase

Q&A Pair
'Question-and-answer' pair – we suggest a response to the question asked

Look for
Phrases you may see on signs, menus etc

Listen for
Phrases you may hear from officials, locals etc

LANGUAGE TIP

An insight into the foreign language

CULTURE TIP

An insight into the local culture

How to read the phrases:

- Coloured words and phrases throughout the book are phonetic guides to help you pronounce the foreign language.
- Lists of phrases with tinted background are options you can choose to complete the phrase above them.

These abbreviations will help you choose the right words and phrases in this book:

f	feminine	m	masculine	sg	singular
inf	informal	pl	plural		
lit	literal	pol	polite		

CONTENTS

ABOUT JAPANESE 6

Learn about Japanese, build your own sentences and pronounce words correctly.

Introduction 6
Top Phrases 8
Pronunciation 10
Grammar 16

TRAVEL PHRASES

Ready-made phrases for every situation – buy a ticket, book a hotel and much more.

BASICS 33

Understanding 34
Numbers & Amounts 36
Time & Dates 40

PRACTICAL 45

Transport 46
Border Crossing 62
Directions 64
Accommodation 68
Shopping 80
Communications 88
Money & Banking 95

Business 98
Sightseeing 102
Accessible Travel 107
Travel with Children 109

SOCIAL 111

Meeting People 112
Interests 122
Feelings & Opinions 126
Going Out 132
Romance 138
Beliefs & Culture 142
Sports 145
Outdoors 153

SAFE TRAVEL 157

Emergencies 158
Police 160
Health 162

FOOD 171

Eating Out 172
Self-Catering 189
Vegetarian & Special Meals 193

MENU DECODER 196

Dishes and ingredients explained – order with confidence and try new foods.

TWO-WAY DICTIONARY 219

Quick reference vocabulary guide – 3500 words to help you communicate.

English–Japanese Dictionary 219
Japanese–English Dictionary 253

INDEX 267

INTRO

Japanese

日本語 NI·HON·GO

Who speaks Japanese?

Why Bother

Japanese people are often too shy or worried about making mistakes to speak to visitors using what English they may know. Even the smallest effort to speak to locals in Japanese will be very warmly received.

Distinctive Sounds

Note the reduced, almost silent u (especially when it appears at the end of a word); and the r, which is pronounced halfway between an 'l' and an 'r'. Japanese has fewer sounds than most other major languages.

123 MILLION speak Japanese as their first language

1 MILLION speak Japanese as their second language

Japanese Script

Written Japanese is a combination of three different scripts. Kanji are ideographs (symbols that represent a concept as well as pronunciation), borrowed from Chinese. Hiragana and katakana are both indigenous, syllabic scripts (each character represents a syllable).

Japanese Lexicon

Japanese has many onomatopoeic expressions (describing something by its sound). For example, pouring rain can be described with zā zā ざあざあ, and a rumbling stomach might go go·ro go·ro ごろごろ.

Borrowings from English

Japanese has borrowed many words from English, often shortening and adapting them, eg pa·so·kon パソコン for 'personal computer' and kom·bi·ni コンビニ for 'convenience store'.

Language Family

It bears some resemblance to Altaic languages such as Mongolian and Turkish, and shows strong grammatical similarities to Korean, but linguists have not been able to prove the origins of Japanese.

Must-Know Grammar

Japanese has various levels of formality, shown with particular words or verb forms. The standard polite ending ·mas ます (given in this book) is the safe middle ground and will be suitable for most situations you'll encounter.

Donations to English

There are several – you may recognise *futon, karaoke, tsunami, bento box* and *manga*, to name a few.

5 Phrases TO LEARN BEFORE YOU GO

01 Is there a Western-/Japanese-style room?

洋室/和室はありますか?

yō·shi·tsu/wa·shi·tsu wa a·ri·mas ka

Some lodgings have only Japanese-style rooms, or a mix of Western and Japanese – ask if you have a preference.

02 Please bring a (spoon/knife/fork).

(スプーン/ナイフ/フォーク)をください。

(spūn/nai·fu/fō·ku) o ku·da·sai

If you haven't quite mastered the art of eating with chopsticks, don't be afraid to ask for cutlery at a restaurant.

03 How do I get to ...?

…へはどう行けばいいですか?

... e wa dō i·ke·ba ī des ka

Finding a place from its address can be difficult in Japan. Addresses usually give an area (not a street) and numbers aren't always consecutive. Practise asking for directions.

04 I'd like a nonsmoking seat, please.

禁煙席をお願いします。

kin·en·se·ki o o·ne·gai shi·mas

There are smoking seats in many restaurants and on some bullet trains so be sure to specify if you want to be smoke-free.

05 What's the local speciality?

地元料理は何がありますか?

ji·mo·to·ryō·ri wa na·ni ga a·ri·mas ka

Throughout Japan most areas have a speciality dish and locals usually love to talk about food.

10 Phrases TO SOUND LIKE A LOCAL

Great!	すごい!	su·goy
Sure.	もちろん。	mo·chi·ron
Hey!	ちょっと、ちょっと!	chot·to chot·to
Just a minute.	ちょっと待って。	chot·to mat·te
It's OK.	いいよ。	ī·yo
No problem.	大丈夫。	dai·jō·bu
Good luck.	頑張って。	gam·bat·te
No kidding?	マジ?	ma·ji
Really?	ほんと?	hon·to
Fat chance!	ありえない!	a·ri·e·nai

JAPANESE

Pronunciation

Japanese pronunciation is not considered difficult for English speakers. Unlike some other Asian languages, it has no tones and most of its sounds are also found in English.

VOWEL SOUNDS

Vowels in Japanese can be either short or long. The long ones should be held twice as long as the short ones and are represented in our pronunciation guides with a horizontal line on top of them.

SYMBOL	ENGLISH	JAPANESE EXAMPLE
a	run	na·ka
ā	father	sak·kā
e	red	sa·ke
ē	reign	pē·ji
i	bit	ni·ji
ī	bee	shī·tsu
o	pot	mot·to
ō	paw	pas·pō·to
u	put	mu·ra
ū	moon	kū·ki

It's important to make the distinction between short and long vowels as vowel length can change the meaning of a word, as in these examples:

彼	ka·re	**he**
カレー	ka·rē	**curry**
おじさん	o·ji·san	**uncle**
おじいさん	o·jī·san	**grandfather**

All vowels in the table on the previous page are 'pure', meaning they're pronounced individually – they do not tend to run together to form vowel sound combinations (diphthongs). Pronounce them clearly and slowly to make yourself understood, eg i·e (家) for 'house' and ī·e (いいえ) for 'no'. There are a few vowel sound combinations, however, that roughly correspond to diphthongs in English:

SYMBOL	ENGLISH	JAPANESE EXAMPLE
ai	aisle	dai·ga·ku
air	pair	air·kon
ow	cow	tow·ru
oy	toy	koy

The vowel u is sometimes not pronounced in Japanese. This so-called 'reduced' vowel most often occurs between k and s and in verb endings like des (です) and mas (ます). Where it's a silent vowel, we haven't included it in the coloured pronunciation guides.

CONSONANT SOUNDS

As the next table shows, most consonant sounds are pretty close to their English counterparts.

To make yourself understood clearly, it's important to make the distinction between single and double consonants as this can produce a difference in meaning, eg:

坂	sa·ka	**slope**
作家	sak·ka	**writer**
過去	ka·ko	**past**
かっこ	kak·ko	**brackets**

Pronounce the double consonants with a slight pause between them.

SYMBOL	ENGLISH	JAPANESE EXAMPLE
b	big	ba·sho
ch	chili	chi·zu
d	din	dai·ga·ku
f	fun (almost like 'fw' with the lips in a rounded position, especially before 'u')	fu·ro
g	go (always a hard sound as in 'go')	gai·jin
h	hit	hi·to
j	jam	jū·su
k	kick	kan·ji
m	man	mu·su·me
n	no	no·ri
p	pig	pan·tsu
r	run (halfway between 'l' and 'r')	ren·ji
s	so	sa·ba·ku
sh	show	shi·ma
t	tin	ta·bi
ts	hits	tsu·na·mi
w	win	wa·sa·bi
y	yes	yu·ki
z	is/zoo	za·ru

WORD STRESS

Syllables are pronounced fairly evenly in Japanese, so there's no need to indicate stressed syllables.

READING & WRITING JAPANESE

Written Japanese is actually a combination of three different scripts. The first, kanji, consists of ideographic characters. The other two, hiragana and katakana, are syllabic scripts – each character represents a syllable.

Kanji

Kanji are ideographs (symbols that each represent a concept, idea or thing as well as pronunciation, rather than a word or set of words) borrowed from Chinese, eg 本 (hon) for 'book', 娘 (mu·su·me) for 'daughter' and 日本語 (ni·hon·go) for 'Japanese language'. Each kanji may be made up of anything from one to over 20 strokes written in a particular order. Some kanji characters have two or more ways of being pronounced depending on the context. For example, the kanji 水 is pronounced mi·zu when it means 'water', but su·i when it's part of another word like 水筒 (pronounced su·i·tō) for 'water bottle'.

There are thousands of kanji in Japanese, with around 2000 considered essential for everyday use. The Ministry of Eduction has designated 1026 characters as basic – these are taught at primary school level.

Hiragana

Hiragana is used to represent particles and grammatical endings particular to Japanese and are placed alongside the ideographic characters – one single Japanese word can contain both scripts. There are 46 basic hiragana characters, each representing a particular syllable. They can be combined to represent over 100 different syllables (see the table, p15).

Where's the market?	市場はどこですか? i·chi·ba wa do·ko des ka

Note that in the phrase above the word for 'market' (i·chi·ba) is written in kanji (市場), but the rest – the particle wa (は), the question word do·ko (どこ), the verb des (です) and the interrogative particle ka (か) – in hiragana.

Katakana

Each hiragana character also has a katakana equivalent. Katakana are used to represent recent borrowings from other languages, especially English. They're also used to write foreign names – you might want to figure out how to write your own name in Japanese.

credit card	クレジットカード ku·re·jit·to·kā·do
My name is Anthony.	私の名前はアンソニーです。 wa·ta·shi no na·ma·e wa an·so·nī des
I'm from Australia.	オーストラリアから来ました。 ō·sto·ra·rya ka·ra ki·mash·ta

Note that the Japanese words for 'credit card', 'Anthony' and 'Australia' are all written in katakana.

The table (p15) shows the basic as well as some of the combined hiragana and katakana characters. For each syllable you'll find the pronunciation (in red) with its hiragana symbol above and katakana symbol below it.

HIRAGANA & KATAKANA SCRIPT TABLE

あ a ア	い i イ	う u ウ	え e エ	お o オ								
か ka カ	き ki キ	く ku ク	け ke ケ	こ ko コ	きゃ kya キャ	きゅ kyu キュ	きょ kyo キョ	が ga ガ	ぎ gi ギ	ぐ gu グ	げ ge ゲ	ご go ゴ
さ sa サ	し shi シ	す su ス	せ se セ	そ so ソ	しゃ sha シャ	しゅ shu シュ	しょ sho ショ	ざ za ザ	じ ji ジ	ず zu ズ	ぜ ze ゼ	ぞ zo ゾ
た ta タ	ち chi チ	つ tsu ツ	て te テ	と to ト	ちゃ cha チャ	ちゅ chu チュ	ちょ cho チョ	だ da ダ	ぢ ji ヂ	づ zu ヅ	で de デ	ど do ド
な na ナ	に ni ニ	ぬ nu ヌ	ね ne ネ	の no ノ	にゃ nya ニャ	にゅ nyu ニュ	にょ nyo ニョ					
は ha ハ	ひ hi ヒ	ふ fu フ	へ he ヘ	ほ ho ホ	ひゃ hya ヒャ	ひゅ hyu ヒュ	ひょ hyo ヒョ	ば ba バ	び bi ビ	ぶ bu ブ	べ be ベ	ぼ bo ボ
ま ma マ	み mi ミ	む mu ム	め me メ	も mo モ	みゃ mya ミャ	みゅ myu ミュ	みょ myo ミョ	ぱ pa パ	ぴ pi ピ	ぷ pu プ	ぺ pe ペ	ぽ po ポ
や ya ヤ		ゆ yu ユ		よ yo ヨ								
ら ra ラ	り ri リ	る ru ル	れ re レ	ろ ro ロ	りゃ rya リャ	りゅ ryu リュ	りょ ryo リョ					
わ wa ワ				を o ヲ	ぎゃ gya ギャ	ぎゅ gyu ギュ	ぎょ gyo ギョ	びゃ bya ビャ		びゅ byu ビュ		びょ byo ビョ
ん n ン					じゃ ja ジャ	じゅ ju ジュ	じょ jo ジョ	ぴゃ pya ピャ		ぴゅ pyu ピュ		ぴょ pyo ピョ

JAPANESE Grammar

This chapter will help you make your own sentences. It's arranged alphabetically for ease of navigation. If you can't find the exact phrase in this book, remember that with just a little grammar, a few gestures, and a couple of well-chosen words, you'll generally get the message across.

Note that we have added literal translations to every phrase to clarify Japanese sentence structures. The use of particles in Japanese – shown in red in the literal translations – has been explained in **particles** (p22) and **prepositions** (p26).

ADJECTIVES & ADVERBS

Describing People/Things • Doing Things

As in English, adjectives come before the noun they describe. There are two types of adjectives: 'i adjectives' that end in a vowel or ·i (い) and 'na adjectives' that end in na (な).

We had a nice meal.	おいしい食事をしました。 (lit: nice meal o did) oy·shī sho·ku·ji o shi·mash·ta
That is a beautiful building.	あれはきれいな建物です。 (lit: that-over-there wa beautiful building is) a·re wa ki·rē na ta·te·mo·no des

Adverbs, which describe a verb or an adjective, can be formed by replacing the ·i (い) ending of 'i adjectives' with the ending

·ku（く）. The adjective ha·yai（速い）'fast', for example, becomes the adverb ha·ya·ku（速く）.

Many adverbs in Japanese, however, exist as a word in their own right. For example, to·te·mo（とても）'very', yuk·ku·ri（ゆっくり）'slowly', and kyō（今日）'today', to name a few.

ARTICLES

Naming People/Things

Japanese doesn't have words equivalent to the English indefinite and definite articles 'a/an' and 'the':

It's a/the hotel.	ホテルです。(lit: hotel is) ho·te·ru des

Words are used without articles and context will tell you whether 'a' or 'the' is meant. If you do want to point out a specific item (indicated by 'the' in English), you can use a demonstrative (see **demonstratives**, p19).

BE

Describing People/Things • Making Statements • Pointing Things Out

The word des（です）roughly corresponds to the English verb 'be' and, like any verb in Japanese, it doesn't change according to who or what it refers to; des can mean 'I am' or 'she is' or 'we are' etc depending on the situation – there's one form only for all subjects. Japanese verbs do change their form when they're expressing the past tense and/or negative. The following table shows how des changes in these cases:

- PRESENT POSITIVE -		- PRESENT NEGATIVE -	
です	des	じゃありません	ja a·ri·ma·sen
- PAST POSITIVE -		**- PAST NEGATIVE -**	
でした	desh·ta	じゃありません でした	ja a·ri·ma·sen desh·ta

I'm Australian.	私はオーストラリア人です。 (lit: I wa Australian is) wa·ta·shi wa ō·sto·ra·rya·jin des
I'm not a medical doctor.	私は医者じゃありません。 (lit: I wa doctor is-not) wa·ta·shi wa i·sha ja a·ri·ma·sen
It was rainy yesterday.	きのうは雨でした。 (lit: yesterday wa rain was) ki·nō wa a·me desh·ta
The person I met last night was not Mr Takagi.	ゆうべ会った人は高木さんじゃありませんでした。 (lit: yesterday met person wa Tagaki-Mister not-was) yū·be at·ta hi·to wa ta·ka·gi·san ja a·ri·ma·sen desh·ta

Note that you drop the particle of the word that immediately precedes a form of the verb des (see **particles**, p22).

There is/There are

There are two ways of expressing that something exists in Japanese. For animate objects (people and animals) the verb i·mas (います) is used. For inanimate objects (things) a·ri·mas (あります) is used.

There are many good restaurants in Tokyo.	東京にはいいレストランがたくさんあります。(lit: Tokyo in wa good restaurant ga many there-are-*inanimate*) tō·kyō ni wa ī res·to·ran ga ta·ku·san a·ri·mas
There are four dogs in the garden.	庭に犬が4匹います。(lit: garden in dog ga four there-are-*animate*) ni·wa ni i·nu ga yon·hi·ki i·mas

COUNTERS/CLASSIFIERS

Counting People/Things

See **numbers & amounts** (p36).

DEMONSTRATIVES

Pointing Things Out • Indicating Location • Making Statements

To refer to or point out a person or object, use one of the words in the table below. Note that the element ko·（こ） refers to someone or something close to the speaker, so·（そ） to someone or something close to the listener and a·（あ） to something far from both the speaker and listener.

NEAR SPEAKER		NEAR LISTENER		FAR FROM BOTH	
this	これ ko·re	that	それ so·re	that over there	あれ a·re
this (book)	この(本) ko·no (hon)	that (book)	その(本) so·no (hon)	that (book) over there	あの(本) a·no (hon)
here	ここ ko·ko	there	そこ so·ko	over there	あそこ a·so·ko
this way	こちら ko·chi·ra	that way	そちら so·chi·ra	that way over there	あちら a·chi·ra

How much does this cost?
これはいくらですか? (lit: this wa how-much is question)
ko·re wa i·ku·ra des ka

That train is full.
その電車は満員です。(lit: that train wa full is)
so·no den·sha wa man·in des

HAVE

Possessing

Possession can be shown in various ways in Japanese. The easiest way is to use the possessive particle no (の) after the noun or pronoun that indicates who or what possesses something:

my friend	私の友達 (lit: I no friend) wa·ta·shi no to·mo·da·chi
It's hers.	これは彼女のです。 (lit: this wa she no is) ko·re wa ka·no·jo no des
Takashi's hotel	たかしのホテル (lit: Takashi no hotel) ta·ka·shi no ho·te·ru

An alternative way of expressing possession is to use the verb mot·te i·mas (持っています), 'have', or the expression ga a·ri·mas (があります), 'there is something':

I have money.	(私は) お金を 持っています。 (lit: (I wa) honourable-money o have) (wa·ta·shi wa) o·ka·ne o mot·te i·mas
I have a car.	(私は) 自動車 があります。 (lit: (I wa) car there-is) (wa·ta·shi wa) ji·dō·sha ga a·ri·mas

NEGATIVES

Negating

To make a verb in the present tense negative, replace the ending ·mas (ます) with ·ma·sen (ません):

I smoke.	タバコを吸います。 (lit: cigarette o inhale) ta·ba·ko o su·i·mas

I don't smoke.	タバコを吸いません。 (lit: cigarette o inhale-not) ta·ba·ko o su·i·ma·sen

To make a verb in the past tense negative, replace ·mash·ta (ました) with ·ma·sen desh·ta (ませんでした):

I came by train.	電車で来ました。 (lit: train by did-come) den·sha de ki·mash·ta
I did not come by train.	電車で来ませんでした。 (lit: train by come did-not) den·sha de ki·ma·sen desh·ta

In Japanese, adjectives also have a negative form. For 'i adjectives' replace the ending ·i (い) with ·ku (く) and negate them by adding a·ri·ma·sen (ありません) or nai des (ないです):

新しい	a·ta·ra·shī	**new**	新しく ありません	a·ta·ra·shi·ku a·ri·ma·sen	**negative form of 'new'**
古い	fu·ru·i	**old**	古く ありません	fu·ru·ku a·ri·ma·sen	**negative form of 'old'**

For 'na adjectives', keep only the stems of the word (ie drop the ending na (な)), then negate them by adding ja a·ri·ma·sen (じゃありません) or ja nai des (じゃないです):

簡単な	kan·tan na	**easy**	簡単じゃ ありません	kan·tan ja a·ri·ma·sen	**negative form of 'easy'**

NOUNS

Naming People/Things • Making Statements

Japanese nouns have no gender (masculine or feminine) or plural forms: you always use the same form of the noun whether you're referring to a masculine or feminine person, object, place or concept, and whether it's singular or plural.

box/boxes	箱	ha·ko
person/people	人	hi·to
ticket/tickets	切符	kip·pu

Make sure you always use a particle after the nouns when using them in a phrase (see **particles**).

PARTICLES

Making Statements • Doing Things • Indicating Location • Possessing • Asking Questions

A Japanese noun or pronoun is almost always followed by a particle. Particles are short elements that display the function of the preceding word in the sentence. They show, for example, whether the preceding word is the subject (who or what is doing something) or the object (the person or thing that's affected by the action expressed by the verb) of the sentence. Sometimes particles act as prepositions, like the English 'to' or 'in'. You'll often come across the following particles in Japanese:

ga (が) **subject particle**
The particle ga (が) indicates the subject of the sentence when this is not omitted (as often happens in Japanese):

This is my address.	これが私の住所です。 (lit: this ga I no address is) ko·re ga wa·ta·shi no jū·sho des

wa (は) **topic particle**
The particle wa (は) marks the topic or the focal point of the sentence. It's often used when clarifying or stressing a particular point.

I'm a teacher.	私は教師です。 (lit: I wa teacher is) wa·ta·shi wa kyō·shi des

When the subject of the sentence is stressed or contrasted, it's also the topic of the sentence, in which case the particle ga will appear.

o（を）**object particle**
The particle o（を）marks the object of the sentence:

I ate sushi.	すしを食べました。 (lit: sushi o eat-did) su·shi o ta·be·mash·ta

no（の）**possessive particle**
The particle no（の）shows that something belongs to someone or something (also see **have**):

Miyuki's house	みゆきさんの家 (lit: Miyuki-Miss no house) mi·yu·ki·san no i·e

ni（に）**particle**
The particle ni（に）can be used in four different ways:

day/month/ year	on Monday	月曜日に	ge·tsu·yō·bi ni
time	at five o'clock	5時に	go·ji ni
location	in the shop	店に	mi·se ni
destination	to the station	駅に	e·ki ni

e（へ）**particle (direction)**
The particle e（へ）indicates direction and is very similar to the destination function of ni.

I'm going to Ginza.	銀座へ行きます。 (lit: Ginza e go) gin·za e i·ki·mas

de (で) particle

The de (で) particle indicates location – it has a similar function to the location function of ni. It can also express the means of doing something:

at the entrance	入口で (lit: entrance de) i·ri·gu·chi de
I'm going by train.	電車で行きます。 (lit: train de go) den·sha de i·ki·mas

ka (か) interrogative particle

The particle ka (か) is added to the end of a statement to turn it into a question. Also see **questions** (p28).

I speak English.	英語が話せます。 (lit: English ga speak) ē·go ga ha·na·se·mas
Do you speak English?	英語が話せますか? (lit: English ga speak ka) ē·go ga ha·na·se·mas ka

PLURALS

Naming People/Things

Japanese nouns are the same whether they refer to one or more persons, objects, places or concepts. If you want to count or express a particular number of items, you'll have to add a classifier (also called a counter) to the noun.

For more details, see **nouns** (p21) and **counters** (p37).

POLITE FORMS

Naming People/Things • Being Polite

Japanese shows different levels of formality with particular words and often by changing the forms of the verbs. This phrasebook uses standard polite ·mas (ます) forms, which will be suitable for most situations you encounter. To keep this safe middle ground, also avoid the use of second person pronouns, as they might sound too direct (see **pronouns**, p27). You'll also notice that the Japanese often add the prefixes o· (お) and go· (ご) to certain nouns to indicate politeness or reverence:

sake	お酒	o·sa·ke
rice/meal	ごはん	go·han
I'll introduce you.	ご紹介します。 (lit: honourable-introduction do)	go·shō·kai shi·mas

Sometimes these prefixes mean 'your honourable ...'. Only use these when talking about or to others, never when talking about yourself or your situation.

your husband	ご主人 (lit: your-honourable-husband) go·shu·jin
my husband	主人 (lit: husband) shu·jin
How are you?	お元気ですか? (lit: your-honourable-healthy is ka) o·gen·ki des ka
I'm fine.	元気です。 (lit: healthy is) gen·ki des

POSSESSIVES

Possessing

To indicate possession, use a pronoun (see **pronouns**, p27) or noun followed by the particle no (の):

This is my book.	これは私の本です。 (lit: this wa I no book is) ko·re wa wa·ta·shi no hon des

Mr Kamimura's suitcase	上村さんのスーツケース (lit: Kamimura-Mister no suitcase) ka·mi·mu·ra·san no sūts·kēs
school teacher	学校の先生 (lit: school no teacher) gak·kō no sen·sē

Also see **have** (p20) and **particles** (p22).

PREPOSITIONS

Giving Instructions • Indicating Location • Pointing Things Out

Japanese particles such as ni (に), e (へ) and de (で) often perform the same function as some English prepositions. Also see **particles** (p22).

above	上に	u·e ni	**in (time)**	なか	na·ka
across	横切って	yo·ko·git·te	**in front of**	前	ma·e
after	あと	a·to	**near**	近く	chi·ka·ku
at (place)	で	de	**over**	むこうに	mu·kō ni
at (time)	に	ni	**on**	上に	u·e ni
before (time)	前	ma·e	**through**	通って	tōt·te
during	あいだ	ai·da	**to**	へ	e
for	ため	ta·me	**under**	下に	shi·ta ni
from	から	ka·ra	**with**	いっしょに	is·sho ni
in (place)	に	ni	**without**	なしで	na·shi de

PRONOUNS

Making Statements • Naming People/Things

Subject pronouns are often omitted in Japanese when the person being spoken about is obvious from context. Japanese pronouns vary based on the level of formality – in this phrasebook we have used an appropriate pronoun for each phrase.

I/me	(polite)	私	wa·ta·shi
	(formal)	わたくし	wa·tak·shi
	(used by men only)	僕/おれ	bo·ku/o·re
you sg	(polite)	あなた	a·na·ta
	(used by men to subordinates)	きみ	ki·mi
she/her		彼女	ka·no·jo
he/him		彼	ka·re
we/us		私たち	wa·ta·shi ta·chi
you pl		あなたたち	a·na·ta ta·chi
they/them	m	彼ら	ka·re ra
	f	彼女たち	ka·no·jo ta·chi

Note that there are no different pronouns for subjects (eg I, she), objects (eg me, her) and possessives (eg my, her). The difference between these is indicated by the particle that follows the pronouns in the sentence: wa (は) for the topic, ga (が) for the subject, o (を) for the object and no (の) for the possessive (for more details see **particles**, p22). See the following examples:

I saw her.	私が彼女を見ました。 (lit: I ga she o see-did) wa·ta·shi ga ka·no·jo o mi·mash·ta
She saw me.	彼女が私を見ました。 (lit: she ga I o see-did) ka·no·jo ga wa·ta·shi o mi·mash·ta
It's hers.	それは彼女のです。 (lit: that wa she no is) so·re wa ka·no·jo no des

Note that often it's better to avoid using second person pronouns altogether, as this might seem too direct.

QUESTIONS

Asking Questions • Answering Questions

To ask a yes/no question, just add ka (か) to the end of a statement and raise your intonation towards the end of the sentence as you would in English.

This is the tourist office.	これは観光案内所です。 (lit: this wa tourist-office is) ko·re wa kan·kō·an·nai·jo des
Is this the tourist office?	これは観光案内所ですか? (lit: this wa tourist-office is ka) ko·re wa kan·kō·an·nai·jo des ka

To ask more specific questions, you can use the Japanese equivalents of 'who', 'where', 'what', 'how', 'why' etc. Note that these words often tend to come towards the end of the sentence, after the subject.

QUESTION WORDS

who	だれ/どなた	da·re/do·na·ta pol
Who is it?	だれですか?	da·re des ka
what	何/なに	nan/na·ni
What is this? What are you doing?	これは何ですか? なにをしますか?	ko·re wa nan des ka na·ni o shi·mas ka
which	どちら	do·chi·ra
Which train goes to Ginza?	どちらの電車が銀座に行きますか?	do·chi·ra no den·sha ga gin·za ni i·ki·mas ka
when	いつ	i·tsu
When's the next bus?	次のバスはいつですか?	tsu·gi no bas wa i·tsu des ka
at what time	何時に	nan·ji ni
At what time does the boat leave?	船は何時に出ますか?	fu·ne wa nan·ji ni de·mas ka
where	どこ	do·ko
Where are the toilets?	トイレはどこですか?	toy·re wa do·ko des ka
how	どのように	do·no yō ni
How does this work?	どのようにしますか?	do·no yō ni shi·mas ka
how much/ how many	どのくらい/いくつ	do·no·ku·rai/i·ku·tsu
How much do you want?	どのくらいほしいですか?	do·no·ku·rai ho·shī des ka
How many are there?	いくつありますか?	i·ku·tsu a·ri·mas ka
how much (money)	いくら	i·ku·ra
How much does it cost?	いくらですか?	i·ku·ra des ka
why	なぜ	na·ze
Why (is that so)?	なぜですか?	na·ze des ka

When answering yes/no questions, the complete verb is often repeated after the 'yes' or 'no'.

yes	はい	hai
no	いいえ	ī·e

Do you understand?	わかりましたか? (lit: understand-did ka) wa·ka·ri·mash·ta ka
Yes, I do (understand).	はい、わかりました。 (lit: yes understand-did) hai wa·ka·ri·mash·ta
No, I don't (understand).	いいえ、わかりません。 (lit: no understand-do-not) ī·e wa·ka·ri·ma·sen

VERBS

Doing Things

Verbs are pretty straightforward in Japanese. First of all, they don't change according to the person. The form shi·mas (します) can mean 'I do', 'you do', 'they do' etc. Secondly, Japanese only has two basic tenses: present and past.

In Japanese dictionaries, verbs will usually be listed in their 'plain form'. This form is not appropriate for most conversations, though. In this phrasebook, we have chosen the polite -mas (ます) form for most phrases, and for ease of use we have also listed the verbs in the dictionary in that form.

VERB	-MAS FORM		PLAIN FORM	
eat	食べます	ta·be·mas	食べる	ta·be·ru
drink	飲みます	no·mi·mas	飲む	no·mu
do	します	shi·mas	する	su·ru
buy	買います	kai·mas	買う	kau
come	来ます	ki·mas	来る	ku·ru
go	行きます	i·ki·mas	行く	i·ku

There are some contexts in which the verb forms change. For example, in negative phrases (see **negatives**, p20), when making a request, or when using the verbs with other verbs such as 'can' and 'must'. These more complex cases have not been included in this chapter, however, as you can make yourself easily understood without knowing the ins and outs of these constructions.

Remember that the verb goes at the end of the sentence.

Future

Future tense is expressed by using the same verb forms as for the present tense – in Japanese it's most often understood from context when you're talking about the future. If you'd like to make it crystal clear, you can also use a word or expression of time in your sentence, such as a·shi·ta（明日）for 'tomorrow', rai·ge·tsu（来月）for 'next month' or su·gu ni（すぐに）for 'soon'.

Past

To form the past tense, simply replace the ending ·mas（ます）(ie the polite verb ending used in this phrasebook) with the ending ·mash·ta（ました）.

I study at university.	大学で勉強します。 (lit: university de study-do) dai·ga·ku de ben·kyō shi·mas
I studied marketing.	マーケティングを 勉強しました。 (lit: marketing o study-did) mā·ke·tin·gu o ben·kyō shi·mash·ta

As with the present tense, Japanese verbs in the past tense don't change according to the subject (ie whether the subject is I, you, he/she/it, we, you (pl) or they).

WORD ORDER

Making Statements

Unlike English, in which word order is typically subject–verb–object, the order of a Japanese sentence is typically subject–object–verb. The subject is often omitted from the sentence if it's clear from context.

I bought a ticket to Hiroshima.	(私は)広島までのチケットを買いました。 (lit: (I wa) Hiroshima to no ticket o bought) (wa·ta·shi wa) hi·ro·shi·ma ma·de no chi·ket·to o kai·mash·ta

When building Japanese phrases it's important to keep each particle (see **particles**, p22) straight after the word it belongs to – no other element should come between a word and its particle. These 'building blocks' – ie words and their particles – can be moved around in a sentence, as long as the basic subject–object–verb order is respected and the verb goes at the end of the sentence. Compare the following phrases, in which the building blocks are ordered in two possible ways:

I write a postcard in Japanese.

(私は)日本語ではがきを書きます。
(lit: (I wa) Japanese de postcard o write)
(wa·ta·shi wa) ni·hon·go de ha·ga·ki o ka·ki·mas
(私は)はがきを日本語で書きます。
(lit: (I wa) postcard o Japanese de write)
(wa·ta·shi wa) ha·ga·ki o ni·hon·go de ka·ki·mas

BASICS

UNDERSTANDING	**34**
NUMBERS & AMOUNTS	**36**
TIME & DATES	**40**

Understanding

KEY PHRASES

Do you speak English?	英語が話せますか?	ē·go ga ha·na·se·mas ka
I don't understand.	わかりません。	wa·ka·ri·ma·sen
What does ... mean?	…はどういう意味ですか?	... wa dō yū i·mi des ka

Q **Do you speak (English)?**	(英語)が話せますか? (ē·go) ga ha·na·se·mas ka
A **I speak (English).**	(英語)が話せます。 (ē·go) ga ha·na·se·mas
A **I don't speak (Japanese).**	(日本語)が 話せません。 (ni·hon·go) ga ha·na·se·ma·sen
Q **Does anyone speak English?**	どなたか英語が話せますか? do·na·ta ka ē·go ga ha·na·se·mas ka
Q **Do you understand?**	わかりましたか? wa·ka·ri·mash·ta ka
A **Yes, I do understand.**	はい、わかりました。 hai wa·ka·ri·mash·ta
A **No, I don't understand.**	いいえ、わかりません。 ī·e wa·ka·ri·ma·sen
I understand.	わかりました。 wa·ka·ri·mash·ta
I don't understand.	わかりません。 wa·ka·ri·ma·sen

I speak a little.	少し話せます。 su·ko·shi ha·na·se·mas
How do you pronounce this?	これはどう発音しますか? ko·re wa dō ha·tsu·on shi·mas ka
How do you write 'shiatsu'?	「指圧」はどう書きますか? shi·a·tsu wa dō ka·ki·mas ka
What does 'deguchi' mean?	「出口」はどういう意味ですか? de·gu·chi wa dō yū i·mi des ka
Could you please write it down?	書いてくれませんか? kai·te ku·re·ma·sen ka
Could you please repeat that?	繰り返してくれませんか? ku·ri·ka·e·shi·te ku·re·ma·sen ka
Could you please speak more slowly?	もっとゆっくり 話してくれませんか? mot·to yuk·ku·ri ha·na·shi·te ku·re·ma·sen ka

Slowly, please!	ゆっくり話して！	yuk·ku·ri ha·na·shi·te

I'd like to learn some of your local dialects.	方言を習いたいのですが。 hō·gen o na·rai·tai no des ga
Would you like to learn some English?	英語を習いたいですか？ ē·go o na·rai·tai des ka

Numbers & Amounts

KEY PHRASES

How many?	どのくらい?	do·no ku·rai
How much?	いくつ?	i·ku·tsu
a little	ちょっと	chot·to
a lot/many	たくさん	ta·ku·san

CARDINAL NUMBERS

The numbers 4, 7 and 9 – and all other numbers containing these numbers – have alternative pronunciations that are completely interchangeable.

1	一	i·chi
2	二	ni
3	三	san
4	四	shi/yon
5	五	go
6	六	ro·ku
7	七	shi·chi/na·na
8	八	ha·chi
9	九	ku/kyū
10	十	jū
11	十一	jū·i·chi
12	十二	jū·ni
20	二十	ni·jū
21	二十一	ni·jū·i·chi

22	二十二	ni·jū·ni
30	三十	san·jū
40	四十	yon·jū
50	五十	go·jū
60	六十	ro·ku·jū
70	七十	na·na·jū
80	八十	ha·chi·jū
90	九十	kyū·jū
100	百	hya·ku
200	二百	ni·hya·ku
300	三百	sam·bya·ku
1,000	千	sen
10,000	一万	i·chi·man
1,000,000	百万	hya·ku·man
100,000,000	一億	i·chi·o·ku

Note that Japanese has no unit for 'a million'. Millions are expressed in units of 10,000, so one million is 100 ten-thousand units.

ORDINAL NUMBERS

To use an ordinal number in Japanese, just add ·ban (番) to the end of the corresponding cardinal number.

1st	一番	i·chi·ban
2nd	二番	ni·ban
3rd	三番	sam·ban

COUNTERS

In Japanese, when expressing a certain number of objects, people or animals, the cardinal number is followed by a counter. Counters, also known as 'classifiers', indicate the size, shape and function of things and distinguish between objects, people and animals.

The following generic counters can be used to count most objects, but not to count people or animals:

1	一つ	hi·to·tsu
2	二つ	fu·ta·tsu
3	三つ	mit·tsu
4	四つ	yot·tsu
5	五つ	i·tsu·tsu
6	六つ	mut·tsu
7	七つ	na·na·tsu
8	八つ	yat·tsu
9	九つ	ko·ko·no·tsu
10	十	tō
numbers higher than 10	…個	…·ko

Note that apart from the last generic counter in the list above, there's no need to add the cardinal number before as this is already part of the counter. For example, the phrase 'Give me an apple, please.' is rin·go o hi·to·tsu ku·da·sai (りんごを一つください), literally 'apple-o one please', not rin·go o i·chi hi·to·tsu ku·da·sai (りんごを一一つください), literally 'apple-o one one please'.

Here are also some basic specific counters frequently used in everyday speech, including the ones for people and animals:

age	…歳	hi·to·tsu
animals*	…匹	fu·ta·tsu
books	…冊	mit·tsu
bottles, pens (long objects)*	…本	yot·tsu
floors (of buildings)	…階	i·tsu·tsu
objects (small)	…個	mut·tsu
people	…人	na·na·tsu
scoops, glasses, cups*	…杯	yat·tsu

sheets (paper, sliced objects)	…枚	ko·ko·no·tsu
time	…時	tō
vehicles	…台	…·ko

*The pronunciation of these three counters changes according to the preceding number. For these, generally use the first option (·hi·ki, ·hon, ·hai) but change to ·pi·ki, ·pon, ·pai after the numbers 1, 6 and 10, and to ·bi·ki, ·bon and ·bai after the number 3. Don't forget to add the cardinal number before each of the specific counters listed above!

USEFUL AMOUNTS

How much?	どのくらい? do·no ku·rai
How many?	いくつ? i·ku·tsu
(100) grams	(100) グラム (hya·ku)·gu·ra·mu
a kilo	1キロ i·chi·ki·ro
a quarter	4分の1 yom·bun no i·chi
a third	3分の1 sam·bun no i·chi
a half	半分 ham·bun
all	全部 zem·bu
none	なし na·shi

For other useful amounts, see **self-catering** (p189).

Time & Dates

KEY PHRASES

What time is it?	何時ですか?	nan·ji des ka
At what time ...?	何時に…	nan·ji ni ...
What date?	何月何日ですか?	nan·ga·tsu nan·ni·chi des ka

TELLING THE TIME

To specify the hour, add the number of the hour before the word ·ji (時) 'o'clock'. Note that four o'clock is an exception: yo·ji (4時), not shi·ji. The minutes come after the hour and are expressed by adding ·fun/·pun (分) after the number – see **numbers & amounts** (p36) for how to form numbers in Japanese. To say 'half past' use ·ji han (時半). For times leading up to the hour (in English 'to') use ma·e des (前です), meaning literally 'before it is' instead of des (です), 'it is'.

Q **What time is it?**	何時ですか? nan·ji des ka
A **It's (ten) o'clock.**	(10)時です。 (jū)·ji des
Five past (ten).	(10)時5分です。 (jū)·ji go·fun des
Quarter past (ten).	(10)時15分です。 (jū)·ji jū·go·fun des
Half past (ten).	(10)時半です。 (jū)·ji han des
Quarter to (ten).	(10)時15分前です。 (jū)·ji jū·go·fun ma·e des

Twenty to (ten).	(10)時20分前です。 (jū)·ji ni·jup·pun ma·e des	
At what time ...?	何時に… nan·ji ni ...	
At (ten).	(10時)に。 (jū·ji) ni	

Combining numbers with minutes produces some special forms:

one minute	1分	ip·pun
two minutes	2分	ni·fun
three minutes	3分	sam·pun
four minutes	4分	yom·pun
five minutes	5分	go·fun
six minutes	6分	rop·pun
seven minutes	7分	na·na·fun
eight minutes	8分	hap·pun
nine minutes	9分	kyū·fun
10 minutes	10分	jup·pun
15 minutes	15分	jū·go·fun
20 minutes	20分	ni·jup·pun

am	午前	go·zen
pm	午後	go·go
morning	朝	a·sa
day	日中	nit·chū
midday	正午	shō·go
afternoon	午後	go·go
evening	夕方	yū·ga·ta
midnight	真夜中	ma·yo·na·ka
night	夜	yo·ru

THE CALENDAR

Monday	月曜日	ge·tsu·yō·bi
Tuesday	火曜日	ka·yō·bi
Wednesday	水曜日	su·i·yō·bi
Thursday	木曜日	mo·ku·yō·bi
Friday	金曜日	kin·yō·bi
Saturday	土曜日	do·yō·bi
Sunday	日曜日	ni·chi·yō·bi
January	1月	i·chi·ga·tsu
February	2月	ni·ga·tsu
March	3月	san·ga·tsu
April	4月	shi·ga·tsu
May	5月	go·ga·tsu
June	6月	ro·ku·ga·tsu
July	7月	shi·chi·ga·tsu
August	8月	ha·chi·ga·tsu
September	9月	ku·ga·tsu
October	10月	jū·ga·tsu
November	11月	jū·i·chi·ga·tsu
December	12月	jū·ni·ga·tsu
summer	夏	na·tsu
autumn	秋	a·ki
winter	冬	fu·yu
spring	春	ha·ru

To express the date, use the cardinal number plus ·ni·chi (日):

What date?

何月何日ですか?
nan·ga·tsu nan·ni·chi des ka

What date is it today?	今日は何月何日ですか?	kyō wa nan·ga·tsu nan·ni·chi des ka
It's (18 October).	(10月18日)です。	(jū·ga·tsu jū·ha·chi·ni·chi) des

There are irregular forms for the 1st to the 10th, the 14th, 20th and 24th when referring to dates:

1st	1日	tsu·i·ta·chi
2nd	2日	fu·tsu·ka
3rd	3日	mik·ka
4th	4日	yok·ka
5th	5日	i·tsu·ka
6th	6日	mu·i·ka
7th	7日	na·no·ka
8th	8日	yō·ka
9th	9日	ko·ko·no·ka
10th	10日	tō·ka
14th	14日	jū·yok·ka
20th	20日	ha·tsu·ka
24th	24日	ni·jū·yok·ka

PRESENT

now	今	i·ma
this afternoon	今日の午後	kyō no go·go
this morning	今朝	ke·sa
this month	今月	kon·ge·tsu
this week	今週	kon·shū
this year	今年	ko·to·shi

today	今日	kyō
tonight	今夜	kon·ya

PAST

(three days) ago	(3日)前	(mik·ka) ma·e
day before yesterday	おととい	o·to·toy
last month	先月	sen·ge·tsu
last night	ゆうべ	yū·be
last week	先週	sen·shū
last year	去年	kyo·nen
since (May)	(5月)から	(go·ga·tsu) ka·ra
yesterday	きのう	ki·nō
yesterday afternoon	きのうの午後	ki·nō no go·go
yesterday evening	きのうの夜	ki·nō no yo·ru
yesterday morning	きのうの朝	ki·nō no a·sa

FUTURE

day after tomorrow	あさって	a·sat·te
in (six days)	(6日)後	(mu·i·ka) go
next ...	来…	rai ...
next month	来月	rai·ge·tsu
next week	来週	rai·shū
next year	来年	rai·nen
tomorrow	明日	a·shi·ta
tomorrow afternoon	明日の午後	a·shi·ta no go·go
tomorrow evening	明日の夜	a·shi·ta no yo·ru
tomorrow morning	明日の朝	a·shi·ta no a·sa
until (June)	(6月)まで	(ro·ku·ga·tsu) ma·de

PRACTICAL

TRANSPORT 46
BORDER CROSSING 62
DIRECTIONS 64
ACCOMMODATION 68
SHOPPING 80
COMMUNICATIONS 88
MONEY & BANKING 95
BUSINESS 98
SIGHTSEEING 102
ACCESSIBLE TRAVEL 107
TRAVEL WITH CHILDREN 109

Transport

KEY PHRASES

What time is the next bus?	次のバスは何時ですか?	tsu·gi no bas wa nan·ji des ka
A ticket to ..., please.	…行きの切符をください。	... yu·ki no kip·pu o ku·da·sai
Please tell me when we get to ...	…に着いたら教えてください。	... ni tsu·i·ta·ra o·shi·e·te ku·da·sai
Please take me to this address.	この住所までお願いします。	ko·no jū·sho ma·de o·ne·gai shi·mas
I'd like to hire a car.	自動車を借りたいのですが。	ji·dō·sha o ka·ri·tai no des ga

GETTING AROUND

Which ... goes to (Nagasaki)?
(長崎)行きの…はどれですか?
(na·ga·sa·ki)·yu·ki no ... wa do·re des ka

boat	船	fu·ne
bullet train	新幹線	shin·kan·sen
bus	バス	bas
plane	飛行機	hi·kō·ki
train	電車	den·sha

Is this the boat to (Kobe)?	(神戸)行きの船は これですか? (kō·be)·yu·ki no fu·ne wa ko·re des ka
Is this the bus to (Kobe)?	(神戸)行きのバスは これですか? (kō·be)·yu·ki no bas wa ko·re des ka
Is this the train to (Kobe)?	(神戸)行きの電車は これですか? (kō·be)·yu·ki no den·sha wa ko·re des ka
What time is the first bus?	始発のバスは 何時ですか? shi·ha·tsu no bas wa nan·ji des ka
What time is the last bus?	最終のバスは何時 ですか? sai·shū no bas wa nan·ji des ka
What time is the next bus?	次のバスは何時 ですか? tsu·gi no bas wa nan·ji des ka
What time does it leave?	何時に出ますか? nan·ji ni de·mas ka
What time does it get to (Nagoya)?	(名古屋)に何時に 着きますか? (na·go·ya) ni nan·ji ni tsu·ki·mas ka
How long will it be delayed?	どのくらい遅れますか? do·no ku·rai o·ku·re·mas ka
That's my seat.	それは私の席です。 so·re wa wa·ta·shi no se·ki des

Is this seat free?	この席は空いていますか? ko·no se·ki wa ai·te i·mas ka

✂ **Is it free?** 空いてますか? ai·te·i·mas ka

Please tell me when we get to (Osaka).	(大阪)に着いたら教えてください。 (ō·sa·ka) ni tsu·i·ta·ra o·shi·e·te ku·da·sai
Please stop here.	ここで停めてください。 ko·ko de to·me·te ku·da·sai
Can we get there by public transport?	そこに公共交通機関で行けますか? so·ko ni kō·kyō·kō·tsū·ki·kan de i·ke·mas ka
I'd prefer to walk there.	歩いて行きたいです。 a·ru·i·te i·ki·tai des

BUYING TICKETS

Where do I buy a ticket?	切符はどこで買えますか? kip·pu wa do·ko de ka·e·mas ka
Do I need to book?	予約が必要ですか? yo·ya·ku ga hi·tsu·yō des ka
A ... ticket (to Tokyo), please.	(東京行きの)…切符をください。 (tō·kyō·yu·ki no) ... kip·pu o ku·da·sai

child's	子ども料金の	ko·do·mo ryō·kin no
green-class (train)	グリーン席	gu·rīn·se·ki
one-way	片道	ka·ta·mi·chi
return	往復	ō·fu·ku
ordinary-class (train)	普通席	fu·tsū·se·ki
student's	学生料金の	gak·sē ryō·kin no

Buying a Ticket

WHAT TIME IS THE NEXT ...?
次の…は何時ですか?
tsu·gi no ... wa nan·ji des ka

BOAT	BUS	TRAIN
船	バス	電車
fu·ne	bas	den·sha

A ... TICKET, PLEASE.
…切符をください。
... kip·pu o ku·da·sai

ONE-WAY	RETURN
片道	往復
ka·ta·mi·chi	ō·fu·ku

I'D LIKE A/AN ... SEAT.
…席をお願いします。
...·se·ki o o·ne·gai shi·mas

AISLE	WINDOW
通路側	窓側
tsū·ro·ga·wa	ma·do·ga·wa

WHICH PLATFORM DOES IT DEPART FROM?
何番のプラットホームから出ますか?
nam·ban no pu·rat·to·fō·mu ka·ra de·mas ka

I'd like a/an ... seat. …席をお願いします。 ...·se·ki o o·ne·gai shi·mas

aisle	通路側	tsū·ro·ga·wa
nonsmoking	禁煙	kin·en
smoking	喫煙	kit·su·en
window	窓側	ma·do·ga·wa

Is there (a toilet)? （トイレ）がありますか? (toy·re) ga a·ri·mas ka

How much is it? いくらですか? i·ku·ra des ka

How long does the trip take? 時間はどのくらいかかりますか? ji·kan wa do·no·ku·rai ka·ka·ri·mas ka

Is it a direct route? 直行便ですか? chok·kō·bin des ka

I'd like to cancel my ticket, please. 切符のキャンセルをお願いします。 kip·pu no kyan·se·ru o o·ne·gai shi·mas

I'd like to change my ticket, please. 切符の変更をお願いします。 kip·pu no hen·kō o o·ne·gai shi·mas

I'd like to confirm my ticket, please. 切符のコンファームをお願いします。 kip·pu no kon·fā·mu o o·ne·gai shi·mas

Can I get a stand-by ticket? スタンドバイチケットはありますか? stan·do·bai·chi·ket·to wa a·ri·mas ka

booklet of tickets 回数券 kai·sū·ken

one-day ticket	1日券 i·chi·ni·chi·ken
one-day free ride ticket	フリー切符 frī·kip·pu

LUGGAGE

Where can I find the left-luggage office?	手荷物預かり所は どこですか? te·ni·mo·tsu·a·zu·ka·ri·sho wa do·ko des ka
Where can I find a luggage locker?	ロッカーはどこですか? rok·kā wa do·ko des ka
Where can I find a trolley?	トロリーはどこですか? to·ro·rī wa do·ko des ka
My luggage has been damaged.	私の手荷物が 壊れました。 wa·ta·shi no te·ni·mo·tsu ga ko·wa·re·mash·ta
My luggage has been lost.	私の手荷物が なくなりました。 wa·ta·shi no te·ni·mo·tsu ga na·ku·na·ri·mash·ta

LISTEN FOR

時刻表	ji·ko·ku·hyō	timetable
キャンセル	kyan·se·ru	cancelled
窓口	ma·do·gu·chi	ticket window
満席	man·se·ki	full
遅れ	o·ku·re	delayed
プラットフォーム	pu·rat·to·fō·mu	platform

My luggage has been stolen.	私の手荷物が ぬすまれました。 wa·ta·shi no te·ni·mo·tsu ga nu·su·ma·re·mash·ta

PLANE

Where's ...?	…はどこですか? ... wa do·ko des ka

the shuttle bus	シャトルバス	sha·to·ru·bas
arrivals	到着便	tō·cha·ku·bin
departures	出発便	shup·pa·tsu·bin
duty-free	免税店	men·zē·ten
gate number (5)	(5)番ゲート	(go)·ban gē·to

BUS & COACH

How often do buses come?	バスはどのくらいひんぱんに 来ますか? bas wa do·no·ku·rai him·pan ni ki·mas ka
Does it stop at (Yokohama)?	(横浜)に停まりますか? (yo·ko·ha·ma) ni to·ma·ri·mas ka
What's the next stop?	次の停車はどこですか? tsu·gi no tē·sha wa do·ko des ka
I'd like to get off at (Kurashiki).	(倉敷)で下車します。 (ku·ra·shi·ki) de ge·sha shi·mas

TRAIN

What station is this?	ここは何駅ですか? ko·ko wa na·ni·e·ki des ka
What's the next station?	次は何駅ですか? tsu·gi wa na·ni·e·ki des ka

LISTEN FOR

超過手荷物	chō·ka te·ni·mo·tsu	excess baggage
機内持込の手荷物	ki·nai·mo·chi·ko·mi no te·ni·mo·tsu	carry-on baggage

Does it stop at (Nagasaki)?	これは(長崎)に停まりますか? ko·re wa (na·ga·sa·ki) ni to·ma·ri·mas ka
Do I need to change?	乗り換えなければいけませんか? no·ri·ka·e·na·ke·re·ba i·ke·ma·sen ka
Which line goes to (Roppongi) station?	(六本木)駅はどの線ですか? (rop·pon·gi)·e·ki wa do·no sen des ka
Can I use this ticket on the (Toei) line?	この切符で(都営)線に乗れますか? ko·no kip·pu de (to·ē)·sen ni no·re·mas ka
I need to pay the excess fare.	のりこし清算したいのですが。 no·ri·ko·shi· sē·san shi·tai no des ga
I'd like to go on a bullet train.	新幹線で行きたいのですが。 shin·kan·sen de i·ki·tai no des ga
Where's exit number (2)?	(２)番出口はどこですか? (ni)·ban de·gu·chi wa do·ko des ka
Where's the (east) exit?	(東)口はどこですか? (hi·ga·shi)·gu·chi wa do·ko des ka
Don't push!	押さないで! o·sa·nai·de

Is it (a/an) ...?*	…ですか? **... des ka**	
direct (nonstop)	直行便	**chok·kō·bin**
limited express train (few stops)	特急	**tok·kyū**
express	急行	**kyū·kō**
rapid train	快速	**kai·so·ku**
local	各駅停車	**ka·ku·e·ki·tē·sha**

* The trains are listed according to how often they stop, starting with the one that stops the least.

Which carriage is for (Hiroshima)?	(広島)行きは 何号車ですか? **(hi·ro·shi·ma)·yu·ki wa nan·gō·sha des ka**
Which is the dining carriage?	食堂車は 何号車 ですか? **sho·ku·dō·sha wa nan·gō·sha des ka**
Which is the green-class (1st-class) carriage?	グリーン車は 何号車ですか? **gu·rīn·sha wa nan·gō·sha des ka**

BOAT

What's the sea like today?	今日の海の様子は どうですか? **kyō no u·mi no yō·su wa dō des ka**
Are there life jackets?	救命胴衣はありますか? **kyū·mē·dō·i wa a·ri·mas ka**
I feel seasick.	船酔いしました。 **fu·na·yoy shi·mash·ta**

LOOK FOR

新幹線	shin·kan·sen	bullet train
モノレール	mo·no·rē·ru	monorail
地下鉄	chi·ka·te·tsu	subway
電車	den·sha	train
市電	shi·den	tram

TAXI

I'd like a taxi at (9) o'clock.	(9)時にタクシーをお願いします。 (ku)·ji ni tak·shī o o·ne·gai shi·mas
I'd like a taxi now.	今タクシーをお願いします。 i·ma tak·shī o o·ne·gai shi·mas
Where's the taxi rank?	タクシー乗り場はどこですか? tak·shī·no·ri·ba wa do·ko des ka
Is this taxi available?	このタクシーは空車ですか? ko·no tak·shī wa kū·sha des ka
How much is it (to ...)?	(…まで)いくらですか? (... ma·de) i·ku·ra des ka
Please take me to (this address).	(この住所)までお願いします。 (ko·no jū·sho) ma·de o·ne·gai shi·mas

To ...	…まで。	... ma·de

Please slow down.	スピードを落としてください。 spī·do o o·to·shi·te ku·da·sai
Please stop here.	ここで停まってください。 ko·ko de to·mat·te ku·da·sai
Please wait here.	ここで待ってください。 ko·ko de mat·te ku·da·sai

For other useful phrases, see **directions** (p64) and **money & banking** (p95).

CAR & MOTORBIKE

I'd like to hire a/an ...	…を借りたいのですが。 ... o ka·ri·tai no des ga

4WD	四駆	yon·ku
automatic	オートマチック	ō·to·ma·chik·ku
car	自動車	ji·dō·sha
(electric) car	(電気)自動車	(den-ki) ji·dō·sha
manual	マニュアル	ma·nyu·a·ru
motorbike	オートバイ	ō·to·bai
scooter	スクーター	skū·tā

How much for daily hire?	1日借りるといくらですか? i·chi·ni·chi ka·ri·ru to i·ku·ra des ka
How much for weekly hire?	1週間借りるといくらですか? is·shū·kan ka·ri·ru to i·ku·ra des ka
Does that include insurance/mileage?	保険料/マイレージが含まれていますか? ho·ken·ryō/mai·rē·ji ga fu·ku·ma·re·te i·mas ka
Do you have a road map?	ロードマップがありますか? rō·do·map·pu ga a·ri·mas ka

Do you have a guide to the road rules in English?	道路交通法の英語のガイドブックがありますか? dō·ro·kō·tsū·hō no ē·go no gai·do·buk·ku ga a·ri·mas ka
What's the speed limit?	制限速度は何キロですか? sē·gen·so·ku·do wa nan·ki·ro des ka
How much is the toll for this road?	この道の通行料はいくらですか? ko·no mi·chi no tsū·kō·ryō wa i·ku·ra des ka
Is this the road to (Sapporo)?	この道は(札幌)まで行きますか? ko·no mi·chi wa (sap·po·ro) ma·de i·ki·mas ka
Where's a petrol station?	ガソリンスタンドはどこですか? ga·so·rin·stan·do wa do·ko des ka

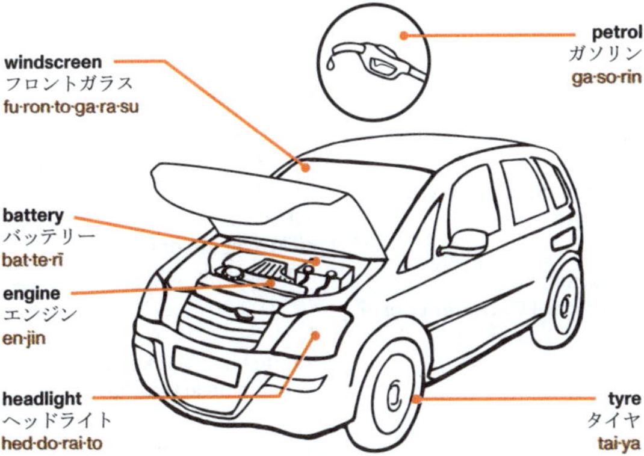

LOOK FOR

一時停止	i·chi·ji·tē·shi	Stop Here
一方通行	ip·pō·tsū·kō	One-way
入口	i·ri·gu·chi	Entrance
工事中	kō·ji·chū	Under Construction
立入り禁止	ta·chi·i·ri·kin·shi	No Entry
駐車	chū·sha	Parking
駐車禁止	chū·sha·kin·shi	No Parking
出口	de·gu·chi	Exit (freeway etc)
止まれ	to·ma·re	Stop
料金所	ryō·kin·jo	Toll

Please fill it up.	満タンにしてください。 man·tan ni shi·te ku·da·sai
I'd like ... litres.	…リットルお願いします。 ... rit·to·ru o·ne·gai shi·mas
Can you check the oil?	オイルのチェックを お願いします。 oy·ru no chek·ku o o·ne·gai shi·mas
Can you check the water?	水のチェックを お願いします。 mi·zu no chek·ku o o·ne·gai shi·mas
Can you check the tyre pressure?	空気圧のチェックを お願いします。 kū·ki·a·tsu no chek·ku o o·ne·gai shi·mas
(How long) Can I park here?	(どのくらい)ここに 駐車できますか? (do·no·ku·rai) ko·ko ni chū·sha de·ki·mas ka

Do I have to pay?	料金を払わなければ なりませんか? **ryō-kin o ha-ra-wa-na-ke-re-ba na-ri-ma-sen ka**
I need a mechanic.	整備士が必要です。 **sē-bi-shi ga hi-tsu-yō des**
I've had an accident.	事故に遭いました。 **ji-ko ni ai-mash-ta**
The car has broken down (at Minato-ku).	車が(港区で) 壊れました。 **ku-ru-ma ga (mi-na-to-ku de) ko-wa-re-mash-ta**
I have a flat tyre.	パンクしました。 **pan-ku shi-mash-ta**
I've run out of petrol.	ガス欠です。 **gas-ke-tsu des**

ここで停まってください。
ko-ko de to-mat-te ku-da-sai
Please stop here.

BICYCLE

Can we get there by bicycle?	そこに自転車で 行けますか? so·ko ni ji·ten·sha de i·ke·mas ka
I'd like to buy a bicycle.	自転車を買いたいのですが。 ji·ten·sha o kai·tai no des ga
I'd like to hire a bicycle.	自転車を借りたいの ですが。 ji·ten·sha o ka·ri·tai no des ga
I'd like a mountain bike.	マウンテンバイクが欲しい のですが。 ma·un·ten·bai·ku ga ho·shī no des ga
I'd like a racing bike.	レース用自転車が欲しい のですが。 rē·su·yō ji·ten·sha ga ho·shī no des ga
I'd like a secondhand bike.	中古の自転車が欲しい のですが。 chū·ko no ji·ten·sha ga ho·shī no des ga
How much is it per day?	1日いくらですか? i·chi·ni·chi i·ku·ra des ka
How much is it per hour?	1時間いくらですか? i·chi·ji·kan i·ku·ra des ka
Do I need a helmet?	ヘルメットは必要 ですか? he·ru·met·to wa hi·tsu·yō des ka
Is there a bicycle-path map?	自転車道の地図が ありますか? ji·ten·sha·dō no chi·zu ga a·ri·mas ka

CULTURE TIP: KEIRIN

An originally Japanese cycling discipline, *keirin* kē·rin (競輪) has made it onto the international stage over the last 20 years. In this 2000m track cycling event, each rider cycles behind a motorised derny (a type of motorcycle specifically designed and built for motor-paced track cycling events) that sets the pace for 1400m, then pulls off the track and leaves the riders to sprint to the finish – fast, furious and spectacular!

I have a puncture.	パンクしました。 pan·ku shi·mash·ta
I'd like my bicycle repaired.	私の自転車を直してもらいたいのですが。 wa·ta·shi no ji·ten·sha o now·shi·te mo·rai·tai no des ga

Border Crossing

KEY PHRASES

I'm here for ... days.	私は…日滞在します。	wa·ta·shi wa ... ni·chi tai·zai shi·mas
I'm staying at ...	…に泊まります。	... ni to·ma·ri·mas
I have nothing to declare.	何も申請するものがありません。	na·ni mo shin·sē su·ru mo·no ga a·ri·ma·sen

PASSPORT CONTROL

I'm in transit.	トランジットです。 to·ran·jit·to des
I'm on business/holiday.	ビジネス/休暇です。 bi·ji·nes/kyū·ka des
I'm here for ... days.	私は…日滞在します。 wa·ta·shi wa ... ni·chi tai·zai shi·mas
I'm here for ... months.	私は…ヶ月滞在します。 wa·ta·shi wa ...·ka·ge·tsu tai·zai shi·mas
I'm here for ... weeks.	私は…週滞在します。 wa·ta·shi wa ...·shū tai·zai shi·mas
I'm going to (Fukuoka).	(福岡)へ行きます。 (fu·ku·o·ka) e i·ki·mas
I'm staying at (Hotel Nikko).	(日航ホテル)に泊まります。 (nik·kō·ho·te·ru) ni to·ma·ri·mas

LOOK FOR

移民	i·min	Immigration
検疫	ken·e·ki	Quarantine
出入国管理	shu·tsu·nyū·ko·ku·kan·ri	Passport Control
税関	zē·kan	Customs
免税	men·zē	Duty-free

AT CUSTOMS

I have nothing to declare.	何も申請するものがありません。 na·ni mo shin·sē su·ru mo·no ga a·ri·ma·sen
I have something to declare.	申請するものがあります。 shin·sē su·ru mo·no ga a·ri·mas
Do I have to declare this?	これを申請しなければなりませんか? ko·re o shin·sē shi·na·ke·re·ba na·ri·ma·sen ka
That's mine.	それは私のです。 so·re wa wa·ta·shi no des
That's not mine.	それは私のじゃありません。 so·re wa wa·ta·shi no ja a·ri·ma·sen
I didn't know I had to declare it.	これを申請しなければならないのを知りませんでした。 ko·re o shin·sē shi·na·ke·re·ba na·ra·nai no o shi·ri·ma·sen desh·ta

For duty-free shopping, see **shopping** (p80) for some handy phrases.

Directions

KEY PHRASES

Where's ...?	…はどこですか?	... wa do·ko des ka
What's the address?	住所は何ですか?	jū·sho wa nan des ka
How far is it?	どのくらいの距離ですか?	do·no ku·rai no kyo·ri des ka

Where's (the tourist office)?	(観光案内所)はどこですか? (kan·kō·an·nai·jo) wa do·ko des ka
How do I get there?	そこへはどう行けばいいですか? so·ko e wa dō i·ke·ba ī des ka
How far is it?	どのくらいの距離ですか? do·no ku·rai no kyo·ri des ka
Can you show me (on the map)?	(地図で)教えてくれませんか? (chi·zu de) o·shi·e·te ku·re·ma·sen ka
What (street) is this?	この(道路)の名前は何ですか? ko·no (dō·ro) no na·ma·e wa nan des ka
What's the address?	住所は何ですか? jū·sho wa nan des ka
Turn left.	左へまがってください。 hi·da·ri e ma·gat·te ku·da·sai

Turn right.	右へまがってください。 mi·gi e ma·gat·te ku·da·sai
It's ...	…です。 ... des

behind ...	…の後ろ	... no u·shi·ro
close	近く	chi·ka·ku
here	ここ	ko·ko
in front of ...	…の前	... no ma·e
near ...	…の近く	... no chi·ka·ku
next to ...	…のとなり	... no to·na·ri
on the corner	角	ka·do
opposite ...	…の向かい側	... no mu·kai·ga·wa
straight ahead	この先	ko·no sa·ki
there	あそこ	a·so·ko

Turn at the corner.	その角をまがってください。 so·no ka·do o ma·gat·te ku·da·sai
Turn at the traffic lights.	その信号をまがってください。 so·no shin·gō o ma·gat·te ku·da·sai
by bus	バスで bas de
on foot	徒歩で to·ho de
by taxi	タクシーで tak·shī de
by train	電車で den·sha de

north	北 ki·ta
south	南 mi·na·mi
east	東 hi·ga·shi
west	西 ni·shi
kilometres	キロ ki·ro
metres	メートル mē·to·ru
minutes	分 fun/pun

LANGUAGE TIP: JAPANESE ADDRESSES

Some useful language for understanding Japanese addresses:

avenue	大通り	ō·dō·ri
lane	路地	ro·ji
street (big, surfaced)	道路	dō·ro
street (smaller than dō·ro**)**	道	mi·chi
city area (a few blocks)	丁目	chō·me
city area (between chō·me **and** ku**)**	町	ma·chi
ward (administrative unit)	区	ku
town	町	ma·chi
city	市	shi
Prefecture	県	ken

Note that Tokyo Prefecture is indicated by adding to (都) to Tokyo – it's often referred to as 'Tokyo Metropolis' – and Osaka and Kyoto Prefectures by adding fu (府) instead of ken (県) to the name of the city. Cities like these with a large population are administratively subdivided in wards, ku (区).

Accommodation

KEY PHRASES

Where's a hotel?	ホテルが ありますか?	ho·te·ru ga a·ri·mas ka
Do you have a double room?	ダブルルームは ありますか?	da·bu·ru·rū·mu wa a·ri·mas ka
How much is it per night?	1泊いくら ですか?	ip·pa·ku i·ku·ra des ka
Is breakfast included?	朝食は 含まれて いますか?	chō·sho·ku wa fu·ku·ma·re·te i·mas ka
What time is checkout?	チェックアウトは 何時ですか?	chek·ku·ow·to wa nan·ji des ka

FINDING ACCOMMODATION

Where's a ...? …がありますか?
... ga a·ri·mas ka

camping ground	キャンプ場	kyam·pu·jō
capsule hotel	カプセルホテル	ka·pu·se·ru·ho·te·ru
guesthouse	民宿	min·shu·ku
hotel	ホテル	ho·te·ru
Japanese-style inn	旅館	ryo·kan
youth hostel	ユースホステル	yū·su·ho·su·te·ru

Can you recommend somewhere cheap?	おすすめの安い ところはありますか? o·su·su·me no ya·su·i to·ko·ro wa a·ri·mas ka
Can you recommend somewhere nearby?	おすすめの近くの ところはありますか? o·su·su·me no chi·ka·ku no to·ko·ro wa a·ri·mas ka

For responses, see **directions** (p64).

BOOKING AHEAD & CHECKING IN

I'd like to book a room, please.	部屋の予約をお願い します。 he·ya no yo·ya·ku o o·ne·gai shi·mas

Are there rooms?	空き部屋は ありますか?	a·ki he·ya wa a·ri·mas ka

I have a reservation.	予約があります。 yo·ya·ku ga a·ri·mas
For (three) nights/weeks.	(3) 泊/週間。 (san)·pa·ku/·shū·kan
From (July 2) to (July 6).	(7月2日)から(7月6日)まで。 (shi·chi·ga·tsu fu·tsu·ka) ka·ra (shi·chi·ga·tsu mu·i·ka) ma·de
Do I need to pay upfront?	前払いですか? ma·e·ba·rai des ka
How much is it per night?	1泊いくらですか? ip·pa·ku i·ku·ra des ka
How much is it per person?	1人いくらですか? hi·to·ri i·ku·ra des ka
How much is it per week?	1週間いくらですか? is·shū·kan i·ku·ra des ka

LOOK FOR

空室	kū·shi·tsu	vacancy
満室	man·shi·tsu	no vacancy

Is breakfast included?	朝食は含まれていますか? chō·sho·ku wa fu·ku·ma·re·te i·mas ka
Can I pay by credit card?	クレジットカードで支払えますか? ku·re·jit·to·kā·do de shi·ha·ra·e·mas ka
Is there wifi here?	ここはワイファイがありますか? ko·ko wa wai·fai ga a·ri·mas·ka
Do you have a double room?	ダブルルームはありますか? da·bu·ru·rū·mu wa a·ri·mas ka
Do you have a single room?	シングルルームはありますか? shin·gu·ru·rū·mu wa a·ri·mas ka
Do you have a twin room?	ツインルームはありますか? tsu·in·rū·mu wa a·ri·mas ka
Can I see the room?	部屋を見てもいいですか? he·ya o mi·te mo ī des ka
I'll take it.	この部屋にします。 ko·no he·ya ni shi·mas
I won't take it.	ちょっと考えます。 (lit: I'll think about it) chot·to kan·ga·e·mas

Finding a Room

DO YOU HAVE A … ROOM?
…ルームはありますか?
…rū·mu wa a·ri·mas ka

DOUBLE
ダブル
da·bu·ru

SINGLE
シングル
shin·gu·ru

HOW MUCH IS IT PER …?
…いくらですか?
… i·ku·ra des ka

NIGHT
1泊
ip·pa·ku

PERSON
1人
hi·to·ri

IS BREAKFAST INCLUDED?
朝食は含まれていますか?
chō·sho·ku wa fu·ku·ma·re·te i·mas ka

CAN I SEE THE ROOM?
部屋を見てもいいですか?
he·ya o mi·te mo ī des ka

I'LL TAKE IT.
この部屋にします。
ko·no he·ya ni shi·mas

I WON'T TAKE IT.
ちょっと考えます。
chot·to kan·ga·e·mas

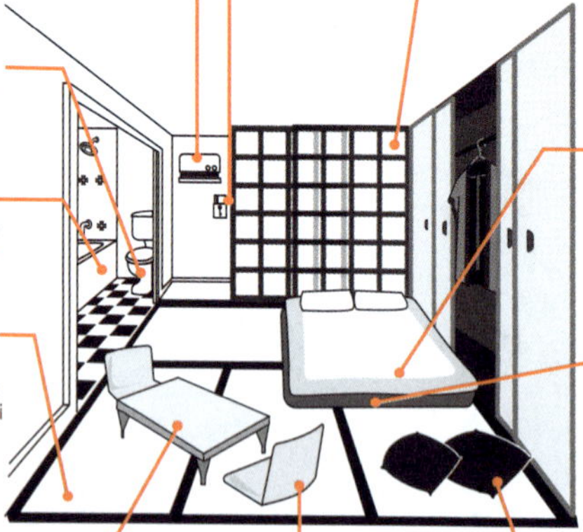

REQUESTS & QUERIES

Do you have an elevator?	エレベーターがありますか? e·re·bē·tā ga a·ri·mas ka
Do you have a laundry service?	洗濯サービスがありますか? sen·ta·ku·sā·bis ga a·ri·mas ka
Do you have a safe?	金庫がありますか? kin·ko ga a·ri·mas ka
Do you change money here?	ここで換金できますか? ko·ko de kan·kin de·ki·mas ka

Can I use the ...?	…を使ってもいいですか? ... o tsu·kat·te mo ī des ka	
kitchen (Japanese)	台所	dai·do·ko·ro
kitchen (Western)	キッチン	kit·chin
laundry	洗濯室	sen·ta·ku·shi·tsu
telephone	電話	den·wa

Could I have an extra blanket, please?	スペアの毛布をお願いします。 spair no mō·fu o o·ne·gai shi·mas
Could I have my key, please?	鍵をお願いします。 ka·gi o o·ne·gai shi·mas
When's breakfast served?	朝食はいつですか? chō·sho·ku wa i·tsu des ka
Where's breakfast served?	朝食はどこですか? chō·sho·ku wa do·ko des ka
Please wake me at (seven) o'clock.	(7)時に起こしてください。 (shi·chi)·ji ni o·ko·shi·te ku·da·sai
There's no need to change my sheets.	シーツを替える必要はありません。 shī·tsu o ka·e·ru hi·tsu·yō wa a·ri·ma·sen
Is there a message for me?	伝言はありますか? den·gon wa a·ri·mas ka
Can I leave a message for someone?	伝言を残したいのですが。 den·gon o no·ko·shi·tai no des ga

Do you arrange tours here?	ここでツアーに 申し込めますか? ko·ko de tsu·ā ni mō·shi·ko·me·mas ka
I'm locked out of my room.	部屋に鍵を残した まま鍵をかけて しまいました。 he·ya ni ka·gi o no·ko·shi·ta ma·ma ka·gi o ka·ke te shi·mai·mash·ta

COMPLAINTS

It's too ...	…すぎます。 ... su·gi·mas

bright	明る	a·ka·ru
cold	寒	sa·mu
dark	暗	ku·ra
noisy	うるさ	u·ru·sa
small	小さ	chī·sa

The (fan) doesn't work.	(扇風機)が 壊れています。 (sem·pū·ki) ga ko·wa·re·te i·mas
Can I get another (blanket)?	(毛布)をもう一つ お願いできますか? (mō·fu) o mō hi·to·tsu o·ne·gai de·ki·mas ka
This (pillow) isn't clean.	この(枕)はきれいじゃ ありません。 ko·no (ma·ku·ra) wa ki·rē ja a·ri·ma·sen

CHECKING OUT

What time is checkout?	チェックアウトは何時 ですか? chek·ku·ow·to wa nan·ji des ka
Can I have a late checkout?	チェックアウトを遅らせたいのですが。 chek·ku·ow·to o o·ku·ra·se·tai no des ga
Can you call a taxi for me?	タクシーを呼んでもらえますか? tak·shī o yon·de mo·ra·e·mas ka
I'd like a taxi at (11) o'clock.	(11)時にタクシーを呼んでください。 (jū·i·chi)·ji ni tak·shī o yon·de ku·da·sai

ホテルがありますか?
ho·te·ru ga a·ri·mas ka
Where's a hotel?

I'm leaving now.	今、出発します。 i·ma shup·pa·tsu shi·mas
Can I leave my bags here?	ここで荷物を預かって もらえますか? ko·ko de ni·mo·tsu o a·zu·kat·te mo·ra·e·mas ka
Could I have my deposit, please?	預かり金を返して いただきたいのですが。 a·zu·ka·ri·kin o ka·e·shi·te i·ta·da·ki·tai no des ga
Could I have my valuables, please?	貴重品を返して いただきたいのですが。 ki·chō·hin o ka·e·shi·te i·ta·da·ki·tai no des ga
Could I have a receipt, please?	レシートをお願いします。 re·shī·to o o·ne·gai shi·mas
I'll be back on (Tuesday).	(火曜日)にもどります。 (ka·yō·bi) ni mo·do·ri·mas
I had a great stay, thank you.	たいへんくつろげました。 tai·hen ku·tsu·ro·ge·mash·ta
I'll recommend it to my friends.	友達に薦めます。 to·mo·da·chi ni su·su·me·mas

CAMPING

Do you have ...?	…がありますか? ... ga a·ri·mas ka

electricity	電気	den·ki
a laundry	コインランドリー	ko·in·ran·do·rī
shower facilities	シャワー	sha·wā
a site	キャンプサイト	kyam·pu·sai·to
tents for hire	貸しテント	ka·shi·ten·to

How much is it per ...?	…いくらですか? ... i·ku·ra des ka	
caravan	キャラバン1台	kya·ra·ban i·chi·dai
person	1人	hi·to·ri
tent	テント1つ	ten·to hi·to·tsu
vehicle	車1台	ku·ru·ma i·chi·dai

Can I camp here?
ここでキャンプしても いいですか?
ko·ko de kyam·pu shi·te mo ī des ka

Can I park next to my tent?
テントのとなりに駐車 してもいいですか?
ten·to no to·na·ri ni chū·sha shi·te mo ī des ka

Is the water drinkable?
水は飲めますか?
mi·zu wa no·me·mas ka

Could I borrow ...?
…を貸してもらえませんか?
... o ka·shi·te mo·ra·e·ma·sen ka

RENTING

If you're planning to stick around for a while in Japan, you might consider staying in a gai·jin hows (外人ハウス), literally meaning 'foreigner house', which offers cheap accommodation for long-term visitors.

Do you have a/an (monthly/weekly) apartment for rent?
賃貸のための (マンスリー/ウィークリー) マンションがありますか?
chin·tai no ta·me no (man·su·rī/wī·ku·rī) man·shon ga a·ri·mas ka

LOOK FOR

(一部)家具付き	(i·chi·bu) ka·gu·tsu·ki	(partly) furnished
家具なし	ka·gu·na·shi	unfurnished

Do you have a house for rent?	賃貸のための家が ありますか? chin·tai no ta·me no i·e ga a·ri·mas ka
Do you have a room for rent?	賃貸のための部屋が ありますか? chin·tai no ta·me no he·ya ga a·ri·mas ka

STAYING WITH LOCALS

Can I stay at your place?	お宅に泊めて いただけませんか? o·ta·ku ni to·me·te i·ta·da·ke·ma·sen ka
I have my own mattress/ sleeping bag.	私はマットレス/ 寝袋を持っています。 wa·ta·shi wa mat·to·res/ ne·bu·ku·ro o mot·te i·mas
Is there anything I can do to help?	何か手伝うことは ありませんか? na·ni ka te·tsu·dow ko·to wa a·ri·ma·sen ka
Can I bring anything for the meal?	食事を運びましょうか? sho·ku·ji o ha·ko·bi·ma·shō ka
Can I clear the table?	テーブルの片付けを しましょうか? tē·bu·ru no ka·ta·zu·ke o shi·ma·shō ka

CULTURE TIP: VISITING ETIQUETTE

It's customary in Japan to bring a small gift when visiting someone's home. Cakes, chocolates, fruit and flowers are common and relatively safe gifts. Something for the kids or from your country will go down a treat and it doesn't need to be big.

Take your shoes off in the entrance hall (gen·kan 玄関), the foyer that specifically serves this purpose. Slippers are usually provided to guests but it's strictly socks only on the ta·ta·mi (たたみ), the straw-mat flooring you'll see in Japanese houses.

For women it's best to sit with the legs to one side rather than cross-legged. The sē·za (正座) position, in which you tuck your knees directly underneath you, is required in very formal situations only. If unsure, simply follow your hosts' example. If you stay over, remember that body-washing takes place before entering the bath – not inside it.

Can I do the dishes?	食器を洗いましょうか? shok·ki o a·rai·ma·shō ka
Thanks for your hospitality.	たいへんお世話になりました。 tai·hen o·se·wa ni na·ri·mash·ta

To compliment your hosts' cooking, see **eating out** (p172).

Shopping

KEY PHRASES

I'd like to buy ...	…をください。	... o ku·da·sai
Can I look at it?	それを見ても いいですか?	so·re o mi·te mo ī des ka
Can I try it on?	試着 できますか?	shi·cha·ku de·ki·mas ka
How much is it?	いくらですか?	i·ku·ra des ka
That's too expensive.	高すぎます。	ta·ka·su·gi·mas

LOOKING FOR ...

Where's a (supermarket)?	(スーパー)はどこですか? (sū·pā) wa do·ko des ka
Where can I buy (a padlock)?	(鍵)はどこで 買えますか? (ka·gi) wa do·ko de ka·e·mas ka
Where can I buy locally produced goods/souvenirs?	地元産の製品/ お土産は、どこで 買えますか? ji·mo·to·san no sē·hin/ o·mi·ya·ge wa do·ko de ka·e·mas ka

To find your way to the shops, see **directions** (p64).

LOOK FOR

営業中	ē·gyō·chū	Open
閉店	hē·ten	Closed
押す	o·su	Push
引く	hi·ku	Pull

MAKING A PURCHASE

I'm just looking.	見ているだけです。 mi·te i·ru da·ke des
I'd like to buy (an adaptor plug).	(電源プラグ)をください。 (den·gen·pu·ra·gu) o ku·da·sai
How much is it?	いくらですか? i·ku·ra des ka

How much?	おいくら?	o·i·ku·ra

Can you write down the price?	値段を書いてもらえますか? ne·dan o kai·te mo·ra·e·mas ka
Do you have any others?	ほかに何かありますか? ho·ka ni na·ni ka a·ri·mas ka
Can I look at it?	それを見てもいいですか? so·re o mi·te mo ī des ka
Could I have it wrapped?	包んでもらえますか? tsu·tsun·de mo·ra·e·mas ka
Does it have a guarantee?	保証はありますか? ho·shō wa a·ri·mas ka
Can I have it sent overseas/abroad?	海外に郵送して もらえますか? kai·gai ni yū·sō shi·te mo·ra·e·mas ka

Can I pick it up later?	受け取りは後でできますか? u·ke·to·ri wa a·to de de·ki·mas ka
It's faulty.	不良品です。 fu·ryō·hin des
Do you accept credit cards?	クレジットカードで支払えますか? ku·re·jit·to· kā·do de shi·ha·ra·e·mas ka
Could I have a bag/ receipt, please?	袋/レシートをください。 fu·ku·ro/re·shī·to o ku·da·sai
I'd like my change, please.	お釣りをお願いします。 o·tsu·ri o o·ne·gai shi·mas
I'd like a refund, please.	払い戻しをお願いします。 ha·rai·mo·do·shi o o·ne·gai shi·mas
I'd like to return this, please.	返品をお願いします。 hem·pin o o·ne·gai shi·mas

BARGAINING

That's too expensive.	高すぎます。 ta·ka·su·gi·mas
Do you have something cheaper?	もっと安いものがありますか? mot·to ya·su·i mo·no ga a·ri·mas ka
Can you give me a discount?	ディスカウントできますか? dis·kown·to de·ki·mas ka
I'll give you (5000 yen).	(5千円)払います。 (go·sen·en) ha·rai·mas

Making a Purchase

I'D LIKE TO BUY …
…をください。
… o ku·da·sai

HOW MUCH IS IT?
いくらですか?
i·ku·ra des ka

CAN YOU WRITE DOWN THE PRICE?
値段を書いてもらえますか?
ne·dan o kai·te mo·ra·e·mas ka

DO YOU ACCEPT CREDIT CARDS?
クレジットカードで支払えますか?
ku·re·jit·to·kā·do de shi·ha·ra·e·mas ka

COULD I HAVE A …, PLEASE?
…をください。
… o ku·da·sai

RECEIPT
レシート
re·shī·to

BAG
袋
fu·ku·ro

☑ CULTURE TIP: JAPANESE SOUVENIRS

Common Japanese souvenirs (o·mi·ya·ge おみやげ) and gifts include folding fans (sen·su 扇子), ceramics (tō·gē 陶芸), tea sets (cha·ki 茶器), lacquerware (shik·ki 漆器), handmade paper (wa·shi 和紙) and Japanese dolls (ni·hon nin·gyō 日本人形). Art lovers will find beautiful scrolls (ka·ke·ji·ku 掛け軸) and woodblock prints (u·ki·yo·e 浮世絵), samurai enthusiasts can look for Japanese swords (ka·ta·na 刀), and the cotton kimono (yu·ka·ta 浴衣) is an ever-popular lightweight souvenir.

CLOTHES

My size is (40).	私のサイズは(40)号です。 wa·ta·shi no sai·zu wa (yon·jū)·gō des
My size is (L/M/S).	私のサイズは(L/M/S)です。 wa·ta·shi no sai·zu wa (e·ru/e·mu/e·su) des
Can I try it on?	試着できますか? shi·cha·ku de·ki·mas ka
It doesn't fit.	体にフィットしません。 ka·ra·da ni fit·to shi·ma·sen

For clothing items, see the **dictionary** (p219). For sizes, see **numbers & amounts** (p36).

BOOKS & READING

Do you have a book by (Yukio Mishima)?	(三島由紀夫)の本はありますか? (mi·shi·ma yu·ki·o) no hon wa a·ri·mas ka
Is there an English-language section?	英語のセクションはありますか? ē·go no sek·shon wa a·ri·mas ka

I'd like a dictionary.	辞書をください。 ji·sho o ku·da·sai
I'd like a newspaper (in English).	(英字)新聞をください。 (ē·ji) shim·bun o ku·da·sai

MUSIC & DVD

I'm looking for something by (Utada).	(宇多田) の曲を探しています。 (u·ta·da) no kyo·ku o sa·ga·shi·te i·mas
What's their best recording?	どの曲がいちばんですか? do·no kyo·ku ga i·chi·ban des ka
Can I listen to this?	これを聴いてもいいですか? ko·re o kī·te mo ī des ka

いくらですか?
i·ku·ra des ka
How much is it?

PHOTOGRAPHY

Do you have batteries for this camera?	このカメラの電池はありますか？ ko·no ka·me·ra no den·chi wa a·ri·mas ka
Do you have memory cards for this camera?	このカメラのメモリーカードはありますか？ ko·no ka·me·ra no me·mo·ri·kā·do wa a·ri·mas ka
I need a passport photo taken.	パスポート用の写真が必要です。 pas·pō·to·yō no sha·shin ga hi·tsu·yō des
Can you print digital photos?	デジタル写真の印刷はできますか? de·ji·ta·ru·sha·shin no in·sa·tsu wa de·ki·mas ka
Can you develop this film?	このフィルムを現像はできますか? ko·no fi·ru·mu o gen·zō wa de·ki·mas ka
When will it be ready?	いつ出来上がりますか? i·tsu de·ki·a·ga·ri·mas ka

REPAIRS

Can I have my (backpack) repaired here?	(バックパック)を直してもらえますか? (bak·ku·pak·ku) o na·o·shi·te mo·ra·e·mas ka
When will my (camera) be ready?	(カメラ)はいつできますか? (ka·me·ra) wa i·tsu de·ki·mas ka

Communications

KEY PHRASES

I want to send a parcel.	小包を送りたいのですが。	ko·zu·tsu·mi o o·ku·ri·tai no des ga
I'd like a SIM card.	SIMカードをお願いします。	shi·mu·kā·do o o·ne·gai shi·mas

POST OFFICE

I want to send a letter.	手紙を送りたいのですが。 te·ga·mi o o·ku·ri·tai no des ga
I want to send a postcard.	はがきを送りたいのですが。 ha·ga·ki o o·ku·ri·tai no des ga
I want to send a parcel.	小包を送りたいのですが。 ko·zu·tsu·mi o o·ku·ri·tai no des ga
I want to buy an envelope.	封筒をください。 fū·tō o ku·da·sai
I want to buy a stamp.	切手をください。 kit·te o ku·da·sai

LOOK FOR

関税申告	kan·zē·shin·ko·ku	customs declaration
国内	ko·ku·nai	domestic
壊れ物	ko·wa·re·mo·no	fragile
国際	ko·ku·sai	international
郵便番号	yū·bin·ban·gō	postcode
郵便局	yū·bin·kyo·ku	post office

Please send it to (Australia).
(オーストラリア)まで お願いします。
(ō·sto·ra·rya) ma·de o·ne·gai shi·mas

Please send it ...
… お願いします。
... o·ne·gai shi·mas

by airmail	航空便で	kō·kū·bin de
by surface mail	普通便で	fu·tsū·bin de
express	速達で	so·ku·ta·tsu de
registered	書留で	ka·ki·to·me de
by sea mail	船便で	fu·na·bin de

It contains (souvenirs).
(お土産)が入っています。
(o·mi·ya·ge) ga hait·te i·mas

Where's the poste restante section?
局留め郵便の セクションはどこですか?
kyo·ku·do·me·yū·bin no sek·shon wa do·ko des ka

Is there any mail for me?
私宛の郵便物 はありますか?
wa·ta·shi·a·te no yū·bin·bu·tsu wa a·ri·mas ka

PHONE

Q What's your phone number?	あなたの電話番号は何番ですか? a·na·ta no den·wa·ban·gō wa nam·ban des ka
A The number is ...	電話番号は…です。 den·wa·ban·gō wa ... des
I want to make a call to (Singapore).	(シンガポール)に電話したいのですが。 (shin·ga·pō·ru) ni den·wa shi·tai no des ga
I want to reverse the charges.	コレクトコールで電話したいのですが。 ko·re·ku·to·kō·ru de den·wa shi·tai no des ga
What's the area code for (Osaka)?	(大阪)の市内局番は何番ですか? (ō·sa·ka) no shi·nai·kyo·ku·ban wa nam·ban des ka
What's the country code for (New Zealand)?	(ニュージーランド)の国番号は何番ですか? (nyū·jī·ran·do) no ku·ni·ban·gō wa nam·ban des ka
It's engaged.	お話中です。 o·ha·na·shi·chū des
I've been cut off.	電話が切れました。 den·wa ga ki·re·mash·ta
The connection's bad.	電話のかかりが悪いです。 den·wa no ka·ka·ri ga wa·ru·i des

LISTEN FOR

ちょっと待ってください。	chot·to mat·te ku·da·sai	One moment.
どなたですか?	do·na·ta des ka	Who's calling?
どなたに代わりましょうか?	do·na·ta ni ka·wa·ri·ma·shō ka	Who do you want to speak to?
…はいません。	... wa i·ma·sen	... is not here.
間違い電話です。	ma·chi·gai·den·wa des	Wrong number.

Hello. It's ...	もしもし。…です。 mo·shi·mo·shi ... des
Is ... there?	…はいらっしゃいますか? ... wa i·ras·shai·mas ka
Please tell them I called.	私が電話したとお伝えください。 wa·ta·shi ga den·wa shi·ta to o·tsu·ta·e ku·da·sai
Can I leave a message?	伝言をお願いできますか? den·gon o o·ne·gai de·ki·mas ka
My number is ...	私の電話番号は…です。 wa·ta·shi no den·wa·ban·gō wa ... des
I'll call back later.	また後で電話します。 ma·ta a·to de den·wa shi·mas

MOBILE/CELL PHONE

I'd like a ... …をお願いします。 ... o o·ne·gai shi·mas

charger for my phone	携帯電話の充電器	kē·tai·den·wa no jū·den·ki
prepaid mobile/ cell phone	プリペイドの携帯電話	pu·ri·pē·do no kē·tai·den·wa
SIM card	SIMカード	shi·mu·kā·do

What are the rates? 通話料金はいくらですか? tsū·wa·ryō·kin wa i·ku·ra des ka

(10) yen per (1) minute. (1)分間(10)円。 (ip)·pun·kan (jū)·en

INTERNET

Do you have internet access here? ここでインターネットは使えますか? ko·ko de in·tā·net·to wa tsu·ka·e·mas ka

Is there wi-fi here?	ここはワイファイがありますか? ko·ko wa wai·fai ga a·ri·mas·ka
Can I connect my laptop here?	私のノートパソコンに接続してもいいですか？ wa·ta·shi no nō·to·pa·so·kon ni se·tsu·zo·ku shi·te mo ī des ka
Do you have PCs?	PCがありますか? pī·shī ga a·ri·mas ka
Do you have Macs?	マッキントッシュがありますか? mak·kin·tos·shu ga a·ri·mas ka
Do you have headphones (with a microphone)?	（マイク付きの）ヘッドフォンがありますか？ (mai·ku tsu·ki no) hed·do·fōn ga a·ri·mas ka

あなたの電話番号は何番ですか?
a·na·ta no den·wa·ban·gō wa nam·ban des ka
What's your phone number?

I'd like to ...	…したいのですが。 ... shi·tai no des ga

check my email	Eメールをチェック	ī·mē·ru o chek·ku
download photos	写真をダウンロード	sha·shin o down·rōd
use a printer	プリント	prin·to
use a scanner	スキャン	skyan

How much per hour?	1時間いくらですか? i·chi·ji·kan i·ku·ra des ka
How much per (five) minutes?	(5)分間いくらですか? (go)·fun·kan i·ku·ra des ka
How much per page?	1ページいくらですか? i·chi·pē·ji i·ku·ra des ka
How do I log on?	どうすればログオンできますか? dō·su·re ba ro·gu·on de·ki·mas ka
Please change it to the English-language setting.	英語のセッティングにしてください。 ē·go no set·tin·gu ni shi·te ku·da·sai
It's crashed.	クラッシュしています。 ku·ras·shu shi·te i·mas
I've finished.	終わりました。 o·wa·ri·mash·ta

Money & Banking

KEY PHRASES

How much is it?	いくらですか?	i·ku·ra des ka
What's the exchange rate?	為替レートはいくらですか?	ka·wa·se·rē·to wa i·ku·ra des ka
Where's an ATM?	ATMはどこですか?	ē·tī·e·mu wa do·ko des ka

Japan is still a cash-based country, although credit cards are becoming more common – carry some yen with you and don't assume you can use credit cards at restaurants, hotels and shops. For more info on the availibility of various methods of payment, see Lonely Planet's guidebook to Japan.

PAYING THE BILL

Q **How much is it?**	いくらですか? i·ku·ra des ka
A **It's free.**	ただです。 ta·da des
A **It's (4000) yen.**	(4000)円です。 (yon·sen)·en des
Do you accept credit cards?	クレジットカードで支払えますか? ku·re·jit·to·kā·do de shi·ha·ra·e·mas ka
Do you accept debit cards?	デビットカードで支払えますか? de·bit·to· kā·do de shi·ha·ra·e·mas ka

I'd like a receipt, please.	レシートをお願いします。 re·shī·to o o·ne·gai shi·mas
I'd like my change, please.	お釣りをお願いします。 o·tsu·ri o o·ne·gai shi·mas
There's a mistake in the bill.	請求書に間違いが あります。 sē·kyū·sho ni ma·chi·gai ga a·ri·mas

BANKING

Where's an ATM?	ATMはどこですか? ē·tī·e·mu wa do·ko des ka
Where's a foreign exchange counter?	外国為替の 窓口はどこですか? gai·ko·ku·ka·wa·se no ma·do·gu·chi wa do·ko des ka
What time does the bank open?	銀行は何時に開きますか? gin·kō wa nan·ji ni hi·ra·ki·mas ka
Where can I ...?	どこで…できますか? do·ko de ... de·ki·mas ka
I'd like to ...	…をお願いします。 ... o o·ne·gai shi·mas

cash a cheque	小切手の現金化	ko·git·te no gen·kin·ka
change money	両替	ryō·ga·e
get a cash advance	キャッシュアドバンス	kyas·shu·a·do·ban·su

LISTEN FOR

身分証明書	mi·bun·shō·mē·sho	identification
ここにサインをお願いします。	ko·ko ni sain o o·ne·gai shi·mas	Sign here.
残高がありません。	zan·da·ka ga a·ri·ma·sen	You have no funds left.

Do you change money here?	ここで両替できますか? ko·ko de ryō·ga·e de·ki·mas ka
What's the charge?	料金はいくらですか? ryō·kin wa i·ku·ra des ka
What's the exchange rate?	為替レートはいくらですか? ka·wa·se·rē·to wa i·ku·ra des ka
The ATM took my card.	ATMにカードを取られてしまいました。 ē·tī·e·mu ni kā·do o to·ra·re·te shi·mai·mash·ta
I've forgotten my PIN.	暗証番号を忘れました。 an·shō·ban·gō o wa·su·re·mash·ta
Can I use my credit card to withdraw money?	クレジットカードで現金を引き出せますか? ku·re·jit·to·kā·do de gen·kin o hi·ki·da·se·mas ka
Has my money arrived yet?	お金は届いていますか? o·ka·ne wa to·doy·te i·mas ka

Business

KEY PHRASES

I'm attending a conference.	会議に出席します。	kai·gi ni shus·se·ki shi·mas
I have an appointment with ...	…とアポがあります。	... to a·po ga a·ri·mas
Can I please have your business card?	名刺をいただけませんか?	mē·shi o i·ta·da·ke·ma·sen ka

DOING BUSINESS

I'm attending a conference.	会議に出席します。 kai·gi ni shus·se·ki shi·mas
I'm attending a meeting.	ミーティングに出席します。 mī·tin·gu ni shus·se·ki shi·mas
I'm attending a trade fair.	展示会に出席します。 ten·ji·kai ni shus·se·ki shi·mas
I'm attending a course.	コースに出席します。 kōs ni shus·se·ki shi·mas
I'm with (Mr Suzuki).	(鈴木さん)といっしょです。 (su·zu·ki·san) to is·sho des
I'm with (two) others.	ほかの(2人)といっしょです。 ho·ka no (fu·ta·ri) to is·sho des
I'm with my colleagues.	同僚といっしょです。 dō·ryō to is·sho des

CULTURE TIP: BUSINESS CARDS

Business cards (mē·shi 名刺) are exchanged at the start of the meeting. Hand over your card with the writing facing the receiver so they can read it, and preferably hold the card with both hands.

Always read the card you're given on the spot, and treat it with care. Never write on the card, fold it or leave it behind as this is interpreted as a sign of disrespect.

During a meeting, it's best to keep the card in front of you on the table – file it away at the end of the meeting.

Q **Can I please have your business card?**	名刺をいただけませんか? mē·shi o i·ta·da·ke·ma·sen ka
A **Here's my business card.**	これが私の 名刺です。 ko·re ga wa·ta·shi no mē·shi des
Q **What's your ...?**	あなたの…は何ですか? a·na·ta no ... wa nan des ka
A **Here's my ...**	これが私の…です。 ko·re ga wa·ta·shi no ... des

address	住所	jū·sho
email address	Eメール アドレス	ī·mē·ru· a·do·res
mobile number	携帯番号	kē·tai·ban·gō
work number	仕事の 電話番号	shi·go·to no den·wa·ban·gō

CULTURE TIP: BUSINESS ETIQUETTE

Always give ample notice of your visit and start a meeting by exchanging business cards. A small present representing your country or company always goes down well.

The seating is linked to status, so wait to be directed to your seat and don't sit (or stand) before the person highest in the pecking order does. Never initiate the use of first names – let your Japanese contacts decide. It's more likely that titles will be used instead.

Don't try to rush or push decisions. Entertainment makes part of the process so try not to skip these occasions. Be aware, though, that talking business during a meal is a no-no and that controversial topics are better avoided.

I have an appointment with ...	…とアポがあります。 ... to a·po ga a·ri·mas
I need ...	…が必要です。 ... ga hi·tsu·yō des

a computer	コンピュータ	kom·pyū·ta
an internet connection	インターネットの接続	in·tā·net·to no se·tsu·zo·ku
an interpreter	通訳	tsū·ya·ku
more business cards	もっと名刺	mot·to mē·shi
some space to set up	セットアップするスペース	set·to·ap·pu su·ru spēs

Where's the business centre?	ビジネスセンターはどこですか? bi·ji·nes·sen·tā wa do·ko des ka

Where's the conference?	会議はどこですか? kai·gi wa do·ko des ka
Where's the meeting?	ミーティングはどこですか? mī·tin·gu wa do·ko des ka
Thank you for your time.	お時間をどうもありがとうございました。 o·ji·kan o dō·mo a·ri·ga·tō go·zai·mash·ta
Shall we go for a drink?	飲みに行きましょうか? no·mi ni i·ki·ma·shō ka
Shall we go for a meal?	食事に行きましょうか? sho·ku·ji ni i·ki·ma·shō ka
It's on me.	私のおごりです。 wa·ta·shi no o·go·ri des

See **eating out** (p172) for more food and drink phrases. See **going out** (p132) for arranging social get-togethers.

Sightseeing

KEY PHRASES

I'd like a guide.	ガイドをお願いします。	gai·do o o·ne·gai shi·mas
Can I take photographs?	写真を撮ってもいいですか?	sha·shin o tot·temo ī des ka
What time does it open?	何時に開きますか?	nan·ji ni a·ki·mas ka
I'm interested in ...	…に興味があります。	... ni kyō·mi ga a·ri·mas

I'd like a/an ...
…をお願いします
... o o·ne·gai shi·mas

audio set	オーディオセット	ō·di·o·set·to
catalogue	パンフレット	pan·fu·ret·to
guide	ガイド	gai·do
(local) map	(市街) 地図	(shi·gai) chi·zu

Do you have information on cultural sights?
文化的見どころについての案内はありますか?
bun·ka·te·ki mi·do·ko·ro ni tsu·i·te no an·nai wa a·ri·mas ka

Do you have information on historical sights?
史跡についての案内はありますか?
shi·se·ki ni tsu·i·te no an·nai wa a·ri·mas ka

LANGUAGE TIP: SAY CHEEEEEESE!

When taking a picture of your Japanese friends and acquaintances, ensure their attention – and best smiles – with hai, chī·zu (ハイ、チーズ), 'Say cheese!'

Do you have information on religious sights?	宗教的見どころについての案内はありますか? shū·kyō·te·ki mi·do·ko·ro ni tsu·i·te no an·nai wa a·ri·mas ka
I'd like to see ...	…を見ようと思います。 ... o mi·yō to o·moy·mas
What's that?	あれは何ですか? a·re wa nan des ka
How old is it?	どのくらい古いですか? do·no ku·rai fu·ru·i des ka
Could you take a photo of me?	私の写真を撮ってもらえませんか? wa·ta·shi no sha·shin o tot·te mo·ra·e·ma·sen ka
Can I take a photograph (of you)?	(あなたの)写真を撮ってもいいですか? (a·na·ta no) sha·shin o tot·te mo ī des ka

GETTING IN

What time does it open?	何時に開きますか? nan·ji ni a·ki·mas ka
What time does it close?	何時に閉まりますか? nan·ji ni shi·ma·ri·mas ka
Can I take photographs?	写真を撮ってもいいですか? sha·shin o tot·temo ī des ka

What's the admission charge?	入場料はいくらですか? nyū·jō·ryō wa i·ku·ra des ka
Is there a discount for ...?	…割引がありますか? ...wa·ri·bi·ki ga a·ri·mas ka

children	子供	ko·do·mo
families	家族	ka·zo·ku
groups	グループ	gu·rū·pu
older people	高齢者	kō·rē·sha
students	学生	gak·sē

GALLERIES & MUSEUMS

Q **What's in the collection?**	所蔵品には何がありますか? sho·zō·hin ni wa na·ni ga a·ri·mas ka
A **It's a/an ... exhibition.**	…の展覧会です。 ... no ten·ran·kai des
I like the works of ...	…の作品が好きです。 ... no sa·ku·hin ga su·ki des
I'm interested in ...	…に興味があります。 ... ni kyō·mi ga a·ri·mas

(Edo) art	(江戸)アート	(e·do) ā·to
calligraphy	書道	sho·dō
ceramics	陶芸	tō·gē
ink painting	水墨画	su·i·bo·ku·ga
ukiyo-e prints	浮世絵	u·ki·yo·e
yamato-e (Japanese painting)	大和絵	ya·ma·to·e

TOURS

Can you recommend a tour?	おすすめのツアーは ありますか? o·su·su·me no tsu·ā wa a·ri·mas ka
When's the next (boat) tour?	次の(ボート)ツアーは いつですか? tsu·gi no (bō·to) tsu·ā wa i·tsu des ka
When's the next day trip?	次の1日観光は いつですか? tsu·gi no i·chi·ni·chi kan·kō wa i·tsu des ka
Is accommodation included?	宿泊料は 含まれていますか? shu·ku·ha·ku·ryō wa fu·ku·ma·re·te i·mas ka

何時に開きますか?
nan·ji ni a·ki·mas ka
What time does it open?

CULTURE TIP: JAPANESE THEATRE

For a night of culture in Japan, choose from the many forms of contemporary or classical theatre. Well-known traditional forms include bun·ra·ku (文楽), puppet theatre involving large puppets manipulated by up to three puppeteers; ka·bu·ki (歌舞伎), a combination of dancing and speaking in conventional intonation patterns and performed exclusively by men; and nō (能), a Zen-influenced classical dance-drama including a chorus, drummers and a flautist. Comedy performances include man·zai (漫才), a dialogue in which witticisms are exchanged on current themes; ra·ku·go (落語) – literally meaning 'dropped word' – a traditional monologue ending in a punch line; and kyō·gen (狂言), comic vignettes in everyday language performed in between *no* performances.

Is food included?	食事代は 含まれていますか? sho·ku·ji·dai wa fu·ku·ma·re·te i·mas ka
Is transport included?	交通費は 含まれていますか? kō·tsū·hi wa fu·ku·ma·re·te i·mas ka
How long is the tour?	ツアーにかかる時間は どのくらいですか? tsu·ā ni ka·ka·ru ji·kan wa do·no ku·rai des ka
I've lost my group.	グループから はぐれました。 gu·rū·pu ka·ra ha·gu·re·mash·ta

Accessible Travel

KEY PHRASES

I need assistance.	手を貸してください。	te o ka·shi·te ku·da·sai
Is there wheel-chair access?	車椅子で入れますか?	ku·ru·ma·i·su de hai·re·mas ka
Are there disabled toilets?	障害者用トイレはありますか?	shō·gai·sha·yō·toy·re wa a·ri·mas ka

I have a disability.	私は障害者です。 wa·ta·shi wa shō·gai·sha des
I need assistance.	手を貸してください。 te o ka·shi·te ku·da·sai
Are there disabled toilets?	障害者用トイレはありますか? shō·gai·sha·yō·toy·re wa a·ri·mas ka
Are there disabled parking spaces?	障害者優先の駐車場はありますか? shō·gai·sha yū·sen no chū·sha·jō wa a·ri·mas ka
Is there wheelchair access?	車椅子で入れますか? ku·ru·ma·i·su de hai·re·mas ka
I have a hearing aid.	補聴器をしています。 ho·chō·ki o shi·te i·mas
Are guide dogs permitted?	盲導犬は入れますか? mō·dō·ken wa hai·re·mas ka

How many steps are there?	段差は何段ありますか? dan·sa wa nan·dan a·ri·mas ka
Is there a lift?	エレベーターはありますか? e·re·bē·tā wa a·ri·mas ka
Are there rails in the bathroom?	バスルームに手すりはありますか? bas·rū·mu ni te·su·ri wa a·ri·mas ka
Could you call me a taxi for the disabled?	障害者用タクシーを呼んでもらえますか? shō·gai·sha·yō·tak·shī o yon·de mo·ra·e·mas ka
Are there train carriages for people with a disability?	障害者のための車両はありますか? shō·gai·sha no ta·me no sha·ryō wa a·ri·mas ka
Could you help me cross the street safely?	道を渡るのを手伝ってもらえますか? mi·chi o wa·ta·ru no o te·tsu·dat·te mo·ra·e·mas ka
Is there somewhere I can sit down?	座れるところはありますか? su·wa·re·ru to·ko·ro wa a·ri·mas ka
guide dog	盲導犬 mō·dō·ken
ramp	スロープ su·rō·pu
walking frame	歩行車 ho·kō·sha
walking stick	杖 tsu·e
wheelchair	車椅子 ku·ru·ma·i·su

Travel with Children

KEY PHRASES

Are children allowed?	子供は入れますか?	ko·do·mo wa hai·re·mas ka
Is there a child discount?	子供割引はありますか?	ko·do·mo·wa·ri·bi·ki wa a·ri·mas ka
Is there a baby change room?	授乳室はありますか?	ju·nyū·shi·tsu wa a·ri·mas ka

Are children allowed?
子供は入れますか?
ko·do·mo wa hai·re·mas ka

Is there a ...?
…はありますか?
... wa a·ri·mas ka

baby change room	授乳室	ju·nyū·shi·tsu
child discount	子供割引	ko·do·mo·wa·ri·bi·ki
child-minding service	託児サービス	ta·ku·ji·sā·bis
children's menu	子供のメニュー	ko·do·mo no me·nyū
crèche	託児所	ta·ku·ji·sho

Do you sell baby wipes?
おしり拭きはありますか?
o·shi·ri·fu·ki wa a·ri·mas ka

Do you sell disposable nappies?
紙おむつはありますか?
ka·mi·o·mu·tsu wa a·ri·mas ka

I need a ... …が必要です。
... ga hi·tsu·yō des

baby seat	ベビーシート	be·bī·shī·to
cot	ベビーベッド	be·bī·bed·do
highchair	ベビーチェア	be·bī·chair
potty	おまる	o·ma·ru
stroller	ベビーカー	be·bī·kā

Where's the nearest toy shop?
この近くの
おもちゃ屋はどこですか?
ko·no chi·ka·ku no
o·mo·cha·ya wa do·ko des ka

Where's the nearest playground?
この近くの遊び場は
どこですか?
ko·no chi·ka·ku no a·so·bi·ba wa
do·ko des ka

Do you hire out strollers?
ベビーカーのレンタルは
ありますか?
be·bī·kā no ren·ta·ru wa
a·ri·mas ka

Where can I change a nappy?
おむつはどこで
換えられますか?
o·mu·tsu wa do·ko de
ka·e·ra·re·mas ka

Do you mind if I breastfeed here?
ここで母乳をあげても
いいですか?
ko·ko de bo·nyū o a·ge·te mo
ī des ka

Is this suitable for ... -year-old children?
これは…歳の
子供向きですか?
ko·re wa ...·sai no
ko·do·mo·mu·ki des ka

To talk about health issues, see **health** (p162).

SOCIAL

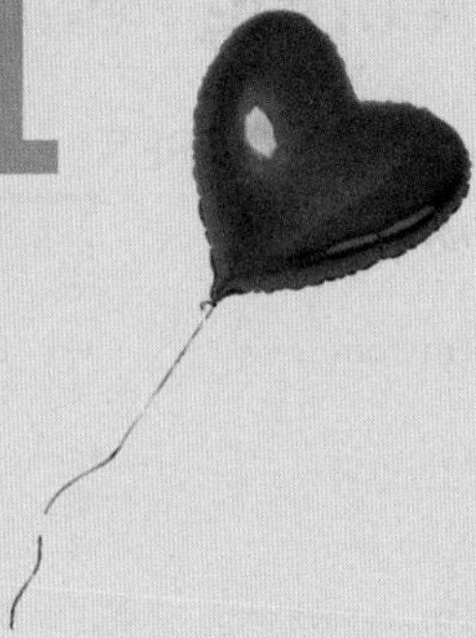

MEETING PEOPLE 112

INTERESTS 122

FEELINGS & OPINIONS 126

GOING OUT 132

ROMANCE 138

BELIEFS & CULTURE 142

SPORTS 145

OUTDOORS 153

Meeting People

KEY PHRASES

My name is ...	私の名前は…です。	wa·ta·shi no na·ma·e wa ... des
I'm from ...	…から来ました。	... ka·ra ki·mash·ta
I work in ...	私は…の仕事をしています。	wa·ta·shi wa ... no shi·go·to o shi·te i·mas
I'm ... years old.	私は…歳です。	wa·ta·shi wa ...·sai des
And you?	あなたは?	a·na·ta wa

BASICS

Yes.	はい。 hai
No.	いいえ。 ī·e
Please. (asking)	ください ku·da·sai
Please. (offering)	どうぞ。 dō·zo
Thank you (very much).	(どうも)ありがとう(ございます)。 (dō·mo) a·ri·ga·tō (go·zai·mas)

You're welcome.	どういたしまして。 dō i·ta·shi·mash·te
Excuse me. (to get attention)	すみません。 su·mi·ma·sen
Sorry.	ごめんなさい。 go·men·na·sai

GREETINGS & GOODBYES

The most common gesture used when greeting is the bow – introducing yourself, greeting, thanking and saying goodbye are all done bowing. Timing, posture and movement of the bow are meant to be a reflection of sincerity, respect and maturity. As a visitor to Japan you're not expected to emulate this ritual faithfully; a gentle nod will do. Kissing and hugging in Japan are rare, except with close friends or family. For handshakes, it's best to wait for the other person to offer their hand if they feel comfortable.

Hello./Hi.	こんにちは。 kon·ni·chi·wa
Good afternoon.	こんにちは。 kon·ni·chi·wa
Good day.	こんにちは。 kon·ni·chi·wa
Good evening.	こんばんは。 kom·ban·wa
Good morning.	おはよう(ございます)。 o·ha·yō (go·zai·mas)
Q **How are you?**	お元気ですか? o·gen·ki des ka
A **Fine. And you?**	はい、元気です。 あなたは? hai, gen·ki des a·na·ta wa

Q (Excuse me,) what's your name?	(失礼ですが、)お名前は何ですか? (shi·tsu·rē des ga) o·na·ma·e wa nan des ka
A My name is ...	私の名前は…です。 wa·ta·shi no na·ma·e wa ... des
I'd like to introduce you to ...	…を紹介します。 ... o shō·kai shi·mas

✂	**This is ...**	こちらは. . . です。	ko·chi·ra wa ... des

This is my ...	こちらは私の…です。 ko·chi·ra wa wa·ta·shi no ... des

child	子供	ko·do·mo
colleague	同僚	dō·ryō
friend	友達	to·mo·da·chi
husband	主人	shu·jin
partner (intimate)	パートナー	pā·to·nā
wife	妻	tsu·ma

For family members, see **family** (p119).

I'm pleased to meet you.	お会いできてうれしいです。 o·ai de·ki·te u·re·shī des
See you later.	また会いましょう。 ma·ta ai·ma·shō
Goodbye.	さようなら。 sa·yō·na·ra

Bye.	じゃ、また。 ja ma·ta
Good night.	おやすみ(なさい)。 o·ya·su·mi (na·sai)
Bon voyage!	よい旅を！ yoy·ta·bi o

ADDRESSING PEOPLE

Avoid using all forms of the second person pronoun 'you' in Japanese speech as it can sound too direct – it will be understood from context who you're referring to when speaking (for more information on pronouns, see **grammar**, p27).

Mr/Ms/Mrs/Miss	…さん ...·san
Sir/Madam	…さま ...·sama

MAKING CONVERSATION

The Japanese love a chat – just avoid criticising aspects of the Japanese culture too vigorously as your comments might be taken quite personally. Never get visibly angry or shout as this leaves a bad impression. For more conversation topics, see **interests** (p122) and **feelings & opinions** (p126).

Isn't it (hot) today?	今日は(暑い)ですね。 kyō wa (a·tsu·i) des ne
What a beautiful day.	素晴らしい日ですね。 su·ba·ra·shī hi des ne
(Nice/Awful/Strange) weather, isn't it?	(いい/ひどい/変な)天気ですね。 (ī/hi·doy/hen·na) ten·ki des ne
Do you live here?	ここに住んでいますか？ ko·ko ni sun·de i·mas ka

☑ LANGUAGE TIP: THE SUFFIX '-SAN'

In Japan people normally call each other by their surname and add the suffix ·san (さん), eg su·zu·ki·san (鈴木さん) – avoid using first names unless invited to do so. It's also common to call people by their title instead of their name, like sha·chō (社長) for a company president and sen·sē (先生) for a doctor or teacher (literally meaning 'master'). You may also notice older people addressing children or young women with the suffix ·chan (ちゃん) as a term of endearment.

Where are you going?	どこに行きますか? do·ko ni i·ki·mas ka
What are you doing?	何をしていますか? na·ni o shi·te i·mas ka
Q **Do you like it here?**	ここが好きですか? ko·ko ga su·ki des ka
I love it here.	ここが大好きです。 ko·ko ga dai·su·ki des
That's (beautiful), isn't it?	(きれい)ですね。 (ki·rē) des ne
Q **Are you here on holidays?**	休暇でここに来ましたか? kyū·ka de ko·ko ni ki·mash·ta ka
A **I'm here for a holiday.**	休暇でここに来ました。 kyū·ka de ko·ko ni ki·mash·ta
A **I'm here on business.**	仕事でここに来ました。 shi·go·to de ko·ko ni ki·mash·ta
A **I'm here to study.**	勉強のためにここに来ました。 ben·kyō no ta·me ni ko·ko ni ki·mash·ta

Ⓠ **How long are you here for?**	いつまでここにいますか? i·tsu ma·de ko·ko ni i·mas ka
Ⓐ **I'm here for (two) weeks.**	ここに(2)週間います。 ko·ko ni (ni)·shū·kan i·mas
Ⓐ **I'm here for (four) days.**	ここに(4)日間います。 ko·ko ni (yok)·ka·kan i·mas

NATIONALITIES

Ⓠ **Where are you from?**	どちらから来ましたか? do·chi·ra ka·ra ki·mash·ta ka
Ⓐ **I'm from (Australia).**	(オーストラリア)から 来ました。 (ō·sto·ra·rya) ka·ra ki·mash·ta

For more countries, see the **dictionary** (p219).

AGE

Talking about age did not use to be a big issue, but the topic is best avoided when speaking to women.

Ⓠ **How old are you?**	おいくつですか? oy·ku·tsu des ka
Ⓐ **I'm ... years old.**	私は…歳です。 wa·ta·shi wa ...·sai des
Ⓠ **How old is your (son/daughter)?**	(息子/娘)さんは おいくつですか? (mu·su·ko/mu·su·me)·san wa oy·ku·tsu des ka
Ⓐ **He's ... years old.**	彼は…歳です。 ka·re wa ...·sai des
Ⓐ **She's ... years old.**	彼女は…歳です。 ka·no·jo wa ...·sai des

(A) Too old!	もう歳です。 mō to·shi des
I'm younger than I look.	私は見た目より 若いです。 wa·ta·shi wa mi·ta·me yo·ri wa·kai des

For your age, see **numbers & amounts** (p36).

OCCUPATIONS & STUDIES

(Q) What's your occupation?	お仕事は何ですか? o·shi·go·to wa nan des ka
(A) I'm a (teacher).	私は(教師)です。 wa·ta·shi wa (kyō·shi) des
I work in (sales).	私は(営業)の 仕事をしています。 wa·ta·shi wa (ē·gyō) no shi·go·to o shi·te i·mas
I'm retired.	私は退職者です。 wa·ta·shi wa tai·sho·ku·sha des
I'm self-employed.	私は自営業者です。 wa·ta·shi wa ji·ē·gyō·sha des
I'm unemployed.	私は失業者です。 wa·ta·shi wa shi·tsu·gyō·sha des
I've been made redundant.	リストラされました。 ri·su·to·ra sa·re·mash·ta
(Q) What are you studying?	何を勉強していますか? na·ni o ben·kyō shi·te i·mas ka
(A) I'm studying (science).	私は(自然科学)を 勉強しています。 wa·ta·shi wa (shi·zen·ka·ga·ku) o ben·kyō shi·te i·mas

FAMILY

Japanese uses different forms for certain words and verbs depending on social context and the specific relationship between the speaker and the listener. One category of such words are the kinship terms, which take different forms depending on whether you're talking about your own family or the listener's family.

	MY		YOUR	
brother	兄弟	**yō·dai**	ご兄弟	**go·kyō·dai**
daughter	娘	**mu·su·me**	娘さん	**mu·su·me·san**
family	家族	**ka·zo·ku**	ご家族	**go·ka·zo·ku**
father	父	**chi·chi**	お父さん	**o·tō·san**
grand-daughter	孫娘	**ma·go·mu·su·me**	孫娘さん	**ma·go·mu·su·me·san**
grand-father	祖父	**so·fu**	おじいさん	**o·jī·san**
grand-mother	祖母	**so·bo**	おばあさん	**o·bā·san**
grandson	孫	**ma·go**	お孫さん	**o·ma·go·san**
husband	夫	**ot·to**	ご主人	**go·shu·jin**
mother	母	**ha·ha**	お母さん	**o·kā·san**
partner	パートナー	**pā·to·nā**	パートナー	**pā·to·nā**
sister	姉妹	**shi·mai**	ご姉妹	**go·shi·mai**
son	息子	**mu·su·ko**	息子さん	**mu·su·ko·san**
wife	妻	**tsu·ma**	奥さん	**o·ku·san**

Q **Do you have a (brother)?** (ご兄弟)がいますか?
(go·kyō·dai) ga i·mas ka

A **I have a (daughter).** (娘)がいます。
(mu·su·me) ga i·mas

A **I don't have a (partner).** (パートナー)がいません。
(pā·to·nā) ga i·ma·sen

Q **Are you married?**	結婚していますか? kek·kon shi·te i·mas ka
A **I'm married.**	私は結婚して います。 wa·ta·shi wa kek·kon shi·te i·mas
A **I'm separated.**	私は離婚しました。 wa·ta·shi wa ri·kon shi·mash·ta
A **I'm single.**	私は独身です。 wa·ta·shi wa do·ku·shin des

TALKING WITH CHILDREN

When's your birthday?	お誕生日はいつ? o·tan·jō·bi wa i·tsu
Do you go to school/ kindergarten?	学校/幼稚園に行っているの? gak·kō/yō·chi·en ni it·te i·ru no
What grade are you in?	何年生? nan·nen·sē
Do you learn English?	英語を勉強してる? ē·go o ben·kyō shi·te·ru
I come from very far away.	私はとても遠く からきたの。 wa·ta·shi wa to·te·mo tō·ku ka·ra ki·ta no

FAREWELLS

Q **What's your (address)?**	あなたの(住所)は何 ですか? a·na·ta no (jū·sho) wa nan des ka
A **Here's my (address).**	これが私の(住所) です。 ko·re ga wa·ta·shi no (jū·sho) des

What's your email address?	あなたのEメールアドレスは何ですか? a·na·ta no ī·mē·ru·a·do·res wa nan des ka
What's your phone number?	あなたの電話番号は何ですか? a·na·ta no den·wa·ban·gō wa nan des ka
Keep in touch.	連絡をとりましょう。 ren·ra·ku o to·ri·ma·shō
It's been great meeting you.	あなたに会えてとてもよかったです。 a·na·ta ni a·e·te to·te·mo yo·kat·ta des

WELL-WISHING

Note that when you're in a more formal situation, you can add go·zai·mas (ございます), 'very much', after some of these wishes.

Bon voyage!	よい旅を! yoy ta·bi o
Congratulations!	おめでとう(ございます)。 o·me·de·tō (go·zai·mas)
Good luck!	がんばって! gam·bat·te
Happy birthday!	誕生日おめでとう(ございます)。 tan·jō·bi o·me·de·tō (go·zai·mas)
Happy New Year!	明けましておめでとう(ございます)。 a·ke·mash·te o·me·de·tō (go·zai·mas)
Look after yourself. (to a sick person)	お大事に。 o·dai·ji ni

Interests

KEY PHRASES

What do you do in your spare time?	ひまなとき何をしますか?	hi·ma na to·ki na·ni o shi·mas ka
Do you like ...?	…が好きですか?	... ga su·ki des ka
I like ...	…が好きです。	... ga su·ki des
I don't like ...	…が好きじゃありません。	... ga su·ki ja a·ri·ma·sen

COMMON INTERESTS

Q **What do you do in your spare time?**	ひまなとき何をしますか? hi·ma na to·ki na·ni o shi·mas ka
A **Do you like (cooking)?**	(料理)が好きですか? (ryō·ri) ga su·ki des ka
A **I like (music).**	(音楽)が好きです。 (on·ga·ku) ga su·ki des
A **I don't like (hiking).**	(ハイキング)が好きじゃありません。 (hai·kin·gu) ga su·ki ja a·ri·ma·sen

For more activities, see **sports** (p145) and the **dictionary**.

MUSIC

What bands do you like?	どんなバンドが好きですか? don·na ban·do ga su·ki des ka

What music do you like?	どんな音楽が好きですか?	**don·na on·ga·ku ga su·ki des ka**
What singers do you like?	どんな歌手が好きですか?	**don·na ka·shu ga su·ki des ka**
Do you ...?	…ますか?	**...·mas ka**

dance	ダンスをし	**dan·su o shi**
go to concerts	コンサートに行き	**kon·sā·to ni i·ki**
listen to music	音楽を聴き	**on·ga·ku o ki·ki**
play an instrument	楽器を演奏し	**gak·ki o en·sō shi**
sing	歌い	**u·tai**

I like...	…が 好きです。	**ga su·ki des**
I don't like...	…が好きじゃありません。	**... ga su·ki ja a·ri·ma·sen**

blues	ブルース	**bu·rū·su**
classical music	クラシック	**ku·ra·shik·ku**
enka (genre of popular ballads)	演歌	**en·ka**
hip hop	ヒップホップ	**hip·pu·hop·pu**
jazz	ジャズ	**ja·zu**
(Japanese) pop	(J-)ポップ	**(jē·)pop·pu**
rock	ロック	**rok·ku**
world music	ワールドミュージック	**wā·ru·do·myū·jik·ku**

See also **going out** (p132).

CULTURE TIP: JAPANESE PASTIMES

While you're in Japan why not try your hand at some local pastimes, such as bon·sai (盆栽; miniature trees), i·ke·ba·na (生け花; flower arranging), o·ri·ga·mi (折り紙; paper folding) or reading man·ga (漫画). Local board games include go (碁) and shō·gi (将棋; Japanese chess).

CINEMA & THEATRE

I feel like going to a ...	…に行こうと思います。 ... ni i·kō to o·moy·mas
What's showing at the cinema/theatre tonight?	今晩はどんな映画/舞台がありますか? kom·ban wa don·na ē·ga/bu·tai ga a·ri·mas ka
Is it in English?	英語ですか? ē·go des ka
Does it have (English) subtitles?	(英語の)字幕がありますか? (ē·go no) ji·ma·ku ga a·ri·mas ka
Is this seat vacant?	この席は空いていますか? ko·no se·ki wa ai·te i·mas ka
Have you seen ...?	…をもう観ましたか? ... o mō mi·mash·ta ka
Q **Who's in it?**	だれが演じていますか? da·re ga en·ji·te i·mas ka
A **It stars ...**	主役は…です。 shu·ya·ku wa ... des
Q **Did you like the film?**	映画はよかったですか? ē·ga wa yo·kat·ta des ka

Ⓠ **Did you like the play?**	劇はよかったですか? ge·ki wa yo·kat·ta des ka
Ⓐ **I thought it was excellent.**	素晴らしかったと思います。 su·ba·ra·shi·kat·ta to o·moy·mas
Ⓐ **I thought it was long.**	長すぎたと思います。 na·ga·su·gi·ta to o·moy·mas
Ⓐ **I thought it was OK.**	まあまあだったと思います。 mā·mā dat·ta to o·moy·mas
I like ...	…が好きです。 ... ga su·ki des
I don't like ...	…が好きじゃ ありません。 ... ga su·ki ja a·ri·ma·sen

action movies	アクションムービー	a·ku·shon·mū·bī
anime films	アニメ	a·ni·me
comedies	コメディ	ko·me·di
drama	ドラマ	do·ra·ma
horror movies	ホラー映画	ho·rā·ē·ga
Japanese cinema	日本映画	ni·hon·ē·ga
sci-fi	SF	e·su·e·fu

Feelings & Opinions

KEY PHRASES

Are you ...?	あなたは…か?	a·na·ta wa ... ka
I'm ...	私は…	wa·ta·shi wa ...
What did you think of it?	どう思いますか?	dō o·moy·mas ka
I thought it was OK.	まあまあだ と思いました。	mā·mā da to o·moy·mash·ta

FEELINGS

Q **Are you ...?**
あなたは…か?
a·na·ta wa ... ka

A **I'm ...**
私は…
wa·ta·shi wa ...

disappointed	がっかり しました	gak·ka·ri shi·mash·ta
embarrassed	恥ずかしいです	ha·zu·ka·shī des
happy	幸せです	shi·a·wa·se des
sad	悲しいです	ka·na·shī des
thirsty	のどが 渇きました	no·do ga ka·wa·ki·mash·ta
tired	疲れました	tsu·ka·re·mash·ta
worried	心配しています	shim·pai shi·te i·mas

I'm (a little) sad.	（ちょっと）悲しいです。 (chot·to) ka·na·shī des
I'm (extremely) sorry.	（本当に）すみません。 (hon·tō ni) su·mi·ma·sen
I feel (very) lucky.	（とても）運が良かったと思います。 (to·te·mo) un ga yo·kat·ta to o·moy·mas

If feeling unwell, see **health** (p162).

OPINIONS

Q **Did you like it?**	好きですか? su·ki des ka
A **I thought it was ...**	…と思いました。 ... to o·moy·mash·ta
Q **What do you think of it?**	どう思いますか? dō o·moy·mas ka
A **It's ...**	…です。 ... des

awful	ひどい	hi·doy
beautiful	美しい	u·tsu·ku·shī
boring	つまらない	tsu·ma·ra·nai
great	素晴らしい	su·ba·ra·shī
interesting	面白い	o·mo·shi·roy

I thought it was OK.	まあまあだと思いました。 mā·mā da to o·moy·mash·ta
I thought it was strange.	変だと思いました。 hen da to o·moy·mash·ta

☑ CULTURE TIP: TAKING A COMPLIMENT

You'll be complimented on your language skills when making even the slightest effort to speak Japanese. If you're able to respond to these pats on the back in a typically modest Japanese fashion, you'll be even more sure to impress. When they say 'Your Japanese is so good' (日本語がお上手ですね。 ni·hon·go ga o·jō·zu des ne), you could answer with 'It's not really' (それほどでも。 so·re·ho·do de·mo).

POLITICS & SOCIAL ISSUES

The Japanese generally tend not to discuss politics openly and avoid mentioning which party they support. Be aware that bold statements regarding Japan and Japanese culture might be taken quite personally and are better avoided.

Q **Who do you vote for?**	だれに投票しますか? da·re ni tō·hyō shi·mas ka
A **I support the ... party.**	私は…党を支持します。 wa·ta·shi wa ...·tō o shi·ji shi·mas

communist	共産	kyō·san
conservative	保守	ho·shu
democratic	民主	min·shu
green	緑の	mi·do·ri no
liberal (progressive)	由	ji·yū
liberal democratic	自民	ji·min
social democratic	社会民主	sha·kai·min·shu
socialist	社会	sha·kai

Did you hear about ...?	…について聞きましたか? ... ni tsu·i·te ki·ki·mash·ta ka
Q Do you agree with it?	それに賛成しますか? so·re ni san·sē shi·mas ka
A I agree with ...	…に賛成します。 ... ni san·sē shi·mas
A I don't agree with ...	…に賛成しません。 ... ni san·sē shi·ma·sen
How do people feel about the economy?	みんなは経済について どう思っていますか? min·na wa kē·zai ni tsu·i·te dō o·mot·te i·mas ka
How do people feel about the environment?	みんなは環境について どう思っていますか? min·na wa kan·kyō ni tsu·i·te dō o·mot·te i·mas ka

美しいです。
u·tsu·ku·shī des
It's beautiful.

How do people feel about the war in ...?	みんなは…戦争について どう思っていますか? min·na wa ...:sen·sō ni tsu·i·te dō o·mot·te i·mas ka
How do people feel about immigration?	みんなは移民について どう思っていますか? min·na wa i·min ni tsu·i·te dō o·mot·te i·mas ka

ENVIRONMENT

Is there a ... problem here?	ここには…の問題が ありますか? ko·ko ni wa ... no mon·dai ga a·ri·mas ka
What should be done about ...?	…について何を しなければなりませんか? ... ni tsu·i·te na·ni o shi·na·ke·re·ba na·ri·ma·sen ka

climate change	気候変動	ki·kō hen·dō
greenhouse effect	温室効果	on·shi·tsu·kō·ka
nuclear energy	原子力	gen·shi·ryo·ku
pollution	公害	kō·gai
recycling	リサイクル	ri·sai·ku·ru
whaling	捕鯨	ho·gē

Where can I recycle this?	これはどこでリサイクル できますか? ko·re wa do·ko de ri·sai·ku·ru de·ki·mas ka

☑ CULTURE TIP: GIVING GIFTS

It's good manners to exchange some niceties when giving or receiving presents. In addition to a simple thank you, the recipient of the present could add 'You shouldn't have bothered' (そんなに気を使わなくてもよかったのに。 son·na ni ki o tsu·ka·wa·na·ku·te mo yo·kat·ta no ni), to which the giver could reply 'It's my pleasure' (どういたしまして。dō i·ta·shi mash·te) or 'It's nothing really' (つまらないものですが。tsu·ma·ra·nai mo·no des ga).

Is this a protected park?	これは保護されている 公園ですか? ko·re wa ho·go sa·re·te i·ru kō·en des ka
Is this a protected species?	これは保護されている 生物ですか? ko·re wa ho·go sa·re·te i·ru sē·bu·tsu des ka
Is this a protected forest?	これは保護されている 森ですか? ko·re wa ho·go sa·re·te i·ru mo·ri des ka

Going Out

KEY PHRASES

What's on tonight?	今夜は何がありますか?	kon·ya wa na·ni ga a·ri·mas ka
What time shall we meet?	何時に会いましょうか?	nan·ji ni ai·ma·shō ka
Where shall we meet?	どこで会いましょうか?	do·ko de ai·ma·shō ka

WHERE TO GO

What's on this weekend?	今週の週末は何がありますか? kon·shū no shū·ma·tsu wa na·ni ga a·ri·mas ka
What's on today?	今日は何がありますか? kyō wa na·ni ga a·ri·mas ka
What's on tonight?	今夜は何がありますか? kon·ya wa na·ni ga a·ri·mas ka
Where can I find ...?	どこに行けば…がありますか? do·ko ni i·ke·ba ... ga a·ri·mas ka

clubs	クラブ	ku·ra·bu
gay venues	ゲイの場所	gē no ba·sho
Japanese-style pubs	居酒屋	i·za·ka·ya
places to eat	食事ができる所	sho·ku·ji ga de·ki·ru to·ko·ro
pubs	パブ	pa·bu

Is there a local entertainment guide?	地元のエンターテイメントガイドはありますか? ji·mo·to no en·tā·tē·men·to gai·do wa a·ri·mas ka
Is there a local film/music guide?	地元の映画/音楽ガイドはありますか? ji·mo·to no ē·ga/on·ga·ku gai·do wa a·ri·mas ka
I feel like going to a ...	…に行きたい気分です。 ... ni i·ki·tai ki·bun des

ballet	バレエ	ba·rē
bar	バー	bā
cafe	カフェ	ka·fe
concert	コンサート	kon·sā·to
film	映画	ē·ga
karaoke bar	カラオケ	ka·ra·o·ke
nightclub	ナイトクラブ	nai·to·ku·ra·bu
party	パーティー	pā·tī
play	劇	ge·ki
restaurant	レストラン	res·to·ran

For more on bars and drinks, see **eating out** (p172).

INVITATIONS

What are you doing now?	これから何をする予定ですか? ko·re·ka·ra na·ni o su·ru yo·tē des ka
What are you doing this weekend?	今週の週末何をする予定ですか? kon·shū no shū·ma·tsu na·ni o su·ru yo·tē des ka

What are you doing tonight?	今夜何をする予定ですか? kon·ya na·ni o su·ru yo·tē des ka
Would you like to go (for a) ...?	…に行きませんか? ... ni i·ki·ma·sen ka
Would you like to go for a coffee?	コーヒーに行きませんか? kō·hī ni i·ki·ma·sen ka
Would you like to go out somewhere?	どこか外に行きませんか? do·ko ka so·to ni i·ki·ma·sen ka
Do you know a good restaurant?	いいレストランを知っていますか? ī res·to·ran o shit·te i·mas ka
Do you want to come to the concert with me?	いっしょにコンサートに行きませんか? is·sho ni kon·sā·to ni i·ki·ma·sen ka
We're having a party.	パーティーをします。 pā·tī o shi·mas
You should come.	来てください。 ki·te ku·da·sai
My round.	私の番です。 wa·ta·shi no ban des

RESPONDING TO INVITATIONS

Sure!	もちろん! mo·chi·ron
Yes, I'd love to.	はい、ぜひとも。 hai, ze·hi to·mo
That's very kind of you.	親切にありがとう。 shin·se·tsu ni a·ri·ga·tō
Where shall we go?	どこに行きましょうか? do·ko ni i·ki·ma·shō ka

No, I'm afraid I can't.	すみませんが、ちょっと 都合が悪いんです。 su·mi·ma·sen ga, chot·to tsu·gō ga wa·ru·in des
What about tomorrow?	明日はどうですか? a·shi·ta wa dō des ka
Sorry, I can't sing.	ごめんなさい、歌えないんです。 go·men·na·sai, u·ta·e·nain des

ARRANGING TO MEET

Q **What time shall we meet?**	何時に会いましょうか? nan·ji ni ai·ma·shō ka
A **Let's meet at (eight) o'clock.**	(8)時に会いましょう。 (ha·chi)·ji ni ai·ma·shō
Where shall we meet?	どこで会いましょうか? do·ko de ai·ma·shō ka
Let's meet at (the entrance).	(入口)で会いましょう。 (i·ri·gu·chi) de ai·ma·shō
I'll pick you up.	迎えに行きます。 mu·ka·e ni i·ki·mas

コーヒーに行きませんか?
kō·hī ni i·ki·ma·sen ka
Would you like to go for a coffee?

CULTURE TIP: KARAOKE

Karaoke boxes (ka·ra·o·ke·bok·kus カラオケボックス) – rooms for karaoke that can be booked on an hourly basis and where you can also be served food and drinks – are hugely popular in Japan. A few phrases that might come in handy while out singing: 'Let's sing together' (いっしょに歌いましょう。is·sho ni u·tai·ma·shō), 'Are there English songs?' (英語の曲がありますか? ē·go no kyo·ku ga a·ri·mas ka), 'I don't know this song' (この曲は知りません。ko·no kyo·ku wa shi·ri·ma·sen), and, for when you'd rather just watch, 'I'm not good at singing' (歌うのが上手じゃありません。u·ta·u no ga jō·zu ja a·ri·ma·sen).

Q **Are you ready?**	準備はいいですか? jum·bi wa ī des ka
A **I'm ready.**	準備はいいです。 jum·bi wa ī des
I'll be coming later.	遅れて行きます。 o·ku·re·te i·ki·mas
Where will you be?	どこにいますか? do·ko ni i·mas ka
If I'm not there by (nine), don't wait for me.	(9)時までに私が行かなかったら待たないでください。 (ku)·ji ma·de ni wa·ta·shi ga i·ka·na·kat·ta·ra ma·ta·nai de ku·da·sai
OK!	OK! ō·kē
I'll see you there.	じゃ、そこで会いましょう。 ja, so·ko de ai·ma·shō

See you later.	あとで会いましょう。 a·to de ai·ma·shō
See you tomorrow.	明日会いましょう。 a·shi·ta ai·ma·shō
I'm looking forward to it.	楽しみにしています。 ta·no·shi·mi ni shi·te i·mas
Sorry I'm late.	遅れてすみません。 o·ku·re·te su·mi·ma·sen
Never mind.	だいじょうぶです。 dai·jō·bu des

DRUGS

I don't take drugs.	麻薬はやりません。 ma·ya·ku wa ya·ri·ma·sen
I take ... occasionally.	ときどき…をやります。 to·ki·do·ki ... o ya·ri·mas
Do you want to have a smoke?	吸いたいですか? su·i·tai des ka
Do you have a light?	火はありますか? hi wa a·ri·mas ka

Romance

KEY PHRASES

Will you go out with me?	付き合いませんか?	tsu·ki·ai·ma·sen ka
I love you.	愛しています。	ai shi·te i·mas
Leave me alone, please.	独りにしておいてください。	hi·to·ri ni shi·te oy·te ku·da·sai
Would you like a drink?	何か飲みませんか?	na·ni ka no·mi·ma·sen ka

ASKING SOMEONE OUT

Q **Would you like to do something (tomorrow)?**	(明日)何かしませんか? (a·shi·ta) na·ni ka shi·ma·sen ka
A **Yes, I'd love to.**	はい、ぜひとも。 hai, ze·hi to·mo
A **Sorry, I can't.**	すみません、行けません。 su·mi·ma·sen, i·ke·ma·sen
Where would you like to go (tonight)?	(今晩)どこに行きたいですか? (kom·ban) do·ko ni i·ki·tai des ka

PICK-UP LINES

Would you like a drink?	何か飲みませんか? na·ni ka no·mi·ma sen ka
What would you like?	何を飲みますか? na·ni o no·mi·mas ka

You look like someone I know.	私の知っている人によく似ています。 wa·ta·shi no shit·te i·ru hi·to ni yo·ku ni·te i·mas
You're a fantastic dancer.	踊りがすごくうまいですね。 o·do·ri ga su·go·ku u·mai des ne
How about some tea?	お茶しませんか? o·cha shi·ma·sen ka
Here's my phone number.	これが私の電話番号。 ko·re ga wa·ta·shi no den·wa·ban·gō
Do you want to come to my place?	うちに来ない? u·chi ni ko·nai
Can I sit here?	ここに座ってもいいですか? ko·ko ni su·wat·te mo ī des ka
Can I dance with you?	いっしょに踊ってもいいですか? is·sho ni o·dot·te mo ī des ka
Can I take you home?	お宅まで送ってもいいですか? o·ta·ku ma·de o·kut·te mo ī des ka

REJECTIONS

I'm here with my boyfriend/girlfriend.	彼氏/彼女と一緒なんです。 ka·re·shi/ka·no·jo to is·sho nan des
I'm with someone.	連れがいますので。 tsu·re ga i·mas no·de
I'm married.	私は結婚しています。 wa·ta·shi wa kek·kon shi·te i·mas

Excuse me, I have to go now.	すみませんが、もう 行かなくてはなりません。 su·mi·ma·sen ga, mō i·ka·na·ku·te wa na·ri·ma·sen
No, thank you.	いいえ、けっこうです。 ī·e, kek·kō des
Leave me alone, please.	独りにしておいてください。 hi·to·ri ni shi·te oy·te ku·da·sai
Go away!	あっちへ行け! at·chi e i·ke
Stop it!	やめて! ya·me·te

GETTING CLOSER

I like you very much.	あなたがとても好き。 a·na·ta ga to·te·mo su·ki
Can I kiss you?	キスしてもいい? ki·su shi·te mo ī
Do you want to come inside for a while?	ちょっと、うちに寄って いきませんか? chot·to u·chi ni yot·te i·ki·ma·sen ka
Can I stay over?	泊まってもいいですか? to·mat·te mo ī des ka

SEX

Let's go to bed.	ベッドに行きましょう。 bed·do ni i·ki·ma·shō
Let's use a (condom).	(コンドーム)を 使いましょう。 (kon·dō·mu) o tsu·kai·ma·shō

I think we should stop now.	これ以上はやめましょう。 ko·re i·jō wa ya·me·ma·shō
That was amazing.	すばらしかったです。 su·ba·ra·shi·kat·ta des

LOVE

I love you.	愛しています。 ai shi·te i·mas
I think we're good together.	いいカップルだと思います。 ī kap·pu·ru da to o·moy·mas
Will you go out with me?	付き合いませんか? tsu·ki·ai·ma·sen ka
Will you marry me?	結婚しませんか? kek·kon shi·ma·sen ka

☑ LANGUAGE TIP: TERMS OF ENDEARMENT

The Japanese are generally more reserved about expressing emotions than some other cultures, so pet names are a lot less used than elsewhere. However, some couples use nicknames derived from their first name. They might affectionately abbreviate each other's first name and add the suffix ·chan (ちゃん) expressing endearment: eg ta·ke·chan (たけちゃん) for ta·ke·shi (たけし) or ha·na·chan (はなちゃん) for ha·na·ko (はなこ).

Beliefs & Culture

KEY PHRASES

What's your religion?	あなたの宗教は何ですか?	a·na·ta no shū·kyō wa nan des ka
I'm ...	私は…です。	wa·ta·shi wa ... des
I'm sorry, it's against my beliefs.	すみませんが、それは私の信仰に反します。	su·mi·ma·sen ga so·re wa wa·ta·shi no shin·kō ni han·shi·mas

RELIGION

Q **What's your religion?**
あなたの宗教は何ですか?
a·na·ta no shū·kyō wa nan des ka

A **I'm not religious.**
私はあまり宗教的ではありません。
wa·ta·shi wa a·ma·ri shū·kyō·te·ki de wa a·ri·ma·sen

A **I'm ...**
私は…です。
wa·ta·shi wa ... des

agnostic	不可知論者	fu·ka·chi·ron·ja
atheist	無神論者	mu·shin·ron·ja
Buddhist	仏教徒	buk·kyō·to
Christian	キリスト教徒	ki·ri·su·to·kyō·to
Hindu	ヒンドゥー教徒	hin·dū·kyō·to
Jewish	ユダヤ教徒	yu·da·ya·kyō·to
Muslim	イスラム教徒	i·su·ra·mu·kyō·to

I believe in (God).	(神)を信じています。 (ka·mi) o shin·ji·te i·mas
I don't believe in (astrology).	(星占い)を信じていません。 (ho·shi·u·ra·nai) o shin·ji·te i·ma·sen
Where can I attend a service?	どこで礼拝に参加できますか? do·ko de rē·hai ni san·ka de·ki·mas ka
Where can I attend mass?	どこでミサに参加できますか? do·ko de mi·sa ni san·ka de·ki·mas ka
Where can I meditate?	どこで瞑想できますか? do·ko de mē·sō de·ki·mas ka
Where can I pray?	どこでお祈りできますか? do·ko de oy·no·ri de·ki·mas ka

CULTURAL DIFFERENCES

Is this a local custom?	これは地元の習慣ですか? ko·re wa ji·mo·to no shū·kan des ka
I don't want to offend you.	不愉快な思いをさせたくありません。 fu·yu·kai na o·moy o sa·se·ta·ku a·ri·ma·sen
I didn't mean to do anything wrong.	悪意でやったわけではありません。 a·ku·i de yat·ta wa·ke de wa a·ri·ma·sen
I'm not used to this.	これに慣れていません。 ko·re ni na·re·te i·ma·sen

I'd rather not join in.	参加を辞退したいと 思います。 san·ka o ji·tai shi·tai to o·moy·mas
I'll try it.	やってみます。 yat·te mi·mas
I'm sorry, it's against my beliefs.	すみませんが、それは 私の信仰に 反します。 su·mi·ma·sen ga so·re wa wa·ta·shi no shin·kō ni han·shi·mas
I'm sorry, it's against my religion.	すみませんが、それは 私の宗教に 反します。 su·mi·ma·sen ga so·re wa wa·ta·shi no shū·kyō ni han·shi·mas
This is different.	これは変わっています。 ko·re wa ka·wat·te i·mas
This is fun.	これは楽しいです。 ko·re wa ta·no·shī des
This is interesting.	これはおもしろいです。 ko·re wa o·mo·shi·roy des

For phrases relating to cultural differences and food, see **vegetarian & special meals** (p193).

Sports

KEY PHRASES

What sport do you play?	どんなスポーツをしますか?	don·na spō·tsu o shi·mas ka
Who's your favourite team?	どのチームがいちばん好きですか?	do·no chī·mu ga i·chi·ban su·ki des ka
What's the score?	スコアはどうですか?	sko·a wa dō des ka

SPORTING INTERESTS

For phrases about hiking, see **outdoors** (p153). For more sports, see the **dictionary**.

Q **What sport do you play?**	どんなスポーツをしますか? don·na spō·tsu o shi·mas ka
Q **What sport do you follow?**	どのスポーツのファンですか? do·no spō·tsu no fan des ka
A **I play/do ...**	…をします。 ... o shi·mas
A **I follow ...**	…のファンです。 ... no fan des

baseball	野球	ya·kyū
basketball	バスケット	bas·ket·to
football (soccer)	サッカー	sak·kā
martial arts	武道	bu·dō
tennis	テニス	te·nis

LISTEN FOR

If you're going to a sumo tournament (場所 ba·sho), here are some of the terms you're likely to hear.

土俵	do·hyō	ring/arena
行司	gyō·ji	referee
引き落とし	hi·ki·o·to·shi	pull down the opponent
まわし	ma·wa·shi	loincloth
押し出し	o·shi·da·shi	push the opponent out of the arena
押し倒し	o·shi·tow·shi	knock or throw down the opponent
力士	ri·ki·shi	wrestler
四股	shi·ko	stomping
つり出し	tsu·ri·da·shi	carry the opponent out of the arena
寄り切り	yo·ri·ki·ri	drive the opponent out of the arena

I cycle.	サイクリングをします。 sai·ku·rin·gu o shi·mas
I run.	ジョギングをします。 jo·gin·gu o shi·mas
I walk.	散歩をします。 sam·po o shi·mas
Q **Do you like (sumo)?**	(相撲)が好きですか? (su·mō) ga su·ki des ka
A **Yes, very much.**	はい、とても好きです。 hai, to·te·mo su·ki des
A **Not really.**	あまり好きじゃありません。 a·ma·ri su·ki ja a·ri·ma·sen
A **I like watching it.**	観るのが好きです。 mi·ru no ga su·ki des

Who's your favourite sportsperson?	どの選手がいちばん好きですか? do·no sen·shu ga i·chi·ban su·ki des ka
Who's your favourite team?	どのチームがいちばん好きですか? do·no chī·mu ga i·chi·ban su·ki des ka

GOING TO A GAME

Would you like to go to a game?	試合に行きたいですか? shi·ai ni i·ki·tai des ka
Who are you supporting?	だれを応援していますか? da·re o ō·en shi·te i·mas ka
What's the score?	スコアはどうですか? sko·a wa dō des ka
Who's playing?	だれがプレーしていますか? da·re ga pu·rē shi·te i·mas ka
Who's winning?	だれが勝っていますか? da·re ga kat·te i·mas ka
That was a great/bad game!	素晴らしい/悪い試合でしたね! su·ba·ra·shī/wa·ru·i shi·ai desh·ta ne
That was a boring game!	つまらない試合でしたね! tsu·ma·ra·nai shi·ai desh·ta ne
What a great team!	素晴らしいチームだ! su·ba·ra·shī chī·mu da
What a terrible team!	だめなチームだ! da·me na chī·mu da

PLAYING SPORT

Ⓠ **Do you want to play?**	プレーしたいですか? pu·rē shi·tai des ka
Ⓐ **That would be great.**	それはいいですね。 so·re wa ī des ne
Ⓐ **I can't.**	できません。 de·ki·ma·sen
Can I join in?	いっしょにやってもいいですか? is·sho ni yat·te mo ī des ka
Your/My point.	あなた/私の点。 a·na·ta/wa·ta·shi no ten
Kick/Pass it to me!	こっちにキック/パス! kot·chi ni kik·ku/pas
You're a good player.	うまいですね。 u·mai des ne
Thanks for the game.	試合、ありがとう。 shi·ai, a·ri·ga·tō
Where's the nearest golf course?	いちばん近いゴルフ場はどこですか? i·chi·ban chi·kai go·ru·fu·jō wa do·ko des ka
Where's the nearest gym?	いちばん近いジムはどこですか? i·chi·ban chi·kai ji·mu wa do·ko des ka
Where's the nearest tennis court?	いちばん近いテニスコートはどこですか? i·chi·ban chi·kai te·nis kō·to wa do·ko des ka
What's the charge per day/hour?	1日/1時間の料金はいくらですか? i·chi·ni·chi/i·chi·ji·kan no ryō·kin wa i·ku·ra des ka

What's the charge per game?	1ゲームの料金はいくらですか? i·chi·gē·mu no ryō·kin wa i·ku·ra des ka
What's the charge per visit?	1回の料金はいくらですか? ik·kai no ryō·kin wa i·ku·ra des ka
Can I hire a ...?	…を貸してもらえませんか? ... o ka·shi·te mo·ra·e·ma·sen ka

ball	ボール	bō·ru
bicycle	自転車	ji·ten·sha
court	コート	kō·to
racquet	ラケット	ra·ket·to

Where are the changing rooms?	更衣室はどこですか? kō·i·shi·tsu wa do·ko des ka
Can I take lessons?	レッスンを受けられますか? res·sun o u·ke·ra·re·mas ka

BASEBALL

base	塁 ru·i
baseball	野球 ya·kyū
batter	バッター bat·tā
curve ball	カーブ kā·bu
dugout	ベンチ ben·chi
fastball	速球 sok·kyū

home run	ホームラン hō·mu·ran
infielder	内野手 nai·ya·shu
inning	イニング i·nin·gu
out a/n	アウト ow·to
outfielder	外野手 gai·ya·shu
pitcher	ピッチャー pit·chā
run n	ラン ran
safe	セーフ sē·fu
strike n	ストライク sto·rai·ku

SKIING

I'd like to hire ...	…を借りたいの ですが。 ... o ka·ri·tai no des ga

boots	ブーツ	bū·tsu
gloves	手袋	te·bu·ku·ro
goggles	ゴーグル	gō·gu·ru
poles	ストック	stok·ku
skis	スキー	skī
a ski suit	スキースーツ	skī·sū·tsu
snowboard	スノーボード	su·nō·bo·do

Is it possible to go ...?	…に行けますか? ... ni i·ke·mas ka

alpine skiing	アルペンスキー	a·ru·pen·skī
cross-country skiing	クロスカントリー	ku·ros·kan·to·rī
snowboarding	スノーボード	su·nō·bō·do
tobogganing	そり	so·ri

How much is a pass?	券はいくらですか? ken wa i·ku·ra des ka
What are the conditions like (at Niseko)?	(ニセコの)コンディションはどうですか? (ni·se·ko no) kon·di·shon wa dō des ka
What level is that slope?	このゲレンデはどのレベルですか? ko·no ge·ren·de wa do·no re·be·ru des ka
Which are the advanced slopes?	上級レベルのゲレンデはどこですか? jō·kyū re·be·ru no ge·ren·de wa do·ko des ka
Which are the beginner slopes?	初級レベルのゲレンデはどこですか? sho·kyū re·be·ru no ge·ren·de wa do·ko des ka
Which are the intermediate slopes?	中級レベルのゲレンデはどこですか? chū·kyū re·be·ru no ge·ren·de wa do·ko des ka
cable car	ケーブルカー kē·bu·ru·kā
chairlift/ski-lift	リフト ri·fu·to

LISTEN FOR

コーナー	kō·nā	corner
ファウル	fow·ru	foul
フリーキック	fu·rī·kik·ku	free kick
ゴール	gō·ru	goal
オフサイド	of·sai·do	offside
ペナルティ	pe·na·ru·tī	penalty
レッドカード	red·do·kā·do	red card
審判	shim·pan	referee
イエローカード	ye·rō·kā·do	yellow card

SOCCER

Who plays for (Urawa Reds)?	だれが(浦和レッズ)でプレーしていますか? da·re ga (u·ra·wa rez·zu) de pu·rē shi·te i·mas ka
Which team is at the top of the league?	どのチームがリーグのトップですか? do·no chī·mu ga rī·gu no top·pu des ka
What a goal!	すごいゴール! su·goy gō·ru
What a kick!	すごいキック! su·goy kik·ku

Outdoors

KEY PHRASES

Do we need a guide?	ガイドが必要ですか?	gai·do ga hi·tsu·yō des ka
I'm lost.	道に迷いました。	mi·chi ni ma·yoy·mash·ta
What's the weather like?	天気はどうですか?	ten·ki wa dō des ka

HIKING

Where can I buy supplies?	どこで食料が買えますか? do·ko·de sho·ku·ryō ga ka·e·mas ka
Where can I get a map?	どこで地図が手に入りますか? do·ko·de chi·zu ga te ni hai·ri·mas ka
Where can I hire hiking gear?	登山用品が どこでレンタルできますか? to-zan-yō-hin ga do-ko de ren-ta-ru de-ki-mas ka
How high is the climb?	どのくらい高度差がありますか? do·no·ku·rai kō·do·sa ga a·ri·mas ka
How long is the trail?	どのくらい距離がありますか? do·no·ku·rai kyo·ri ga a·ri·mas ka

Do we need to take bed linen?	シーツを持っていく必要がありますか? shī·tsu o mot·te i·ku hi·tsu·yō ga a·ri·mas ka
Do we need to take food/ water?	食料/水を持っていく必要がありますか? sho·ku·ryō/mi·zu o mot·te i·ku hi·tsu·yō ga a·ri·mas ka
Do we need a guide?	ガイドが必要ですか? gai·do ga hi·tsu·yō des ka
Are there guided treks?	ガイドが同行してくれるルートがありますか? gai·do ga dō·kō shi·te ku·re·ru rū·to ga a·ri·mas ka
Is it safe?	安全ですか? an·zen des ka
Is there a hut?	山小屋がありますか? ya·ma·go·ya ga a·ri·mas ka
Is the track (well) marked?	山道は標識が(きちんと)ありますか? ya·ma·mi·chi wa hyō·shi·ki ga (ki·chin·to) a·ri·mas ka
Is the track open?	山道は開通していますか? ya·ma·mi·chi wa kai·tsū shi·te i·mas ka
Is the track scenic?	山道は眺めがいいですか? ya·ma·mi·chi wa na·ga·me ga ī des ka
Which is the easiest route?	どのルートがいちばん簡単ですか? do·no rū·to ga i·chi·ban kan·tan des ka
Which is the shortest route?	どのルートがいちばん短いですか? do·no rū·to ga i·chi·ban mi·ji·kai des ka

LISTEN FOR

地震	ji·shin	earthquake
雨季	u·ki	rainy season
津波	tsu·na·mi	tsunami
台風	tai·fū	typhoon
噴火	fun·ka	volcanic eruption
火山	ka·zan	volcano

Where can I find the camping ground?	キャンプ場はどこにありますか? kyam·pu·jō wa do·ko ni a·ri·mas ka
Where can I find the showers/toilets?	シャワー/トイレはどこにありますか? sha·wā/toy·re wa do·ko ni a·ri·mas ka
Does this path go to ...?	この道は…に行きますか? ko·no mi·chi wa ... ni i·ki·mas ka
Can I go through here?	ここを通り抜けできますか? ko·ko o tō·ri·nu·ke de·ki·mas ka
Is the water OK to drink?	水を飲んでもだいじょうぶですか? mi·zu o non·de mo dai·jō·bu des ka
I'm lost.	道に迷いました。 mi·chi ni ma·yoy·mash·ta

BEACH

Where's the best beach?	いちばんいいビーチはどこですか? i·chi·ban ī bī·chi wa do·ko des ka

Where's the nearest beach?	いちばん近いビーチはどこですか? i·chi·ban chi·kai bī·chi wa do·ko des ka
Is it safe to dive here?	ここは安全に飛び込めますか? ko·ko wa an·zen ni to·bi·ko·me·mas ka
Is it safe to swim here?	ここは安全に泳げますか? ko·ko wa an·zen ni o·yo·ge·mas ka
What time is high/low tide?	満潮/干潮は何時ですか? man·chō/kan·chō wa nan·ji des ka

WEATHER

What will the weather be like tomorrow?	明日の天気はどうですか? a·shi·ta no ten·ki wa dō des ka
Q **What's the weather like?**	天気はどうですか? ten·ki wa dō des ka
A **It's ...**	…です。 ... des

cloudy	曇り	ku·mo·ri
cold	寒い	sa·mu·i
hot	暑い	a·tsu·i
humid	蒸し暑い	mu·shi·a·tsu·i
raining	雨	a·me
snowing	雪	yu·ki
sunny	晴れ	ha·re
warm	暖かい	a·ta·ta·kai
windy	風が強い	ka·ze ga tsu·yoy

SAFE TRAVEL

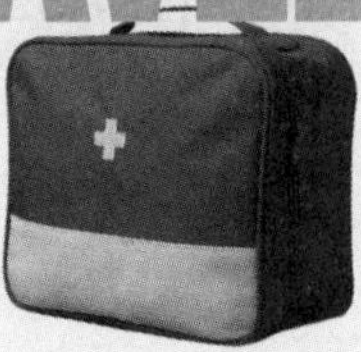

EMERGENCIES	**158**
POLICE	**160**
HEALTH	**162**

Emergencies

KEY PHRASES

Help!	たすけて！	tas·ke·te
There's been an accident.	事故です。	ji·ko des
It's an emergency.	緊急です。	kin·kyū des

Help!	たすけて！ tas·ke·te
Stop!	止まれ！ to·ma·re
Go away!	離れろ！ ha·na·re·ro
Thief!	どろぼう！ do·ro·bō
Fire!	火事だ！ ka·ji da
Watch out!	危ない！ a·bu·nai
Careful!	気をつけて！ ki o tsu·ke·te
It's an emergency.	緊急です。 kin·kyū des
There's been an accident.	事故です。 ji·ko des
Call the police.	警察を呼んで。 kē·sa·tsu o yon·de
Call a doctor.	医者を呼んで。 i·sha o yon·de

LOOK FOR

病院	byō·in	Hospital
警察	kē·sa·tsu	Police
警察署	kē·sa·tsu·sho	Police Station
交番	kō·ban	Police Box
救急	kyū·kyū	Emergency Department

Call an ambulance.	救急車を呼んで。 kyū·kyū·sha o yon·de
Could you please help?	たすけてください。 tas·ke·te ku·da·sai
Can I use your phone?	電話を貸して くれませんか? den·wa o ka·shi·te ku·re·ma·sen ka
I'm lost.	道に迷いました。 mi·chi ni ma·yoy·mash·ta
Where are the toilets?	トイレはどこですか? toy·re wa do·ko des ka
Is it safe at night?	夜は安全ですか? yo·ru wa an·zen des ka
Is it safe for women?	女性にとって安全ですか? jo·sē ni tot·te an·zen des ka
Is it safe on your own?	独りで安全ですか? hi·to·ri de an·zen des ka
Is it safe for travellers?	旅行者にとって安全 ですか? ryo·kō·sha ni tot·te an·zen des ka

Police

KEY PHRASES

Where's the police station?	警察署はどこですか?	kē·sa·tsu·sho wa do·ko des ka
I want to contact my embassy/ consulate.	領事館/大使館に連絡したいです。	ryō·ji·kan/tai·shi·kan ni ren·ra·ku shi·tai des
My bags were stolen.	私のバッグが盗まれました。	wa·ta·shi no bag·gu ga nu·su·ma·re·mash·ta

Where's the police station?	警察署はどこですか? kē·sa·tsu·sho wa do·ko des ka
I want to report an offence.	犯罪を報告したいのですが。 han·zai o hō·ko·ku shi·tai no des ga
I've been assaulted.	私は暴行を受けました。 wa·ta·shi wa bō·kō o u·ke·mash·ta
I've been raped.	私はレイプされました。 wa·ta·shi wa rē·pu sa·re·mash·ta
I've been robbed.	私は強盗に遭いました。 wa·ta·shi wa gō·tō ni ai·mash·ta
It was him/her.	やったのは彼/彼女です。 yat·ta no wa ka·re/ka·no·jo des
My ... was/were stolen.	私の…が盗まれました。 wa·ta·shi no ... ga nu·su·ma·re·mash·ta

I've lost my ...	…をなくしました。	... o na·ku·shi·mash·ta
backpack	バックパック	bak·ku·pak·ku
bags	バッグ	bag·gu
handbag	ハンドバッグ	han·do·bag·gu
money	お金	o·ka·ne
passport	パスポート	pas·pō·to
wallet	財布	sai·fu

What am I accused of?	どんな理由で告訴されるのですか? don·na ri·yū de ko·ku·so sa·re·ru no des ka
I didn't realise I was doing anything wrong.	違法行為をしているつもりはありませんでした。 i·hō·kōy o shi·te i·ru tsu·mo·ri wa a·ri·ma·sen desh·ta
I didn't do it.	私はやっていません。 wa·ta·shi wa yat·te i·ma·sen
Can I make a phone call?	電話をかけてもいいですか? den·wa o ka·ke·te mo ī des ka
Can I have a lawyer (who speaks English)?	(英語ができる)弁護士をお願いします。 (ē·go ga de·ki·ru) ben·go·shi o o·ne·gai shi·mas
I want to contact my consulate/embassy.	領事館/大使館に連絡したいです。 ryō·ji·kan/tai·shi·kan ni ren·ra·ku shi·tai des

Health

KEY PHRASES

Where's the nearest hospital?	この近くの病院はどこですか?	ko·no chi·ka·ku no byō·in wa do·ko des ka
I'm sick.	私は病気です。	wa·ta·shi wa byō·ki des
I need a doctor.	お医者さんが必要です。	oy·sha·san ga hi·tsu·yō des
I'm on medication for ...	…の薬を飲んでいます。	... no ku·su·ri o non·de i·mas
I'm allergic to ...	私は…アレルギーです。	wa·ta·shi wa ... a·re·ru·gī des

Where's the nearest ...? この近くの…はどこですか?
ko·no chi·ka·ku no ... wa do·ko des ka

(24-hour) chemist	(24時間営業の)薬局	(ni·jū·yo·ji·kan ē·gyō no) yak·kyo·ku
dentist	歯医者	ha·i·sha
doctor	医者	i·sha
hospital	病院	byō·in

I need a doctor (who speaks English). (英語ができる)お医者さんが必要です。
(ē·go ga de·ki·ru) oy·sha·san ga hi·tsu·yō des

Could I see a female doctor?	女性のお医者さんをお願いできますか? jo·sē no oy·sha·san o o·ne·gai de·ki·mas ka
Could the doctor come here?	お医者さんはこちらに来ることができますか? oy·sha·san wa ko·chi·ra ni ku·ru·ko·to ga de·ki·mas ka
I've run out of my medication.	薬が切れました。 ku·su·ri ga ki·re·mash·ta
I don't want a blood transfusion.	輸血はしたくないです。 yu·ke·tsu wa shi·ta·ku·nai des
Please use a new syringe.	新しい注射器を使ってください。 a·ta·ra·shī chū·sha·ki o tsu·kat·te ku·da·sai
I've been vaccinated against tetanus.	私は破傷風の予防注射をしました。 wa·ta·shi wa ha·shō·fū no yo·bō·chū·sha o shi·mash·ta
I've been vaccinated against typhoid.	私はチフスの予防注射をしました。 wa·ta·shi wa chif·su no yo·bō·chū·sha o shi·mash·ta
I've been vaccinated against hepatitis A/B/C.	私はA/B/C型肝炎の予防注射をしました。 wa·ta·shi wa ē/bī/shī· ga·ta·kan·en no yo·bō·chū·sha o shi·mash·ta
He/She has been vaccinated against ...	彼/彼女は…の予防注射をしました。 ka·re/ka·no·jo wa ... no yo·bō·chū·sha o shi·mash·ta

SYMPTOMS & CONDITIONS

I'm sick.	私は病気です。 wa·ta·shi wa byō·ki des
My friend/child is (very) sick.	友達/子供は (ひどい)病気です。 to·mo·da·chi/ko·do·mo wa (hi·doy) byō·ki des
He/She is having a/an ...	彼/彼女は…を 起こしています ka·re/ka·no·jo·wa ... o o·ko·shi·te i·mas

allergic reaction	アレルギー反応	a·re·ru·gī·han·nō
asthma attack	喘息発作	zen·so·ku·hos·sa
epileptic fit	てんかん発作	ten·kan·hos·sa
heart attack	心臓発作	shin·zō·hos·sa

I feel ...	私は… wa·ta·shi wa ...

better	良く なりました	yo·ku na·ri·mash·ta
dizzy	めまいがします	me·mai ga shi·mas
hot and cold	暑くなったり 寒くなったり します	a·tsu·ku nat·ta·ri sa·mu·ku nat·ta·ri shi·mas
nauseated	吐き気が します	ha·ki·ke ga shi·mas
weak	ちからが ありません	chi·ka·ra ga a·ri·ma·sen
worse	悪くなって います	wa·ru·ku nat·te i·mas

LISTEN FOR

どうしましたか?	dō shi·mash·ta ka What's the problem?
どこが痛いですか?	do·ko ga i·tai des ka Where does it hurt?
熱がありますか?	ne·tsu ga a·ri·mas ka Do you have a temperature?
いつからこのような状態ですか?	i·tsu ka·ra ko·no yō·na jō·tai des ka How long have you been like this?
前にもなったことがありますか?	ma·e ni mo nat·ta ko·to ga a·ri·mas ka Have you had this before?

I've been injured.	私はけがをしました。 wa·ta·shi wa ke·ga o shi·mash·ta
I've been vomiting.	私はもどしています。 wa·ta·shi wa mo·do·shi·te i·mas
It hurts here.	ここが痛いです。 ko·ko ga i·tai des
I can't sleep.	眠れません。 ne·mu·re·ma·sen
I'm on medication for ...	…の薬を飲んでいます。 ... no ku·su·ri o non·de i·mas
I have ...	私は…があります。 wa·ta·shi wa ... ga a·ri·mas
I have asthma.	私は喘息があります wa·ta·shi wa zen·so·ku ga a·ri·mas
I have diarrhoea.	私は下痢があります。 wa·ta·shi wa ge·ri ga a·ri·mas

LISTEN FOR

お酒を飲みますか?	o·sa·ke o no·mi·mas ka Do you drink?
タバコを吸いますか?	ta·ba·ko o su·i·mas ka Do you smoke?
麻薬を使用していますか?	ma·ya·ku o shi·yō shi·te i·mas ka Do you take drugs?
アレルギーがありますか?	a·re·ru·gī ga a·ri·mas ka Are you allergic to anything?
薬を使用していますか?	ku·su·ri o shi·yō shi·te i·mas ka Are you on medication?
最近、性交渉がありましたか?	sai·kin sē·kō·shō ga a·ri·mash·ta ka Are you sexually active?
コンドームなしの性交渉がありましたか?	kon·dō·mu·na·shi no sē·kō·shō ga a·ri·mash·ta ka Have you had unprotected sex?
入院する必要があります。	nyū·in su·ru hi·tsu·yō ga a·ri·mas You need to be admitted to hospital.

I have a headache.	私は頭痛があります。 wa·ta·shi wa zu·tsū ga a·ri·mas
I've recently had ...	私は最近…がありました。 wa·ta·shi wa sai·kin ... ga a·ri·mash·ta
He/She has ...	彼/彼女は…があります。 ka·re/ka·no·jo wa ... ga a·ri·mas

For more symptoms and conditions, see the **dictionary** (p219)

ALLERGIES

I'm allergic to ...	私は…アレルギーです。 wa·ta·shi wa ... a·re·ru·gī des
He's/She's allergic to ...	…アレルギーです。 ... a·re·ru·gī des

antibiotics	抗生物質	kō·sē·bus·shi·tsu
anti-inflammatories	抗炎症薬	kō·en·shō·ya·ku
aspirin	アスピリン	as·pi·rin
bees	蜂	ha·chi
codeine	コデイン	ko·de·in
penicillin	ペニシリン	pe·ni·shi·rin
pollen	花粉	ka·fun

I have a skin allergy.	皮膚アレルギーです。 hi·fu·a·re·ru·gī des

For food-related allergies, see **vegetarian & special meals** (p193).

WOMEN'S HEALTH

(I think) I'm pregnant.	私は妊娠してい(ると思い)ます。 wa·ta·shi wa nin·shin shi·te i (ru to o·moy)·mas
I need a pregnancy test.	妊娠テストをお願いします。 nin·shin·tes·to o o·ne·gai shi·mas
I'm on the pill.	ピルを飲んでいます。 pi·ru o non·de i·mas

I haven't had my period for (six) weeks.	(6)週間月経が ありません。 (ro·ku)·shū·kan gek·kē ga a·ri·ma·sen
I've noticed a lump here.	ここにしこりがあります。 ko·ko ni shi·ko·ri ga a·ri·mas
I need contraception.	避妊薬をお願いします。 hi·nin·ya·ku o o·ne·gai shi·mas
I need the morning-after pill.	モーニングアフターピルを お願いします。 mō·nin·gu·af·tā·pi·ru o o·ne·gai shi·mas

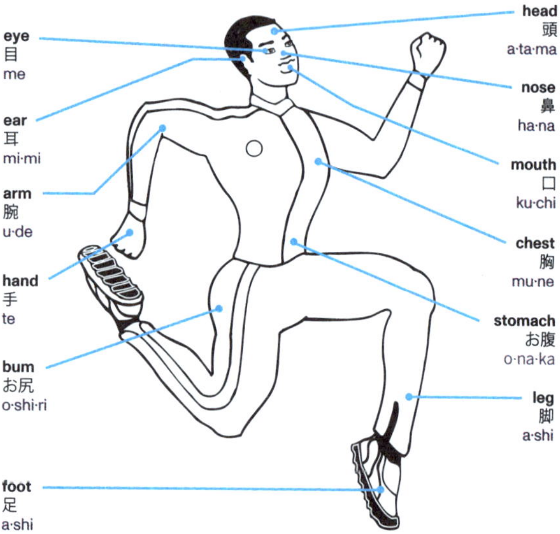

PARTS OF THE BODY

My ... hurts.	…が痛いです。 ... ga i·tai des
I can't move my ...	…を動かせません。 ... o u·go·ka·se·ma·sen
I have a cramp in my ...	…がつりました。 ... ga tsu·ri·mash·ta
My ... is swollen.	…が腫れています。 ... ga ha·re·te i·mas

DENTIST

I have a broken tooth.	歯が折れました。 ha ga o·re·mash·ta
I have a toothache.	歯が痛いです。 ha ga i·tai des
I've lost a filling.	歯の詰め物が とれました。 ha no tsu·me·mo·no ga to·re·mash·ta
My dentures are broken.	入れ歯がこわれました。 i·re·ba ga ko·wa·re·mash·ta
My gums hurt.	歯茎が痛いです。 ha·gu·ki ga i·tai des
I don't want it extracted.	抜かないでください。 nu·ka·nai·de ku·da·sai

LISTEN FOR

大きく開いて。	ō·ki·ku hi·rai·te	Open wide.
うがいをして ください。	u·gai o shi·te ku·da·sai	Rinse.

LISTEN FOR

1日2回(食事時)。	i·chi·ni·chi ni·kai (sho·ku·ji·do·ki) Twice a day (with food).
これを使ったことがありますか?	ko·re o tsu·kat·ta ko·to ga a·ri·mas ka Have you taken this before?

I need a filling.	詰め物をしてください。 tsu·me·mo·no o shi·te ku·da·sai
Ouch!	痛い! i·tai

CHEMIST

I need something for (a headache).	なにか(頭痛)に効くものが必要です。 na·ni ka (zu·tsū) ni ki·ku·mo·no ga hi·tsu·yō des
Do I need a prescription for (antihistamines)?	(抗ヒスタミン剤)の処方箋が必要ですか? (kō·his·ta·min·sai) no sho·hō·sen ga hi·tsu·yō des ka
I have a prescription.	処方箋があります。 sho·hō·sen ga a·ri·mas
How many times a day?	1日何回ですか? i·chi·ni·chi nan·kai des ka
Will it make me drowsy?	眠くなりますか? ne·mu·ku na·ri·mas ka

FOOD

EATING OUT 172

SELF-CATERING 189

VEGETARIAN & SPECIAL MEALS 193

Eating Out

KEY PHRASES

Can you recommend a restaurant?	どこかいいレストランを知っていますか?	do·ko ka ī res·to·ran o shit·te i·mas ka
I'd like to reserve a table for two people.	2人の予約をお願いします。	fu·ta·ri no yo·ya·ku o o·ne·gai shi·mas
I'd like the menu, please.	メニューをお願いします。	me·nyū o o·ne·gai shi·mas
I'd like a beer, please.	ビールをお願いします。	bī·ru o o·ne·gai shi·mas
Please bring the bill.	お勘定をください。	o·kan·jō o ku·da·sai

BASICS

Alternative terms are commonly used for meals – the first options given below being slightly more formal.

breakfast	朝食/朝ごはん chō·sho·ku/a·sa·go·han
lunch	昼食/昼ごはん chū·sho·ku/hi·ru·go·han
dinner	夕食/晩ごはん yū·sho·ku/ban·go·han
snack	間食/スナック kan·sho·ku/su·nak·ku
to eat	食べます ta·be·mas

to drink	飲みます no·mi·mas
I'd like ...	…をください。 ... o·ku·da·sai
I'm starving!	お腹がすいた。 o·na·ka ga su·i·ta

FINDING A PLACE TO EAT

Can you recommend a cafe?	どこかいいカフェを 知っていますか? do·ko ka ī ka·fe o shit·te i·mas ka
Can you recommend a restaurant?	どこかいいレストランを 知っていますか? do·ko ka ī res·to·ran o shit·te i·mas ka
Where would you go for a cheap meal?	安い食事をするなら どこに行きますか? ya·su·i sho·ku·ji o su·ru na·ra do·ko ni i·ki·mas ka

☑ CULTURE TIP: JAPANESE MEALS

Traditional Japanese breakfasts usually consist of rice (go·han ご飯), miso soup (mi·so·shi·ru 味噌汁), raw egg (na·ma·ta·ma·go 生卵), dried fish (hi·mo·no 干物), dried seaweed (no·ri 海苔) and pickles (tsu·ke·mo·no 漬物). Some eat fermented soy beans (nat·tō 納豆) at breakfast. Western-style breakfasts are also common. Lunch boxes (ben·tō 弁当) often include rice, soup, pickles, a main dish and fruit. Noodles – so·ba (そば), sō·men (そうめん), rā·men (ラーメン) or u·don (うどん) – are also common fare for lunch. Dinner will usually include rice, soup and a side dish (o·ka·zu おかず). For more Japanese dishes and ingredients, see the **menu decoder** (p196).

Where would you go for local specialities?	名物を食べるなら どこに行きますか? mē·bu·tsu o ta·be·ru na·ra do·ko ni i·ki·mas ka
Where would you go for a celebration?	お祝いをするなら どこに行きますか? oy·wai o su·ru na·ra do·ko ni i·ki·mas ka
I'd like to reserve a table for one person/two people.	1人/2人の予約を お願いします。 hi·to·ri/fu·ta·ri no yo·ya·ku o o·ne·gai shi·mas
I'd like to reserve a table for (eight) o'clock.	(8)時の予約を お願いします。 (ha·chi)·ji no yo·ya·ku o o·ne·gai shi·mas
Are you still serving food?	まだ食事が できますか? ma·da sho·ku·ji ga de·ki·mas ka
How long is the wait?	どのくらい待ちますか? do·no ku·rai ma·chi·mas ka

AT THE RESTAURANT

When you book for more than three, you'll always be seated at a table. When you make a booking for two or less, make sure you request a table if you don't want to end up at the counter. You can say 'at a table, please': tē·bu·ru de o·ne·gai shi·mas.

I'd like a table for (five), please.	(5)人分のテーブルを お願いします。 (go)·nim·bun no tē·bu·ru o o·ne·gai shi·mas

For five, please.	5名です。	go mē des

Eating Out

CAN I SEE THE MENU, PLEASE?
メニューをお願いします。
me·nyū o o·ne·gai shi·mas

WHAT WOULD YOU RECOMMEND FOR ...?
お勧めの. . . は何ですか？
o·su·su·me no ... wa nan des ka

THE MAIN MEAL
メインディッシュ
mēn dish

DESSERT
デザート
de·zā·to

DRINKS
飲み物
no·mi·mo·no

CAN YOU BRING ME ..., PLEASE?
…をください。
... o ku·da·sai

I'D LIKE THE BILL, PLEASE.
お勘定をください。
o·kan·jō o ku·da·sai

LISTEN FOR

閉店です。	hē·ten des	We're closed.
満席です。	man·se·ki des	We're full.
何名様?	nan·mē·sa·ma	How many people?
少々お待ちください。	shō·shō o·ma·chi ku·da·sai	One moment, please.

I'd like nonsmoking, please.	禁煙席をお願いします。 kin·en·se·ki o o·ne·gai shi·mas
I'd like smoking, please.	喫煙席をお願いします。 ki·tsu·en·se·ki o o·ne·gai shi·mas
I'd like ..., please.	…をお願いします。 ... o o·ne·gai shi·mas

the menu (in English)	(英語の)メニュー	(ē·go no) me·nyū
a children's menu	子供のメニュー	ko·do·mo no me·nyū
the drink list	飲み物のメニュー	no·mi·mo·no no me·nyū
a half portion	半人前	han·nim·ma·e

What would you recommend?	なにがお勧めですか? na·ni ga o·su·su·me des ka
What's in that dish?	あの料理に何が入っていますか? a·no ryō·ri ni na·ni ga hait·te i·mas ka

Can you tell me what traditional foods I should try?	伝統的な食べ物は どんなものがおすすめ ですか？ den·tō·te·ki na ta·be·mo·no wa don·na mo·no ga o·su·su·me des ka
I'll have that.	あれをください。 a·re o ku·da·sai
Please decide for me.	おまかせします。 o·ma·ka·se shi·mas
Does it take long to prepare?	料理に時間が かかりますか? ryō·ri ni ji·kan ga ka·ka·ri·mas ka
Is service included in the bill?	サービス料込みですか? sā·bis·ryō ko·mi des ka
Are these complimentary?	これはただですか? ko·re wa ta·da des ka
I'd like (the chicken).	(鶏肉)をお願いします。 (to·ri·ni·ku) o o·ne·gai shi·mas
I'd like a local speciality.	地元の名物を お願いします。 ji·mo·to no mē·bu·tsu o o·ne·gai shi·mas

REQUESTS

Please bring ...	…をください。 ... o ku·da·sai

a knife/fork	ナイフ/フォーク	nai·fu/fō·ku
a glass	グラス	gu·ra·su
a serviette	ナプキン	na·pu·kin
a spoon	スプーン	spūn
a wineglass	ワイングラス	wain·gu·ra·su

LISTEN FOR

お決まりでしょうか?	o·ki·ma·ri de·shō ka What can I get for you?
…がお好きですか?	... ga o·su·ki des ka Do you like ...?
…をおすすめします。	... o o·su·su·me shi·mas I suggest the ...
どのように料理 いたしましょうか?	do·no yō ni ryō·ri i·ta·shi·ma·shō ka How would you like that cooked?
どうぞ。	dō·zo Here you go!

I'd like it ... …ください。 ... ku·da·sai

boiled (in hot water)	ゆでて	yu·de·te
boiled (in stock)	煮て	ni·te
deep fried	揚げて	a·ge·te
fried	炒めて	i·ta·me·te
grilled	グリルして	gu·ri·ru shi·te
medium	ミディアムにして	mi·dya·mu ni shi·te
rare	レアにして	rair ni shi·te
re-heated	温めなおして	a·ta·ta·me·now·shi·te
steamed	蒸して	mu·shi·te
well done	ウェルダンにして	we·ru·dan ni shi·te
with the dressing on the side	ドレッシングを別にして	do·res·shin·gu o be·tsu ni shi·te

I don't want it deep fried.	揚げないでください。 a·ge·nai·de ku·da·sai
I don't want it fried.	炒めないでください。 i·ta·me·nai·de ku·da·sai
I don't want it re-heated.	温めなおさないでください。 a·ta·ta·me·now·sa·nai·de ku·da·sai
I'd like it with ...	…を付けてお願いします。 ... o tsu·ke·te o·ne·gai shi·mas
I'd like it without ...	…を抜きでお願いします。 ... o nu·ki de o·ne·gai shi·mas

chilli	唐辛子	tō·ga·ra·shi
garlic	ニンニク	nin·ni·ku
ginger	ショウガ	shō·ga
sauce	ソース	sō·su
seaweed	のり	no·ri
soy sauce	しょう油	shō·yu
horseradish	わさび	wa·sa·bi

See also **vegetarian & special meals** (p193).

COMPLIMENTS & COMPLAINTS

Bon appetit!	いただきます (lit: I receive) i·ta·da·ki·mas
I love this dish.	この料理が大好きです。 ko·no ryō·ri ga dai·su·ki des
I love the local cuisine.	地元料理が大好きです。 ji·mo·to·ryō·ri ga dai·su·ki des
That was delicious!	おいしかった。 oy·shi·kat·ta

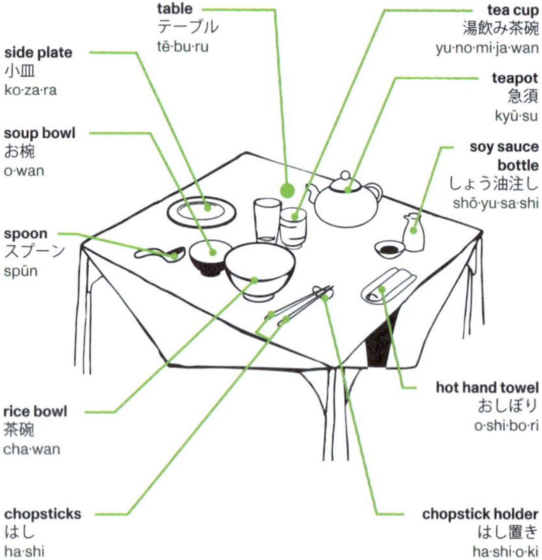

It was a real feast.	ごちそうさま go·chi·sō·sa·ma
I'm full.	お腹がいっぱいです。 o·na·ka ga ip·pai des
This is cold.	これは冷たいです。 ko·re wa tsu·me·tai des
This is spicy.	これはスパイシーです。 ko·re wa spai·shī des
This is superb.	これは素晴らしいです。 ko·re wa su·ba·ra·shī des

PAYING THE BILL

I'd like the bill, please.	お勘定をください o·kan·jō o ku·da·sai
There's a mistake in the bill.	請求書に間違いがあります。 sē·kyū·sho ni ma·chi·gai ga a·ri·mas

NONALCOHOLIC DRINKS

sparkling mineral water	炭酸ミネラルウォーター tan·san·mi·ne·ra·ru·wō·tā
still mineral water	炭酸なしのミネラルウォーター tan·san·na·shi no·mi·ne·ra·ru·wō·tā
hot water	お湯 o·yu
lemonade	レモネード re·mo·nē·do

LOOK FOR

前菜	zen·sai	appetisers
スープ	sū·pu	soups
アントレー	an·to·rē	entrees
サラダ	sa·ra·da	salads
メインコース	mēn·kō·su	main courses
デザート	de·zā·to	desserts
一品料理	ip·pin·ryō·ri	à la carte
飲み物	no·mi·mo·no	drinks

For more menu items, see the **menu decoder** (p196).

milk	ミルク mi·ru·ku
orange juice	オレンジジュース o·ren·ji·jū·su
soft drink	ソフトドリンク so·fu·to·do·rin·ku
water	水 mi·zu
(cup of) tea ...	…紅茶(1杯) ... kō·cha (ip·pai)
(cup of) coffee ...	…コーヒー(1杯) ... kō·hī (ip·pai)
with (milk)	(ミルク)入り (mi·ru·ku)·i·ri
without (sugar)	(砂糖)なし (sa·tō)·na·shi
... coffee	…コーヒー ... kō·hī

black	ブラック	bu·rak·ku
iced	アイス	ai·su
strong	濃い	koy
weak	薄い	u·su·i
white	ホワイト	ho·wai·to

Japanese green tea	お茶 o·cha
barley tea	麦茶 mu·gi·cha
green leaf tea	煎茶 sen·cha
oolong tea	ウーロン茶 ū·ron·cha

CULTURE TIP: JAPANESE EATERIES

Many eating places specialise in serving up one particular type of dish. Look for the -ya (屋) after the name of a dish and that's usually where you'll find it. For example, ton·ka·tsu·ya (とんかつ屋) specialise in *tonkatsu* (pork cutlet), sha·bu·sha·bu·ya (しゃぶしゃぶ屋) in *shabu shabu* hotpot, so·ba·ya (そば屋) in *soba* (buckwheat noodles) and su·shi·ya (すし屋) in sushi. Other popular alternatives are ro·ba·ta·ya·ki (ろばた焼き), where food is grilled, ya·ki·to·ri (焼き鳥) restaurants specialising in variations of skewered chicken, and o·den (おでん) shops, whipping up stewed hotpot. For a quick bite and booze, try the i·za·ka·ya (居酒屋), or a kis·sa·ten (喫茶店) cafe-style establishment. Other options are the sho·ku·dō (食堂), cheap restaurants or dining halls dishing up filling and inexpensive food, or kai·ten·zu·shi (回転ずし), where sushi comes on a rotating conveyer belt.

powdered green tea	抹茶 **mat·cha**
roasted rice tea	玄米茶 **gem·mai·chai**
roasted tea	焙じ茶 **hō·ji·cha**
cappucino	カプチーノ **ka·pu·chī·no**
decaffeinated	デカフェ **de·ka·fe**
espresso	エスプレッソ **es·pres·so**
latte	カフェラテ **ka·fe·ra·te**

☑ CULTURE TIP: CHOPSTICK ETIQUETTE

Don't wave your chopsticks (ha·shi はし) around. Put them down if you need to make hand gestures. Never leave them standing up in your food either – this position is associated with death because of the similarity with incense sticks offered to the dead. Also note that chopsticks are usually referred to with the honorific o (お), ie o·ha·shi (おはし).

ALCOHOLIC DRINKS

beer	ビール bī·ru
brandy	ブランデー bu·ran·dē
champagne	シャンペン sham·pen
chilled sake	冷酒 rē·shu
cocktail	カクテル ka·ku·te·ru
plum wine	梅酒 u·me·shu
sake	酒 sa·ke
shochu highball	酎ハイ chū·hai
shochu spirit	焼酎 shō·chū
warm sake	お燗 o·kan
a shot of rum	ラムをワンショット ra·mu o wan·shot·to

a shot of vodka	ウォッカをワンショット **wok·ka o wan·shot·to**
a shot of whisky	ウィスキーをワンショット **wis·kī o wan·shot·to**
a bottle of ... wine	…ワインをボトルで **...·wain o bo·to·ru de**
a glass of ... wine	…ワインをグラスで **...·wain o gu·ra·su de**

dessert	デザート	**de·zā·to**
red	赤	**a·ka**
rosé	ロゼ	**ro·ze**
sparkling	スパークリング	**spā·ku·rin·gu**
white	白	**shi·ro**

a ... of beer	ビールを…で **bī·ru o ... de**

glass	グラス	**gu·ra·su**
jug	ジャグ	**ja·gu**
large bottle	大ビン	**ō·bin**
large mug	大ジョッキ	**dai·jok·ki**
small bottle	中ビン	**chū·bin**

あれをください。
a·re o ku·da·sai
I'll have that.

IN THE BAR

When going out, keep in mind that some bars impose a 'table charge' (tē·bu·ru·chā·ji テーブルチャージ). At the bar, if you fancy a bite with your drinks, check out which bar snacks (o·tsu·ma·mi おつまみ) are on offer.

Excuse me.	すみません。 su·mi·ma·sen
I'm next.	次は私です。 tsu·gi wa wa·ta·shi des
Q **What would you like?**	何を飲みますか? na·ni o no·mi·mas ka
A **I'll have ...**	…をお願いします。 ... o o·ne·gai shi·mas
Same again, please.	同じのをお願いします。 o·na·ji no o o·ne·gai shi·mas
No ice, thanks.	氷なしでお願いします。 kō·ri·na·shi de o·ne·gai shi·mas
I'll buy you a drink.	1杯おごります。 ip·pai o·go·ri·mas
It's my round next.	次は私の番です。 tsu·gi wa wa·ta·shi no ban des

CULTURE TIP: TEA CEREMONY

The sha·no·yu (茶の湯), or sa·do (茶道), as they're more commonly known, are quite elaborate tea ceremonies governed by a set of centuries-old rules and conventions. Guests are served the powdered green tea in a tea bowl that's larger than the standard tea cup, often a special piece of art in itself. Drink it by taking three or four large sips of tea, ensuring nothing remains in the bowl. You're allowed to make a slurping noise when drinking hot tea. Sweets are also served.

Do you serve meals here?	食事はできますか? sho·ku·ji wa de·ki·mas ka
How much is the table charge?	テーブルチャージはいくらですか? tē·bu·ru·chā·ji wa i·ku·ra des ka

DRINKING UP

Cheers!	乾杯! kam·pai
This is hitting the spot.	お腹に染みます。 o·na·ka ni shi·mi·mas
I feel fantastic!	気分がいいです。 ki·bun ga ī des
I think I've had one too many.	ちょっと飲みすぎました。 chot·to no·mi·su·gi·mash·ta
I'm feeling drunk.	酔いました。 yoy·mash·ta
I feel ill.	気分が悪いです。 ki·bun ga wa·ru·i des
Where's the toilet?	トイレはどこですか? toy·re wa do·ko des ka

LISTEN FOR

何にしますか?	nan ni shi·mas ka	What are you having?
もうじゅうぶんでしょう。	mō jū·bun de shō	I think you've had enough.
ラストオーダーです。	ras·to·ō·dā des	Last orders.

I'm tired. I'd better go home.	疲れました。うちに帰ります。 tsu·ka·re·mash·ta u·chi ni ka·e·ri·mas
Can you call a taxi for me?	タクシーを呼んでくれますか? tak·shī o yon·de ku·re·mas ka
I don't think you should drive.	運転しないほうがいいと思います。 un·ten shi·nai hō ga ī to o·moy·mas

Self-Catering

KEY PHRASES

What's the local speciality?	地元料理は何がありますか?	ji·mo·to·ryō·ri wa na·ni ga a·ri·mas ka
Where can I find the ... section?	…のコーナーはどこですか?	... no kō·nā wa do·ko des ka
I'd like ...	…ください。	... ku·da·sai

BUYING FOOD

What's the local speciality?	地元料理は何がありますか? ji·mo·to·ryō·ri wa na·ni ga a·ri·mas ka
Do you sell locally produced food?	地元産の食べ物はありますか? ji·mo·to·san no ta·be·mo·no wa a·ri·mas ka
Do you sell organic produce?	オーガニックの食べ物はありますか? ō·ga·nik·ku no ta·be·mo·no wa a·ri·mas ka
What's that?	それは何ですか? so·re wa nan des ka
Can I taste it?	味見してもいいですか? a·ji·mi shi·te mo ī des ka
Can I have a bag, please?	1袋ください。 hi·to·fu·ku·ro ku·da·sai

LISTEN FOR

いらっしゃいませ。	i·ras·shai·ma·se Welcome./Can I help you?
なにをお探しですか?	na·ni o o·sa·ga·shi des ka What would you like?
他に何か お探しですか?	ho·ka ni na·ni ka o·sa·ga·shi des ka Anything else?
ございません。	go·zai·ma·sen There isn't any.
(5千円)です。	(go·sen·en) des That's (5000 yen).

How much is a kilo of (rice)?	(米)1キロいくらですか? (ko·me) i·chi·ki·ro i·ku·ra des ka
How much?	いくら? i·ku·ra
I'd like this/that one.	これ/あれをください。 ko·re/a·re o ku·da·sai
I'd like ...	…ください。 ... ku·da·sai

(200) grams	(200)グラム	(ni·hya·ku)·gu·ra·mu
half a dozen	半ダース	han·dās
a dozen	1ダース	i·chi·dās
(two) kilos	(2)キロ	(ni)·ki·ro
a bottle	ビン1本	bin ip·pon
a packet	1パック	hi·to·pak·ku
(three) pieces	(3)個	(san)·ko
(six) slices	(6)枚	(ro·ku)·mai
(just) a little	(ほんの)少し	(hon·no) su·ko·shi
more	もっと	mot·to
some ...	…をいくらか	... o i·ku·ra ka

Less.	少なく。 su·ku·na·ku	
A bit more.	もうちょっと多く。 mō chot·to ō·ku	
Enough.	充分です。 jū·bun des	
Do you have anything cheaper?	安いものがありますか? ya·su·i mo·no ga a·ri·mas ka	
Do you have other kinds?	他のものがありますか? ho·ka no mo·no ga a·ri·mas ka	
Where can I find the ... section?	…のコーナーはどこですか? ... no kō·nā wa do·ko des ka	

dairy	乳製品	nyū·sē·hin
fish	魚	sa·ka·na
frozen goods	冷凍食品	rē·tō·sho·ku·hin
fruit and vegetable	果物と野菜	ku·da·mo·no to ya·sai
meat	肉	ni·ku
poultry	鳥肉	to·ri·ni·ku

COOKING

Could I please borrow a (bottle opener)?	(栓抜き)を貸してもらえませんか? (sen·nu·ki) o ka·shi·te mo·ra·e·ma·sen ka
I need a (can opener).	(缶切り)が必要です。 (kan·ki·ri) ga hi·tsu·yō des
bowl	ボール bō·ru
chopping knife	包丁 hō·chō

corkscrew	コークスクリュー kō·ku·sku·ryū
miso-soup bowl	お椀 o·wan
pair of chopsticks	箸 ha·shi
pair of disposable chopsticks	割り箸 wa·ri·ba·shi
rice cooker	炊飯器 su·i·han·ki
wok	中華鍋 chū·ka·na·be
cooked	火が通った hi ga tōt·ta
cured	保存 ho·zon
dried	乾燥 kan·sō
fresh	新鮮 shin·sen
frozen	冷凍 rē·tō
raw	なま na·ma
smoked	燻製 kun·sē

For more cooking implements, see the **dictionary** (p219).

Vegetarian & Special Meals

KEY PHRASES

I'm a vegetarian.	私は ベジタリアンです。	wa·ta·shi wa be·ji·ta·ri·an des
Could you prepare a meal without ...?	…抜きの 料理をお願い できますか?	...·nu·ki no ryō·ri o o·ne·gai de·ki·mas ka
I'm allergic to ...	私は… にアレルギーが あります。	wa·ta·shi wa ... ni a·re·ru·gī ga a·ri·mas

SPECIAL DIETS & ALLERGIES

Halal and kosher food might be hard to come by, even in the big cities, but you might want to try your luck with these phrases.

Is there a halal restaurant?	イスラム教徒のための ハラルレストランは ありますか? i·su·ra·mu·kyō·to no ta·me no ha·ra·ru res·to·ran wa a·ri·mas ka
Is there a kosher restaurant?	ユダヤ教徒のための コーシャーレストランは ありますか? yu·da·ya·kyō·to no ta·me no kō·shā res·to·ran wa a·ri·mas ka

Is there a vegetarian restaurant?	ベジタリアンレストランはありますか? be·ji·ta·ri·an res·to·ran wa a·ri·mas ka
I'm on a special diet.	私は特殊な食餌制限をしています。 wa·ta·shi wa to·ku·shu na sho·ku·ji·sē·gen o shi·te i·mas
I'm a vegan.	私は厳格な菜食主義者です。 wa·ta·shi wa gen·ka·ku na sai·sho·ku·shu·gi·sha des
I'm a vegetarian.	私はベジタリアンです。 wa·ta·shi wa be·ji·ta·ri·an des
I'm allergic to ...	私は…にアレルギーがあります。 wa·ta·shi wa ... ni a·re·ru·gī ga a·ri·mas

dairy produce	乳製品	nyū·sē·hin
eggs	卵	ta·ma·go
gelatine	ゼラチン	ze·ra·chin
gluten	グルテン	gu·ru·ten
honey	蜂蜜	ha·chi·mi·tsu
MSG	グルタミン酸ソーダ	gu·ru·ta·min·san·sō·da
nuts	ナッツ類	nat·tsu·ru·i
peanuts	ピーナッツ	pī·nat·tsu
seafood	海産物	kai·sam·bu·tsu

To explain your dietary restrictions with reference to religious beliefs, see **beliefs & culture** (p142).

ORDERING FOOD

I don't eat ...	…は食べません。 ... wa ta·be·ma·sen
Could you prepare a meal without ...?	…抜きの料理をお願いできますか? ...nu·ki no ryō·ri o o·ne·gai de·ki·mas ka

butter	バター	ba·tā
eggs	卵	ta·ma·go
fish	魚	sa·ka·na
fish stock	魚のだし	sa·ka·na no da·shi
meat stock	肉のだし	ni·ku no da·shi
oil	油	a·bu·ra
pork	豚肉	bu·ta·ni·ku
poultry	鳥肉	to·ri·ni·ku
red meat	赤身の肉	a·ka·mi no ni·ku

Is this ...?	これは…食品ですか? ko·re wa ... sho·ku·hin des ka

free of animal produce	動物性成分抜きの	dō·bu·tsu·sē sē·bun·nu·ki no
free-range	放し飼いの	ha·na·shi·gai no
genetically modified	遺伝子組み替えの	i·den·shi·ku·mi·ka·e no
gluten-free	グルテン抜きの	gu·ru·ten·nu·ki no
low fat	脂肪分が低い	shi·bō·bun ga hi·ku·i
low in sugar	糖分が低い	tō·bun ga hi·ku·i
organic	オーガニックの	ō·ga·nik·ku no
salt-free	塩分抜きの	em·bun·nu·ki no

MENU Decoder

料理読本

The Japanese dishes and ingredients in this menu decoder are listed alphabetically, by pronunciation, so you can easily understand what's on offer in Japanese eateries and ask for what takes your fancy.

A

a·ba·ra あばら ribs
a·be·ka·wa·mo·chi 安倍川もち rice cakes covered with ki·na·ko & sugar (Shizuoka Prefecture)
a·bo·ga·do アボガド avocado
a·bu·ra 油 oil
a·bu·ra·a·ge 油揚げ deep-fried, thinly sliced tō·fu
... a·e …和え dishes dressed with ..., eg go·ma·a·e (dish dressed with sesame seeds)
a·e·mo·no 和え物 food blended with a dressing
...·a·ge …揚げ fried ...
a·ge·da·shi·dō·fu 揚げだし豆腐 deep-fried tō·fu in fish stock
a·ge·mo·no 揚げ物 deep-fried food
a·hi·ru アヒル duck
ai·ga·mo 合鴨 Japanese duck
ai·na·me あいなめ green ling • ling cod (type of fish)
ais·ku·rī·mu アイスクリーム ice cream
a·ji アジ horse mackerel • scad (type of fish)
a·ka·a·ma·dai 赤アマダイ red a·ma·dai
a·ka·chi·ko·rī 赤チコリー radicchio
a·ka·gai 赤貝 ark shell • bearded clam • red clam
a·ka·ga·rē アカガレイ plaice
a·ka·in·gen 赤インゲン red kidney bean
a·ka·ji·so 赤じそ red shi·so
a·ka·kya·be·tsu 赤キャベツ red cabbage
a·ka·ren·zu·ma·me 赤レンズマメ red lentil
a·ka·ta·ma·ne·gi 赤たまねぎ red onion
a·ka·wain 赤ワイン red wine
a·ka·za·ke 赤酒 reddish wine made of rice, barley and/or wheat, to which wood ash is added (Kumamoto Prefecture)
a·ki·a·ji 秋味 see a·ra·ma·ki·za·ke
a·ki·ta·gai アキタ貝 north Japan term for scallop
a·ma·dai アマダイ blanquillo (type of fish) • ocean whitefish • tilefish (also called gu·ji)
a·ma·e·bi 甘エビ sweet prawn
a·mai 甘い sweet (taste)
a·ma·nat·tō 甘納豆 sugar-coated beans boiled in syrup
a·ma·za·ke 甘酒 sweet, warm sa·ke

a·ma·zu 甘酢 vinegar sweetened with sugar
am·bai 塩梅 literally 'salt-plum', meaning 'balance' – a term used by the older generation in reference to food
a·me 飴 candy • lolly
a·mi·ga·sa·ta·ke アミガサタケ morel (type of mushroom)
a·mi·ya·ki 網焼き cooked on a griddle
am·mi·tsu あんみつ a dessert made from fruit, boiled red peas, diced Japanese gelatine & an·ko with syrup on top
am·pan アンパン baked bun filled with an·ko
an あん sweet bean paste
a·na·kyū アナキュウ no·ri-rolled su·shi with conger eel & cucumber
a·na·go アナゴ conger eel
an·cho·bi アンチョビ anchovy
an·ka·ke あんかけ dishes topped with a sauce thickened with cornstarch
an·ko 餡子 a·zu·ki beans boiled with sugar
an·kō アンコウ angler • goosefish • monkfish
an·ko·ro·mo·chi あんころ餅 rice cake filled with sweetened a·zu·ki beans
an·zu あんず apricot
an·zu·ta·ke アンズタケ chanterelle
a·o·ji·so 青じそ green beefsteak plant
a·o·no·ri あおのり a strong green type of no·ri seaweed, produced in flake form & sprinkled on o·ko·no·mi·ya·ki & ya·ki·so·ba
a·o·to あおと green peppers
a·o·ya·gi あおやぎ sunray surf clam • trough shell
a·o·yu あおゆ green yu·zu
a·ra アラ grouper • type of sea bass • rock cod that reaches up to 1m in length
a·ra あら left-over fish head, bones & offal used in hotpot, clear soups & stock
a·rai あらい a style of sa·shi·mi for which raw, white-fleshed fish is thinly sliced & washed in cold water to keep the meat firm
a·ra·ma·ki·za·ke 新巻鮭 salted whole salmon
a·ra·na·be アラ鍋 hotpot made with sea bass (Kyūshū)
a·ra·re あられ baked cracker made from mo·chi
a·sa no mi 麻の実 hemp seed
a·sa·ri あさり baby clam
a·sa·tsu·ki あさつき very thin spring onion
a·sa·zu·ke 浅漬け lightly salted pickles
as·sa·ri あっさり general term for light (not greasy)
a·ta·ma·ryō·ri 頭料理 'head cuisine' using fish entrails (Taketa City)
ā·ti·chō·ku アーティチョーク artichoke
a·tsu·a·ge 厚揚げ fried tō·fu
a·wa アワ Italian millet • foxtail millet (rice substitute)
a·wa·bi あわび abalone
a·wa·bi no ka·su·zu·ke あわびの粕漬け abalone pickled in sa·ke·ka·su (Iwate Prefecture)
a·wa·mo·ri 泡盛 alcoholic spirit made from rice (Okinawa Prefecture)
a·yu アユ sweetfish • smelt (salmonoid food fish)
a·yu·ryō·ri アユ料理 sweetfish cuisine
a·zu·ki 小豆 red bean – ingredient for the sweet paste used as a filling in many Japanese cakes & confections

B

bai·gai バイ貝 bloody clam
ba·ka·gai バカ貝 see a·o·ya·gi
ban·cha 番茶 everyday green tea made from the second tea harvest
ba·ni·ra バニラ vanilla
ba·ni·ku 馬肉 horse meat
ba·ra no mi·cha バラの実茶 rosehip tea
bas バス bass • sea perch

ba·sa·shi 馬刺し horse meat sa·shi·mi (Nagano Prefecture)
ba·tā バター butter
ba·tā·mi·ru·ku バターミルク buttermilk
bat·te·ra·zu·shi バッテラずし vinegared fish on pressed su·shi
be·bī·kōn ベビーコーン baby corn
bē·kon ベーコン bacon
bē·ku·do·po·te·to ベークドポテト baked potatoes
be·ni·ba·na·in·gen ベニバナインゲン runner bean
be·ni·shō·ga 紅しょうが red pickled ginger
be·ni·ta·de 紅たで water pepper, a dark red peppery garnish
ben·tō 弁当 lunch box normally containing rice with different vegetables, meat, fish & sometimes fruit
be·ra べら wrasse (type of fish)
be·rī ベリー berries
bet·ta·ra·zu·ke べったらづけ pickled dai·kon
bī·fu ビーフ beef
bī·fu·jā·kī ビーフジャーキー beef jerky
bī·fu·ka·tsu ビーフカツ beef cutlet
bi·fu·te·ki ビフテキ beef steak
bin·na·ga ビンナガ longfin tuna
bī·ru ビール beer • ale
bī·to·rū·to ビートルート beetroot
bi·wa びわ loquat (small yellow plum-like fruit)
bo·ra ボラ mullet
bo·ta·mo·chi 牡丹もち rice cake made from half sticky rice & half nonglutinous rice
bu·chi·in·gem·ma·me ブチインゲンマメ pinto bean
bu·dō ブドウ grapes
bu·na·shi·me·ji ぶなしめじ a small, yellow mushroom variety
bu·rak·ku·be·rī ブラックベリー blackberry
bu·rak·ku·pu·din·gu ブラックプディング black pudding
bu·ri ブリ amberjack • yellowtail (types of fish)
bu·ri·ko ブリコ ha·ta·ha·ta eggs (Akita Prefecture)
bu·rok·ko·rī ブロッコリー broccoli
bu·rū·be·rī ブルーベリー blueberry
bu·ta·ni·ku 豚肉 pork
bu·ta·ni·ku no shi·o·zu·ke 豚肉の塩漬け salted pork
bu·ta no shō·ga·ya·ki 豚の生姜焼き pork sautéed in ginger & shō·yu
bu·tsu·ji 仏事 Buddhist funerary cuisine

C

chā·han チャーハン fried rice
chai·bu チャイブ chive
cha·kai·se·ki 茶懐石 tea kai·se·ki
cham·pon チャンポン noodle soup
chan·ko·na·be ちゃんこ鍋 sumo wrestler's stew of meat & vegetables
cha no yu 茶の湯 tea ceremony
chā·shū·men チャーシュー麺 rā·men topped with sliced roast pork
cha·sō·men 茶そうめん noodles containing green tea
cha·wan·mu·shi 茶碗蒸 savoury steamed custard containing fish stock, chicken & gingko nuts
che·rī·to·ma·to チェリートマト cherry tomatoes • plum tomatoes
chi·dai チダイ 'blood tai' fish (smaller than the ma·dai)
chi·kin チキン chicken
chi·ko·rī チコリー chicory
chi·ku·wa ちくわ sausage-shaped fish cake made from fish paste
chi·ku·zen·ni 筑前煮 chicken, taro, carrots, go·bō, lotus root, kon·nya·ku, dried shī·ta·ke mushroom & snow peas stewed in a stock made of sugar, shō·yu & mi·rin
chi·ma·ki ちまき nonglutinous-rice cake wrapped in large leaves
chim·pi 陳皮 citrus zest

chin·gen·sai チンゲンサイ bok choy
chip·pu チップ chips (crisps)
chi·ra·shi·zu·shi ちらしずし su·shi·me·shi topped with raw fish, a·bu·ra·a·ge & vegetables
chi·ri(·na·be) ちり（鍋） hotpot with white fish & vegetables
chi·ri·sō·su チリソース chilli sauce
chī·zu チーズ cheese
chō·ji チョウジ clove
cho·ko·rē·to チョコレート chocolate
chō·mi·ryō 調味料 seasoning
chop·pu チョップ chops
chow·dā チャウダー chowder
chō·za·me チョウザメ sturgeon
chū·go·ku·cha 中国茶 Chinese tea
chū·hai 酎ハイ shō·chū served with various nonalcoholic mixers
chū·ka·so·ba 中華そば an old-fashioned term for rā·men – now suggests rā·men in a lighter, predominantly shō·yu-based da·shi

D

da·ga·shi 駄菓子 'no good' sweets – cheap and OK but a bit junky
dai·fu·ku·mo·chi 大福もち rice cake with an·ko inside
dai·gin·jō·shu 大吟醸酒 highest grade sa·ke – fruitier than gin·jō·shu
dai·kon 大根 Chinese radish (giant white radish)
dai·kon·o·ro·shi 大根おろし grated dai·kon
dai·ō ダイオウ rhubarb
dai·to·ku·ji·nat·tō 大徳寺納豆 soy beans fermented with yeast
dai·zu 大豆 soy bean
dan·go だんご balls made from rice & flour
dan·sha·ku·i·mo 男爵芋 type of potato, especially common on Hokkaidō
da·ru·ma·ka·re·i ダルマカレイ turbot (type of fish)
da·shi だし stock, usually made from ka·tsu·o·bu·shi & kom·bu
da·shi·ji·ru だし汁 broth
da·te·ma·ki だて巻 sweetened rolled omelette, often served at New Year
de·be·ra でべら dried cinnamon flounder (Hiroshima Prefecture)
de·ka·fe no kō·cha デカフェの紅茶 decaffeinated tea
dem·bu でんぶ boiled & roasted snapper or cod flavoured with sugar & shō·yu & made into pink flakes that are used in su·shi rolls
den·ga·ku 田楽 dishes in which grilled fish, vegetables & tō·fu are topped with mi·so sauce
...·don …丼 rice with savoury topping
do·jō ドジョウ loach • oriental weatherfish (type of fish)
do·rai·bī·ru ドライビール 'dry beer' – it has a higher alcohol content & is more aerated than standard beer
do·rai·fu·rū·tsu ドライフルーツ dried fruit
do·ra·ya·ki どら焼き sweet a·zu·ki bean paste between two pancakes
do·te·na·be 土手鍋 hotpot with mi·so paste stock to which vegetables & seafood are added

E

e·bi エビ general term for prawn, shrimp, lobster & crayfish
e·bi·fu·rai エビフライ battered prawn
e·bi·sō·men エビそうめん shrimp sō·men
e·da·ma·me 枝豆 young soy bean – a favourite snack with beer
e·do·mi·so 江戸味噌 dark, fiery red & slightly sweet mi·so from Tokyo
e·i エイ ray fish
e·i·hi·re エイヒレ dried stingray fin served grilled as a snack with sa·ke
e·ki·ben 駅弁 station lunchbox
en·dai·bu エンダイブ endive

en·dō エンドウ field pea (type of green pea)
en·ga·wa えんがわ base of the dorsal fin of flounder & sole
e·no·ki·da·ke えのきだけ velvet shank mushroom • winter mushroom
e·ra えら gill
ē·ru エール ale

F

fen·ne·ru フェンネル fennel
fu 麸 shapes made from gluten flour used in clear soup
fu·cha·ryō·ri 普茶料理 Chinese Zen cuisine
fu·e·dai フエダイ snapper
fu·gu フグ puffer(fish) • globefish – famous fish that contains the deadly nerve toxin tetrodotoxin – its flesh is eaten as u·su·zu·ku·ri or in fu·gu·chi·ri & the milt (ie the testes of the fish) is regarded as a delicacy
fu·gu·chi·ri フグチリ hotpot with fu·gu
fu·gu·shi·ra·ko フグ白子 milt (ie the testes) of the fu·gu
fu·ka·ga·wa·na·be 深川鍋 hotpot with baby clam & spring onion
fu·ka·hi·re フカヒレ shark fin
fu·ki フキ Japanese butterbur (vegetable)
fu·ki·no·tō フキノトウ bud of fu·ki plant symbolising the beginning of spring
fu·ku·ro·ta·ke ふくろたけ paddy straw mushroom
fu·na フナ crucian carp – eaten as kan·ro·ni, tsu·ku·da·ni or a·rai
fu·na·zu·shi フナずし female crucian carp with eggs that are salted then pickled whole in fermented cooked rice (Shiga Prefecture)
fu·ri·ka·ke ふりかけ dried topping for rice
fu·rū·tsu·jū·su フルーツジュース fruit juice
fu·rū·tsu·kē·ki フルーツケーキ fruit cake
fu·rū·tsu·pan·chi フルーツパンチ fruit punch
fu·su·ma ふすま bran
fu·to·ma·ki 太巻き various ingredients rolled in no·ri seaweed (large su·shi rolls)

G

gai·mai 外米 foreign-produced rice
gam·mo·do·ki がんもどき minced tō·fu fried with finely chopped vegetables & seaweed – used in hotpots
gan ガン goose
ga·ri がり pickled pinkish-red ginger usually served as an accompaniment for su·shi
gek·kē·ju 月桂樹 bay
gem·mai 玄米 brown rice
gem·mai·cha 玄米茶 roasted tea with roasted & popped rice
ge·so げそ squid tentacles
gī ギー ghee
gin·jō 吟醸 sa·ke made of rice ground back to 60% of its weight before soaking and steaming
gin·jō·shu 吟醸酒 a type of sa·ke with a clean, fruity taste
gin·nan ぎんなん gingko nut
go·bō ごぼう burdock root
go·bu·zu·ki 五分づき mix of half white & half brown rice
go·ham·mo·no ご飯もの rice dishes
go·han ご飯 cooked rice • general term for 'a meal'
go·ma ごま sesame seeds
go·ma·a·bu·ra ごま油 sesame oil
go·ma·a·e ごま和え dishes mixed with sesame, salt & sugar sauce
go·ma·da·re ごまだれ sesame sauce
go·ma·dō·fu ごま豆腐 tō·fu-like food made of ground white sesame & starch

go·ma·me ゴマメ a small sardine cooked in shō·yu & sugar
go·mo·ku·so·ba 五目そば rā·men topped with vegetables, seafood & meat
go·ri·ryō·ri ゴリ料理 refers to dishes using ka·ji·ka (a type of fish) – a speciality of Kanazawa Prefecture
gu 具 filling • topping
gu·a·va グアヴァ guava
gu·ji ぐじ see a·ma·dai
gu·rap·pa グラッパ grappa (type of spirit)
gu·rē·pu·fu·rū·tsu グレープフルーツ grapefruit
gu·rīn·o·rī·bu グリーンオリーブ green olive
gu·ru·ta·min·san·sō·da グルタミン酸ソーダ MSG
gyo·ku·ro 玉露 highest-quality Japanese green tea
gyō·nyū 凝乳 curd
gyo·shō 魚醤 fish sauce
gyō·za ギョウザ Chinese-style dumplings, normally made from minced pork, cabbage, garlic, ginger & garlic chives
gyū·don 牛丼 thinly sliced beef simmered in sweetened shō·yu & served on rice
gyū·ni·ku 牛肉 beef
gyū·nyū 牛乳 milk
gyū·tan 牛タン beef tongue

H

ha 葉 leaf
hā·bu·tī ハーブティー herbal tea
ha·dok·ku ハドック haddock
hak·ka ハッカ mint • peppermint
ha·ku·mai 白米 plain, white rice
ha·ku·sai 白菜 Chinese cabbage
ha·ma·chi ハマチ yellowtail • amberjack (see bu·ri)
ha·ma·gu·ri ハマグリ clam
ha·mo ハモ conger • daggertooth (type of eel)
ham·pen はんぺん sponge-like fish cake made of ground shark meat mixed with grated yam & rice flour
ha·mu ハム ham
ha·na·dai·kon ハナダイコン rocket
ha·na·ma·me 花豆 flower bean
ha·na·sa·ki·ga·ni 花咲ガニ type of king crab • 'flower opening' crab that opens up when dipped into hot water
hap·pa 葉っぱ leaf
hap·pō·sai 八宝菜 stir-fry with assorted vegetables, meat & seafood & thickened with a Chinese-style sauce
ha·ra·pe·nyo ハラペニョ jalapeño chilli
ha·ra·wa·ta はらわた gizzards • offal
ha·ru·sa·me はるさめ bean-starch vermicelli
ha·sa·mi はさみ crab claws
ha·ta ハタ grouper (type of fish)
ha·ta·ha·ta ハタハタ sailfin sandfish used to make fermented fish sauce called shot·tsu·ru (Akita Prefecture)
ha·ta·ha·ta·zu·shi ハタハタずし pickled ha·ta·ha·ta
hat·chō·mi·so 八丁味噌 a dark mi·so originally created in Okazaki
ha·to 鳩 pigeon
ha·ya·shi·rai·su ハヤシライス stewed meat & vegetables with rice
ha·ya·to·u·ri ハヤトウリ chayote (fruit of a particular tropical climbing plant)
ha·ze ハゼ goby fish
hē·ku ヘイク hake
hē·ze·ru·nat·tsu ヘーゼルナッツ hazelnut
hi·bo·shi·to·ma·to 日干しトマト sun-dried tomatoes
hi·da·ra 干ダラ dried cod
hi·ga·shi 干菓子 dried sweets eaten during the tea ceremony
hi·ji·ki ひじき a type of seaweed
hi·ji·ki no ni·mo·no ひじきの煮物 hi·ji·ki simmered with shō·yu, sugar, fried tō·fu & boiled soy beans

hi·ki·ni·ku ひき肉 mince
hi·ki·wa·ri·mu·gi 挽き割り麦 cracked wheat
hi·ki·wa·ri·tō·mo·ro·ko·shi 挽き割りトウモロコシ hominy (boiled ground maize)
hī·ku·do·ri 肥育鶏 capon (castrated cock fowl fattened for eating)
hi·me·ma·su ヒメマス see ka·wa·ma·su
hi·mo·no 干物 dried fish
hi·ra·ki ひらき fully open ma·tsu·ta·ke mushroom
hi·ra·ma·sa ヒラマサ yellowtail • amberjack • kingfish
hi·ra·me ヒラメ bastard halibut • brill • flatfish • flounder • plaice • turbot
hi·ra·ta·ke ヒラタケ oyster mushroom
hi·re·ka·tsu ヒレカツ fried pork fillet
hi·to·ku·chi·to·ma·to 一口トマト cherry tomatoes • plum tomatoes
hi·tsu·ji 羊 sheep • lamb
hi·ya·mu·gi 冷麦 cold noodles dipped in cold sauce
hi·ya·shi·chū·ka 冷やし中華 cold noodles in sweet & sour soup with cucumber, chicken & egg on top
hi·ya·shi·u·don 冷やしうどん simple cold u·don
hi·ya·yak·ko 冷奴 cold tō·fu
hi·yo·ko·ma·me ヒヨコマメ chickpeas
hi·za·ni·ku ひざ肉 knuckle
hō·bō ホウボウ gurnard • bluefin • sea robin (types of fish)
hō·ji·cha ほうじ茶 roasted ban·cha
hok·kai·dō·ryō·ri 北海道料理 Hokkaidō cuisine
hok·ke ホッケ atka mackerel
hok·ki·gai ホッキ貝 hen clam (also known as u·ba·gai)
ho·ko·ri·ta·ke ホコリタケ puffball (fungus)
hom·mi·rin 本みりん good quality mi·rin
hon·jō·zō·shu 本醸造酒 Japanese rice wine, ground back to 70% of its original size & blended with alcohol & water
hon·shi·me·ji 本しめじ type of mushroom
hō·ren·sō ホウレンソウ spinach
ho·shi·en·dō 干しエンドウ green split pea
ho·shi·ga·ki 干し柿 dried persimmon
ho·so·ma·ki 細まき thin su·shi roll
ho·ta·ru·i·ka ホタルイカ firefly squid
ho·ta·te(·gai) ホタテ(貝) scallop
ho·ta·te·ryō·ri ホタテ料理 scallop cuisine
ho·wai·to·pu·din·gu ホワイトプディング white pudding
ho·ya ホヤ sea squirt mixed with cucumber & vinegar & eaten raw
ho·zon·ryō 保存料 preservative
hya·ku·hi·ro 百尋 boiled whale intestine (Hakata City)

I

i·chi·go イチゴ strawberry
i·chi·ji·ku イチジク fig
ī·da·ko いいだこ 'rice octopus' – a small octopus with lots of eggs inside, which look like rice
i·gai 貽貝 mussel (also known as mū·ru·gai)
i·ka イカ squid • cuttlefish
i·ki·zu·ku·ri 活き作り a method of presentation of fish & lobster, where the fish is served alive
i·ku·ra イクラ salted salmon eggs
i·na·go イナゴ rice locust – a type of rice-eating grasshopper, often eaten as tsu·ku·da·ni
i·na·ka·ryō·ri 田舎料理 rustic cuisine
i·na·man·jū いな饅頭 cleaned mullet stuffed with mi·so paste (Nagoya Prefecture) – see also bo·ra
i·na·ri·zu·shi 稲荷ずし vinegared rice in a fried tō·fu pouch
in·gem·ma·me インゲンマメ kidney bean

i·non·do イノンド dill
i·no·shi·shi いのしし wild boar
i·ri·do·ri 煎り鳥 stirfried chicken, dried shī·ta·ke, go·bō, ta·ro, kon·nya·ku, lotus root, carrots & bamboo shoots stewed in shō·yu & mi·rin
i·ri·ko いりこ sea cucumber • dried trepang (sea cucumber) • dried sardine
i·se·e·bi イセエビ Japanese spiny lobster • crayfish
i·shi·ka·ri·na·be 石狩鍋 Hokkaidō salmon & vegetable hotpot
i·so·be·ma·ki 磯辺巻き grilled rice cakes dipped in shō·yu & wrapped in no·ri
... i·ta·me …炒め stir-fried ...
i·ta·me·mo·no 炒め物 stir-fried dishes
i·ta·ya·gai いたや貝 a small scallop (also known as sha·ku·shi·gai)
i·to·kon·nya·ku 糸こんにゃく thinly sliced kon·nya·ku
i·to·na 糸菜 a pot-herb mustard, used as a leafy green vegetable
i·to·sō·men 糸そうめん thinnest type of sō·men
i·wa·na イワナ char (troutlike fish)
i·wa·shi いわし pilchard • sardine

J

ja·ga·ba·tā ジャガバター baked potatoes with butter
ja·ga·i·mo ジャガイモ potatoes
ja·po·ni·ka·mai ジャポニカ米 short-grain rice
jin·jā ジンジャー ginger
...ji·ru …汁 ... juice • ... soup
ji·za·ke 地酒 local sa·ke
jō·ryū·shu 蒸留酒 spirits
jū·bu·zu·ki 十分づき plain white rice
jum·mai·shu 純米酒 Japanese rice wine made by grinding rice back to 70% of its original weight
jun·sai じゅんさい water shield (small water plant)

K

ka·ba·ya·ki 蒲焼 grilled fish or eel dipped in shō·yu-based sauce, eg u·na·gi no ka·ba·ya·ki
ka·bo·cha かぼちゃ Japanese pumpkin
ka·bu かぶ turnip
ka·bu·na·me·ko かぶなめこ wild, slightly larger variety of na·me·ko mushroom
ka·bu·to·mu·shi かぶと蒸し steamed head of large fish varieties
ka·bu·to·ni かぶと煮 stewed head of large fish varieties
ka·e·ru カエル frog
ka·e·ru no a·shi カエルの足 frog legs
kai(·ru·i) 貝(類) shellfish
kai·sam·bu·tsu 海産物 seafood
kai·se·ki 懐石 see kai·se·ki·ryō·ri
kai·se·ki·ryō·ri 懐石料理 multicourse set meal including many small dishes – also known as kai·se·ki
kai·sō 海藻 generic term for edible seaweed and sea vegetables
kai·wa·re·dai·kon 貝割れ大根 spicy salad sprout from the mustard family
kai·zo·ku·ryō·ri 海賊料理 'pirate food' – live seafood put on the BBQ (Tokushima Prefecture)
ka·ji·ka カジカ similar to goby (fresh-water fish) – dishes using ka·ji·ka are called go·ri·ryō·ri & are a speciality of Kanazawa Prefecture
ka·ji·ki カジキ marlin
ka·ke·so·ba かけそば buckwheat noodles in broth
ka·ke·u·don かけうどん wheat flour noodles in broth
ka·ki 柿 persimmon
ka·ki カキ oyster
ka·ki·a·ge かき揚げ finely chopped seafood & vegetables fried in tem·pu·ra batter
ka·ki·me·shi かき飯 oyster rice
ka·ki·mo·chi かきもち see a·ra·re

ka·ki·na·be カキ鍋 oyster hotpot (Hiroshima Prefecture)
ka·ma·bo·ko かまぼこ white-fish paste that's steamed & sold in blocks
ka·ma·su カマス barracuda • sea pike
ka·mi·re·ru·cha カミレル茶 chamomile tea
ka·mo 鴨 duck
kam·pa·chi カンパチ amberjack (type of fish best eaten in summer)
kam·pyō かんぴょう dried fruit of bottle gourd, flavoured with shō·yu
kam·pyō·ma·ki かんぴょう巻き su·shi rolls made using kam·pyō
ka·ni カニ crab
ka·ni·ba·sa·mi カニばさみ see ha·sa·mi
ka·ni·mi·so カニ味噌 crab reproductive organs, often eaten as an hors d'oeuvre
kan·ki·tsu·ru·i 柑橘類 citrus
kan·ko·ku·ryō·ri 韓国料理 Korean cuisine
kan·zō カンゾウ liquorice
kan·ro·ni 甘露煮 small fish boiled in & sweetly flavoured with shō·yu & mi·rin • chestnuts boiled in syrup
kan·to·da·ki かんと炊き the name used for o·den in the Kansai region
kap·pa·ma·ki かっぱ巻き cucumber su·shi rolled in no·ri seaweed
ka·ra 殻 shell
ka·ra·a·ge から揚げ meat or fish dusted in flour & deep-fried
ka·ra·me·ru カラメル caramel (baked sugar)
ka·ra·mi·mo·chi からみもち rice cake with grated dai·kon
ka·ra·shi からし mustard
ka·ra·shi·men·tai·ko 辛子明太子 salted cod roe pickled in chilli (Kyūshū) – also just men·tai·ko
ka·ra·shi·na からし菜 brown mustard
ka·ra·shi·zu·ke からし漬け pickled vegetables flavoured with mustard
ka·ra·su·mi からすみ dried mullet roe (Nagasaki & Kyūshū) – see also bo·ra
ka·rē カレー curry
ka·re·i カレイ dab • flatfish • flounder
ka·rē·nam·ban カレー南蛮 buckwheat noodles with chicken or pork curry
ka·rē·rai·su カレーライス Japanese-style curry & rice
ka·rē·u·don カレーうどん u·don noodles with curry roux sauce (ie sauce based on equal amounts of fat and flour)
ka·ri·fu·ra·wā カリフラワー cauliflower
ka·rin かりん Chinese quince
ka·rin·tō かりんとう sweet made of flour & baking powder, deep-fried & coated with brown sugar
ka·ru·da·mon カルダモン cardamom
ka·ru·don カルドン cardoon (thistle-like plant with edible stalks)
ka·ru·kan かるかん a confection made from ya·ma·i·mo, rice powder & sugar (Kagoshima)
ka·shi·wa·mo·chi 柏もち rice cake wrapped in oak leaf – eaten on 5 May (Children's Day)
ka·su 粕 lees (sediment) from sa·ke
ka·su·ji·ru 粕汁 thick soup flavoured with lees (sediment) from sa·ke
ka·su·te·ra カステラ yellow sponge cake (Nagasaki Prefecture)
ka·su·zu·ke 粕漬け vegetables pickled in lees (sediment) from sa·ke
ka·ta·ku·chi·i·wa·shi カタクチイワシ anchovy • Japanese anchovy
ka·ta·ku·ri·ko 片栗粉 arrowroot flour
ka·ta·ya·ki·so·ba 固焼きそば crunchy fried noodles topped with vegetables
ka·ta·yu·de·ta·ma·go 固ゆで卵 hard-boiled egg
ka·tsu カツ cutlets
ka·tsu·don カツ丼 fried pork cutlet & egg on rice
ka·tsu·o カツオ bonito • skipjack (fish)

ka·tsu·o·bu·shi カツオ節 dried bonito (fish) flakes
ka·wa·ha·gi カワハギ leatherjacket • filefish
ka·wa·hi·me·ma·su カワヒメマス grayling (salmonoid fish)
ka·wa·ma·su 川マス freshwater red salmon • pike
ka·wa·za·ka·na 川魚 river fish • lake fish
ka·zu·no·ko かずのこ dried herring roe, usually served as part of o-se-chi-ryo-ri
ke·chap·pu ケチャップ (tomato) ketchup
ke·ga·ni 毛がに bristly crab • horsehair crab (best in winter)
kē·ki ケーキ cake(s)
ke·shi no mi ケシの実 poppy seed
kē·sho·ku 軽食 snacks
ki·dai キダイ yellowish tai, a cheap fish served as shi·o·ya·ki
ki·en·dō 黄エンドウ yellow split pea
ki·ha·da キハダ yellowfin tuna
ki·i·chi·go キイチゴ raspberry
ki·ji 雉 pheasant
ki·ku·i·mo キクイモ Jerusalem artichoke
ki·ku·ko きくこ cod milt (fish testes) used in hotpot
ki·ku·ra·ge きくらげ wood ear mushroom
ki·mi·sō·men 黄身そうめん noodles with egg yolk
kim·ma キンマ betel (plant with edible leaves and nuts)
kim·me(·dai) キンメ (ダイ) redfish
ki·na·ko きなこ soy bean flour
ki·na·ko·mo·chi きなこもち rice cake covered with sweetened soy bean flour
kin·kan キンカン kumquat
kin·ko きんこ dried trepang (sea cucumber)
ki no mi 木の実 berries
kim·me(·dai) キンメ (ダイ) redfish • alfonsino
kim·pi·ra·go·bō きんぴらごぼう thinly cut go·bō, normally eaten flavoured with shō·yu
ki·no·ko きのこ mushroom
kin·to·ki 金時 large red bean
ki·nu·go·shi·dō·fu 絹ごし豆腐 smooth, soft tō·fu (see also mo·men·dō·fu)
ki·ri·mi 切り fish or meat fillet
ki·shi·men きしめん flat noodles (Nagoya)
ki·su キス whiting
ki·tsu·ne·so·ba きつねそば buckwheat noodles with fried tō·fu
ki·tsu·ne·u·don きつねうどん wheat flour noodles with fried tō·fu
ki·yu·zu 黄ゆず yellow yu·zu
kō·be·gyū 神戸牛 beef from Kobe renowned as marble beef
ko·bu·cha 昆布茶 tea made of kom·bu seaweed (also called kom·bu·cha)
ko·bu·da·shi 昆布だし kelp stock
ko·bu·ma·ki 昆布巻き small fish or go·bō wrapped in kom·bu & boiled
kō·cha 紅茶 (black) tea
ko·chi·jan コチジャン a Korean sweet, spicy, pepper-mi·so paste
ko·e·bi 小エビ shrimp
ko·en·do·ro コエンドロ cilantro (also called Chinese parsley and coriander)
ko·ha·da こはだ threadfin shad • gizzard shad (herringlike types of fish also known as ko·no·shi·ro)
kō·hī コーヒー coffee
ko·hi·tsu·ji 子羊 lamb
ko·ko·a ココア cocoa
ko·ko·na·tsu ココナツ coconut
ko·ma·tsu·na 小松菜 mustard spinach (green leafy vegetable)
kom·bu 昆布 kelp (seaweed)
kom·bu·cha 昆布茶 see ko·bu·cha
ko·me 米 uncooked rice
ko·me·mi·so 米味噌 mi·so made from rice

kōm·mī·ru コーンミール cornmeal
ko·mu·gi 小麦 wheat
ko·mu·gi·hai·ga 小麦胚芽 wheat germ
kō·na·go こうなご sand eel
ko·na·za·tō 粉砂糖 icing sugar
kon·nya·ku こんにゃく devil's tongue – a tuber used to make a gelatinous paste that is used in hotpots & stewed foods (Gunma, Tochigi & Fukushima Prefectures)
ko·no·ko このこ dried trepang roe eaten as a snack with sa·ke (Ishikawa Prefecture)
kō no mo·no 香の物 pickled vegetables, served during a cha·kai·se·ki
ko·no·shi·ro コノシロ see ko·ha·da
ko no wa·ta コノワタ salted trepang (sea cucumber) intestine
kon·sai 根菜 root vegetables
ko·ri·an·da コリアンダ coriander
kō·ri·dō·fu 凍り豆腐 freeze-dried tō·fu used in stewed dishes
kō·ri·mi·zu 氷水 ice water
ko·ro ころ young, fully closed ma·tsu·ta·ke
ko·ro·ha コロハ fenugreek
ko·rok·ke コロッケ croquette
ko·ro·mo ころも coating of deep-fried food • batter
kō·ryō·kyō コウリョウキョウ galangal
ko·shi·ni·ku 腰肉 loin
kō·shin·ryō 香辛料 condiments
ko·shō 胡椒 pepper
ko·shō·sō コショウソウ cress
ko·tsu·zu·i 骨髄 marrow
kot·te·ri こってり general term for rich or thick (see also as·sa·ri)
ko·u·shi no ni·ku 仔牛の肉 veal
koy コイ carp used for mi·so soup or a·rai
kō·ya·dō·fu こうや豆腐 see kō·ri·dō·fu
koy·cha 濃茶 thick tea
koy·ku·chi·shō·yu 濃い口しょう油 dark shō·yu
ku·chi·ko クチコ salted trepang roe
ku·da·mo·no くだもの fruit
ku·ji·ra くじら whale
ku·mi·a·ge·dō·fu くみ上げ豆腐 freshly made tō·fu
ku·min クミン cumin
kun·sē 燻製 smoked
kun·sē·sa·ke 燻製サケ kipper
ku·ra·ge クラゲ jellyfish
ku·rak·kā クラッカー cracker
ku·ram·be·rī クランベリー cranberry
ku·ram·be·rī·sō·su クランベリーソース cranberry sauce
ku·res クレス cress
ku·re·son クレソン watercress
ku·ri 栗 chestnut
ku·ri·jō·chū 栗焼酎 shō·chū made from chestnuts
ku·ri·kin·ton 栗きんとん chestnuts boiled in syrup & covered with mashed sweet potatoes
ku·ro·a·na·go クロアナゴ black conger eel
ku·ro·bī·ru 黒ビール stout (beer)
ku·rō·bu クローブ clove
ku·ro·dai クロダイ black bream or porgy
ku·ro·go·ma 黒ごま black sesame seed
ku·ro·ma·gu·ro クロマグロ bluefin tuna
ku·ro·ma·me 黒豆 black soy bean
ku·ro·o·rī·bu 黒オリーブ black olive
ku·ro·was·san クロワッサン croissant
ku·ru·ma·ba·sō クルマバソウ sweet woodruff (plant whose leaves are used to flavour wine and liqueurs)
ku·ru·ma·e·bi 車えび kuruma prawn • tiger prawn • scampi
ku·ru·mi クルミ walnut
ku·ru·zet·to クルゼット courgette • zucchini
ku·sa·mo·chi 草もち green rice cake mixed with mugwort (a herbal plant)
ku·sa·ya くさや strong-smelling dried fish (island of Niijima & Izu archipelago)

kū·sū 古酒 or クースー aged a·wa·mo·ri alcohol
ku·wai クワイ arrowhead (water plant)
ku·wa no mi くわの実 mulberry
ku·zu 葛 the starch extracted from the root of the kudzu vine
ku·zu·ki·ri 葛きり thin, vermicelli-like noodles made from ku·zu
kya·be·tsu キャベツ (white) cabbage
kya·bya キャビア caviar
kya·ra·me·ru キャラメル caramel (lolly)
kya·ra·wē キャラウェー caraway seed
kyō·do·ryō·ri 郷土料理 regionalised speciality cuisine
kyō·na 京菜 a pot-herb mustard plant, used as leafy green vegetable
kyō·ri·ki·ko 強力粉 strong wheat flour
kyō·ryō·ri 京料理 Kyoto specialist cuisine
kyō·to·shi·ro·mi·so 京都白味噌 a delicate, sweet, white mi·so used in kyo·ryō·ri
kyū·ri キュウリ cucumber
kyū·ri·mo·mi キュウリもみ thinly sliced cucumber mixed & softened with salt
kyū·ri no pi·ku·ru·su キュウリのピクルス gherkin
kyū·shū·ryō·ri 九州料理 cuisine of the island of Kyūshū
kyū·tē·ryō·ri 宮廷料理 palace cuisine

M

ma·a·ji マアジ horse mackerel • jack mackerel • scad (type of fish)
ma·a·na·go マアナゴ conger eel
ma·dai マダイ red sea bream • silver sea bream • snapper
ma·ga·mo マガモ mallard (a duck)
ma·gu·ro マグロ tuna – caught mostly outside Japan
mai·ta·ke まいたけ hen-of-the-woods mushroom
ma·i·wa·shi まいわし sardine • pilchard
ma·ki·zu·shi 巻きずし general term for no·ri-rolled su·shi
ma·me 豆 beans, including pea & soy beans
ma·me·mi·so 豆味噌 mi·so made from soy beans
ma·me·ru·i 豆類 legume
man·gō マンゴー mango
man·jū 饅頭 steamed bun filled with sweet a·zu·ki beans
ma·ri·ne マリネ marinade
ma·ru·me·ro マルメロ quince
mas·shu·po·te·to マッシュポテト mashed potatoes
mas·tā·do マスタード mustard
ma·su マス pink salmon • generic term for trout
mat·cha 抹茶 powdered green tea
mat·cha·ai·su 抹茶アイス green tea ice cream
mat·cha·shi·o 抹茶塩 salt & powdered green tea, used for dipping tem·pu·ra
ma·tō·dai マトウダイ John Dory (fish)
ma·ton マトン mutton
ma·tsu·ka·wa·zu·ku·ri 松皮づくり a type of sa·shi·mi made from unskinned tai – the skin is tasty & looks like pine bark
ma·tsu no mi 松の実 pine nut
ma·tsu·ta·ke マツタケ expensive & highly fragrant mushroom variety
ma·yo·nē·zu マヨネーズ mayonnaise
me·ba·chi メバチ bigeye tuna
me·ba·ru メバル brown rockfish
me·bō·ki メボウキ sweet basil
me·da·ma·ya·ki 目玉焼き fried egg
men 麺 noodles
men·chi·ka·tsu メンチカツ crumbed & fried mince meat patties
men·ru·i 麺類 generic term for noodles
men·tai·ko 明太子 see ka·ra·shi·men·tai·ko
me·ron メロン melon • cantaloupe
mēs メース mace (a spice)

mi 身 generic term for flesh (of fish & shellfish)
mi·ga·ki·ni·shin 身欠きにしん dried herring
mi·kan みかん mandarin orange
mi·na·mi·ma·gu·ro ミナミマグロ southern bluefin tuna
min·to ミント mint
mi·rin みりん sweet rice wine used for cooking
mi·ru·gai みる貝 otter shell
mi·ru·ku ミルク milk
mi·ru·ku·tī ミルクティー milk tea
mi·so 味噌 fermented soy-bean paste – can also be made from rice or barley
mi·so·ni 味噌煮 fish simmered in mi·so stock
mi·so·rā·men 味噌ラーメン rā·men with mi·so-flavoured broth
mi·so·shi·ru 味噌汁 soup made from mi·so paste with da·shi – often includes vegetables, tō·fu & wa·ka·me
mi·so·zu·ke 味噌漬 meat, fish & vegetables pickled in mi·so
mi·tsu·ba みつば Japanese wild chervil, used to add flavour to hotpots, cha·wan·mu·shi & o·ya·ko·don
mi·tsu·ma·me みつまめ Japanese dessert made from boiled red peas, diced Japanese gelatine (agar-agar) & fruit topped with syrup – similar to am·mi·tsu, but does not include an·ko
mi·zu 水 water
mi·zu·na ミズナ a pot-herb mustard plant, used as leafy green vegetable
mi·zu·ta·ki 水炊き hotpot with chicken & vegetables boiled in their own stock – eaten with dipping sauce made from shō·yu & pon·zu
mi·zu·yō·kan 水羊羹 mild, sweet yō·kan jelly
mo·chi もち rice cake made from glutinous rice
mo·chi·go·me もち米 glutinous rice, used to make mo·chi
mo·dan·ya·ki モダン焼き Japanese-style savoury pancake with noodles
mo·men·dō·fu 木綿豆腐 rough, firm tō·fu (see also ki·nu·go·shi·dō·fu)
mo·mi·ji·o·ro·shi もみじおろし relish from grated dai·kon & chilli
mo·mo 桃 peach
mo·na·ka 最中 a sweet made of an·ko inside a thin wafer shell
mo·ri·so·ba もりそば cold buckwheat noodles served in a bamboo steamer & dipped into a cold sauce before eating
mo·tsu モツ chicken, pork or beef offal
mo·tsu·na·be モツ鍋 hotpot made of chicken, pork or beef offal
mo·tsu·ni モツ煮 simmered chicken, pork or beef offal
mo·ya·shi モヤシ bean sprouts
mo·zu·ku モズク type of seaweed served mixed with vinegar
mo·zu·ku·ga·ni モズクガニ small freshwater crab
mu·gi 麦 general term for wheat, oat, barley & rye
mu·gi·cha 麦茶 cold tea made from roasted barley
mu·gi·jō·chū 麦焼酎 shō·chū made from wheat (Oita Prefecture)
mu·gi·mi·so 麦味噌 barley mi·so popular in Kyūshū
mu·gi·to·ro 麦とろ cooked rice & wheat with grated yam on top
mu·ne·ni·ku 胸肉 brisket (meat from the breast of a four-legged animal, especially beef)
mu·ni·e·ru ムニエル meunière (describes a dish fried lightly in butter)
mū·ru·gai ムール貝 mussel (also known as i·gai)
mu·shi·gyō·za 蒸しギョウザ steamed gyō·za dumpling
mu·shi·mo·no 蒸し物 steamed dishes
mu·tsu·go·rō ムツゴロウ a kind of goby • mud skipper
myō·ga ミョウガ Japanese ginger
myū·zu·rī ミューズリー muesli

N

na 菜 leaf vegetables (see also nap·pa)
...·na·be …鍋 hotpot made of ...
na·be(·mo·no) 鍋(物) general term for hotpot – the diner selects the raw ingredients & cooks them in the na·be pot
na·be·ya·ki·u·don 鍋焼きうどん u·don noodles, seafood, meat & vegetables cooked in a small pot
na·ma·ga·shi 生菓子 uncooked sweet paste confections filled with red an
na·ma·ko ナマコ trepang (sea cucumber)
na·ma·su なます thinly cut, raw seafood or uncooked vegetables steeped in vinegar
na·ma·ta·ma·go 生卵 raw egg
na·ma·za·ke 生酒 sa·ke that has not been pasteurised
na·ma·zu ナマズ catfish
na·me·ko なめこ a small, golden-brown mushroom related to the ma·tsu·ta·ke
nam·ban·zu·ke 南蛮漬け fried fish marinated in vinegar with sliced onions & chilli
na·no·ha·na·zu·ke 菜の花漬け rape shoot pickle (Kyoto)
nap·pa 菜っ葉 leaf vegetables (see also na)
na·re·zu·shi なれずし salted a·yu pickled in vinegar & cooked rice
na·ru·to·ma·ki なると巻き thinly sliced fish cakes served in noodles, such as rā·men & u·don – contains the same ingredients as ka·ma·bo·ko
na·shi ナシ Japanese pear
na·su ナス eggplant • aubergine
na·ta·ne 菜種 rape seed
na·ta·ne·fu·gu 菜種フグ end-of-season fu·gu, at its tastiest & most poisonous
na·tsu·me なつめ date
na·tsu·me·gu ナツメグ nutmeg
na·tsu·me·ya·shi ナツメヤシ date (fruit)
nat·tō 納豆 sticky, fermented soy beans
ne·gi ねぎ spring onion • scallion • welsh onion
ne·gi·ma ねぎま tuna & spring onion stewed in a hotpot (Tokyo) • grilled spring onion & chicken meat on skewers served in ya·ki·to·ri restaurants
ne·ku·ta·rin ネクタリン nectarine
ni·bo·shi 煮干 dried anchovies used to make stock
ni·ga·u·ri にがうり balsam pear • bitter melon
ni·gi·ri·zu·shi にぎりずし hand-pressed su·shi
ni·go·ri·za·ke にごり酒 cloudy sa·ke
ni·hon·cha 日本茶 Japanese tea
ni·hon·ryō·ri 日本料理 Japanese cuisine
ni·hon·shu 日本酒 another word for sa·ke
ni·ji·ma·su ニジマス see ka·wa·ma·su
ni·ki·ri·mi·rin 煮きりみりん mi·rin with alcohol that is burned off prior to use
nik·kē 肉桂 see nik·ki
nik·ki ニッキ cinnamon
nik·ko·ro·ga·shi 煮っころがし potatoes or ta·ro stewed in shō·yu-based stock
ni·ku 肉 meat
ni·ku·dan·go 肉団子 meatball
ni·ku·ja·ga 肉じゃが potato & meat stew
ni·ku·ji·ru 肉汁 gravy
ni·ku·zu·ku ニクズク nutmeg
ni·mai·gai 二枚貝 clam
ni·mo·no 煮物 simmered dishes
nin·jin ニンジン carrot
nin·ni·ku ニンニク garlic
ni·ra にら Chinese chives • garlic chives
ni·shin にしん herring (best in spring

ni·tsu·ke 煮つけ fish or vegetables simmered in savoury stock until almost all the liquid evaporates
ni·wa·to·ri にわとり chicken
no·bu·ta 野豚 wild boar
no·mi·ya 飲み屋 Japanese-style bar
no·ri 海苔 sea laver (particular type of seaweed) • type of seaweed formed into sheets & used to wrap su·shi
no·ri·ma·ki 海苔巻 su·shi rolled in seaweed
no·shi·i·ka のしいか dried, hand-rolled squid
no·u·sa·gi 野ウサギ hare
nu·ka 糠 (rice) bran
nu·ka·mi·so 糠味噌 fermented rice bran used as a base to make pickles
nu·ka·zu·ke 糠漬け vegetables pickled in nu·ka·mi·so
nu·ta ぬた clam or tuna with spring onion covered in vinegared mi·so
nyū·men にゅうめん sō·men noodles in hot soup

O

o·a·ge おあげ thinly sliced, thick tō·fu fried in sesame oil
o·ben·tō お弁当 see ben·tō
o·cha お茶 Japanese green tea
o·cha·zu·ke お茶漬け white rice with green tea poured onto it
o·den おでん hotpot with tō·fu, kon·nya·ku, fish-cake balls & potato stewed in stock
o·do·ri·gu·i おどり食い shrimps or small fish eaten live & dipped in vinegar or shō·yu
ō·gi·gai 扇貝 scallop
o·ha·gi おはぎ see bo·ta·mo·chi
o·hi·ta·shi おひたし boiled green-leaf vegetables served cold with shō·yu
o·kan お燗 warm sa·ke
o·ka·ra おから lees from soy milk eaten with finely chopped vegetables
o·ka·shi お菓子 sweets • lollies
o·ka·shi·ra·tsu·ki 尾頭付き dish consisting of a whole fish
o·ka·yu おかゆ rice porridge • congee (gruel of boiled rice and water)
o·ka·zu おかず a dish accompanying rice, mi·so, soup & pickles
o·ko·no·mi·ya·ki お好み焼き Japanese-style savoury pancake
o·ku·ra オクラ okra
ō·mu·gi 大麦 barley
o·mu·rai·su オムライス dish consisting of omelette with a rice filling
o·mu·re·tsu オムレツ omelette
o·ni·ga·ra·ya·ki 鬼殻焼き prawns in the shell, grilled over hot coals
o·ni·gi·ri おにぎり rice ball
on·sen·ta·ma·go 温泉たまご egg boiled in a natural hot spring
o·re·ga·no オレガノ oregano
o·ren·ji オレンジ orange
o·rī·bu オリーブ olive
o·rī·bu·oy·ru オリーブオイル olive oil
...·o·ro·shi …おろし grated ...
o·ro·shi·shō·ga おろししょうが grated ginger
ō·ru·spais オールスパイス allspice
o·se·chi·ryō·ri おせち料理 various preserved dishes stored in layered lacquerware dishes & served at New Year
o·sa·ke お酒 Japanese wine (see also sa·ke)
o·shi·ru·ko お汁粉 grilled rice cake served with sweet, stewed a·zu·ki bean
o·shi·zus·hi 押しずし su·shi made by pressing vinegared rice into a square box & layering su·shi ingredients on top (Kansai region)
ō·to·mī·ru オートミール oatmeal
o·ya·ko·don 親子丼 chicken & egg on rice

P

pā·chi パーチ perch
pai パイ pie
pai·nap·pu·ru パイナップル pineapple

pan パン bread • bread roll
pan·ga·ta パン型 loaf
pan·ko パン粉 breadcrumbs
pa·pa·i·ya パパイヤ papaya
pa·pu·ri·ka パプリカ paprika
pa·se·ri パセリ parsley
pās·nip·pu パースニップ parsnip
pas·ta パスタ pasta
pas·to·ra·mi パストラミ pastrami
pe·kan ペカン pecan
pe·pā·min·to ペパーミント peppermint
pe·pā·min·to·tī ペパーミントティー peppermint tea
pe·pa·rō·ni ペパローニ pepperoni
pes·to·rī ペストリー pastry
pī·man ピーマン capsicum (usually green) • bell pepper
pī·nats ピーナツ groundnut • peanut
pis·ta·chi·o ピスタチオ pistachio
pō·chi·do·eg·gu ポーチド・エッグ poached egg
pō·ku ポーク pork (also called bu·ta·ni·ku)
pō·ku·sō·sē·ji ポークソーセージ pork sausages
pō·ku·so·tē ポークソテー sautéed pork
pon·kan ポンカン a large type of citrus fruit
pon·zu ポン酢 juice from citrus fruits • a mix of shō·yu, da·shi, citrus juices & sometimes vinegar used as a dipping sauce & in salad dressings
pop·pu·kōn ポップコーン popcorn
po·te·to ポテト potatoes
po·te·to·fu·rai ポテトフライ fried potatoes • French fries
pō·to·wain ポートワイン port
pu·ra·mu·to·ma·to プラムトマト plum tomatoes
pu·rūn プルーン prune

R

ra·dis·shu ラディッシュ radish
rā·do ラード lard
ra·gā·bī·ru ラガービール lager
rak·kyō ラッキョウ scallion • baker's garlic
rā·men ラーメン yellow wheat noodles
ra·mu ラム lamb
rā·yu ラー油 chilli oil
re·ba·sa·shi レバ刺し liver sa·shi·mi
re·mon レモン lemon
re·mon·tī レモンティー lemon tea
ren·kon れんこん lotus root
ren·zu·ma·me レンズマメ lentil
rē·shi レイシ lychee
rē·shu 冷酒 chilled sa·ke
re·tas レタス lettuce
rē·tō 冷凍 frozen
rē·zun レーズン raisin • sultana
ri·kyū·ru リキュール liqueur
rin·go りんご apple
ro·bus·tā ロブスター lobster
rō·ru·do·ō·to ロールドオート rolled oats
rō·ru·kya·be·tsu ロールキャベツ cabbage rolls
rō·ru·pan ロールパン bread roll
rōs(·to) ロース(ト) roast
rōz·ma·rī ローズマリー rosemary
ryō·chō 猟鳥 game (birds)
ryō·jū 猟獣 game (other animals)
ryo·ku·cha 緑茶 green tea
(...) ryō·ri (…)料理 (...-style) cuisine

S

sa·ba サバ chub mackerel • Pacific mackerel
sa·ba no mi·so·ni サバの味噌煮 mackerel simmered with mi·so
sa·ba no ni·tsu·ke サバの煮付け mackerel simmered with shō·yu
sa·dō 茶道 tea ceremony
sa·fu·ran サフラン saffron
sa·go サゴ sago
sa·ka·na 魚 fish
sa·ka·na no pē·sto 魚のペースト fish paste
sa·ka·na no ta·ma·go 魚の卵 fish roe

sa·ke 酒 alcohol made from a fermenting process that uses grain (also known as rice wine) • general term for alcoholic drinks (also called o·sa·ke & ni·hon·shu)
sa·ke 鮭 salmon • chum salmon • dog salmon (also known as sha·ke)
sa·ke·a·te 酒あて accompaniments to sa·ke & beer
sa·ke·ka·su 酒粕 lees (sediment) from rice wine
sa·ku·ra·ma·su 桜マス/琵琶マス cherry salmon
sa·ku·ra·mo·chi 桜もち pink rice cake wrapped in a cherry leaf
sa·ku·ram·bo さくらんぼ cherry
sa·ku·ra·ni·ku さくら肉 horse meat
sam·ma さんま Pacific saury • saury pike (types of fish)
san·do·rai·to·ma·to サンドライトマト sun-dried tomatoes
san·jin·ryō·ri 山人料理 'mountain man food' (Fukushima Prefecture & Tohoku region)
san·sai 山菜 edible, wild mountain vegetables
san·sai·ryō·ri 山菜料理 mountain vegetable cuisine
san·shō 山椒 Japanese prickly ash pod • Sichuan pepper
sa·ra·shi·ne·gi さらしねぎ Welsh onion, soaked in water, drained & thinly sliced
sā·ro·in サーロイン sirloin
sa·sa·ge ささげ black-eyed peas
sa·shi·mi 刺身 raw fish or meat
sa·tō 砂糖 sugar
sa·to·i·mo サトイモ taro
sa·tsu·ma·a·ge さつま揚げ fish paste mixed with finely chopped vegetables, then fried in sesame oil – used in ni·mo·no & o·den
sa·tsu·ma·i·mo サツマイモ sweet potato
sa·wa·chi·ryō·ri 皿鉢料理 celebratory cuisine with vegetables, seafood, ni·mo·no & a·ge·mo·no piled on one large platter (Kōchi Prefecture & Shikoku)
sa·wa·ga·ni 沢がに freshwater crab, often served deep-fried in ka·ra·a·ge
sa·wā·ku·rī·mu サワークリーム sour cream
sa·wa·ra さわら spotted mackerel • Spanish mackerel
sa·ya·en·dō サヤエンドウ snow pea
sa·ya·in·gen サヤインゲン string beans
sa·yo·ri サヨリ garfish • halfbeak • snipe fish
sa·za·e サザエ whelk (mollusc)
sa·za·e no tsu·bo·ya·ki サザエのつぼ焼き whelk (mollusc) grilled in the shell
sē·ji セージ sage
se·ki·han 赤飯 'red rice' with a·zu·ki beans
sem·bē せんべい rice cracker
sem·mai·zu·ke 千枚漬け large turnips pickled in sweet vinegar (Kyoto)
sen·cha 煎茶 a typical Japanese green tea
sen·dai·mi·so 仙台味噌 salty mi·so (Miyagi Prefecture)
sen·gi·ri 千切 vegetables thinly sliced lengthways • julienne
se·ri せり water dropwort (type of plant) – used in su·ki·ya·ki, soups & salads
se·ro·ri セロリ celery
sē·shu 清酒 sa·ke • generic term for clear rice wine
sha·bu·sha·bu しゃぶしゃぶ thinly sliced beef dipped into a boiling hotpot, then into sesame or pon·zu sauces
sha·ko しゃこ mantis shrimp • squilla (type of mantis shrimp)
sha·ku·shi·gai 杓子貝 see i·ta·ya·gai
sham·pen シャンペン sparkling wine

shan·dī シャンディー shandy
she·rī シェリー sherry
shi·ba·e·bi 芝エビ shiba shrimp • prawn
shi·bō 脂肪 fat
shi·bo·ri·ta·te jū·su しぼりたてジュース fresh juice
shi·chi·bu·zu·ki 七分づき a mixture of 70% white & 30% brown rice
shi·chi·men·chō 七面鳥 turkey
shi·chi·mi·tō·ga·ra·shi 七味唐辛子 a blend of seven spices used as a condiment for noodle dishes & na·be·mo·no
shi·chū シチュー stew
shī·fū·do シーフード seafood
shi·ka 鹿 deer
shi·ka·ni·ku 鹿肉 venison
shi·ki·mi シキミ star anise
shi·ma·a·ji シマアジ crevalle jack (type of fish)
shi·ma·dō·fu しまどうふ hard tō·fu suited to frying (Okinawa Prefecture)
shi·me·ji しめじ a type of mushroom
shi·me·sa·ba しめサバ vinegared mackerel
shi·mo·fu·ri(·gyū·ni·ku) 霜降り（牛肉） marbled (beef)
shi·na·chi·ku シナチク pickled Chinese bamboo sprouts
shi·na·mon シナモン cinnamon
shin·cha 新茶 new-season green tea – usually available in stores in early summer
shin·shū·mi·so 信州味噌 mi·so from Nagano Prefecture
shi·o 塩 salt
shi·o·bo·shi·wa·ka·me 塩干しワカメ wa·ka·me washed in salt water, then dried
shi·o·ka·ra 塩辛 seafood pickled with salt
shi·o·nu·ki·wa·ka·me 塩抜きワカメ wa·ka·me washed in plain, unsalted water & dried
shi·o·ya·ki 塩焼き salted & grilled food
shi·o·zu·ke 塩漬け vegetables, meat or seafood pickled in salt
ship·po·ku·ryō·ri 卓袱料理 a refined banquet cuisine from Nagasaki Prefecture
shi·ra·ko 白子 milt (testes from fish)
shi·ra·shi·me·yu 白絞め油 salad oil, normally rape seed oil
shi·ra·su シラス whitebait
shi·ra·su·bo·shi しらす干し boiled & dried young anchovies or pilchards
shi·ra·ta·ki しらたき kon·nya·ku in noodle form
shi·ra·u·o しらうお a type of fish eaten live & known in English as ice goby or icefish (Fukuoka Prefecture)
shi·ri·ni·ku 尻肉 rump
shi·ro·a·e 白和え vegetables mixed with sauce made from tō·fu
shi·ro·a·ma·dai 白アマダイ white a·ma·dai
shi·ro·go·ma 白ごま white sesame seed
shi·ro·ke·shi no mi 白ケシの実 white poppy seed
shi·ro·mi·so 白味噌 white mi·so
shi·ro·mi·za·ka·na 白身魚 white-fleshed fish
shi·ro·wain 白ワイン white wine
shi·ro·za·ke 白酒 white, cloudy rice wine
shi·rya·ru シリアル cereal
shi·sha·mo ししゃも capelin • longfin smelt • night smelt (types of fish)
shi·so しそ beefsteak plant • perilla (a member of the mint family) – used as a condiment, a colouring or as a flavouring for pickles
shi·ta 舌 tongue
shi·ta·bi·ra·me シタビラメ sole
shī·ta·ke しいたけ shiitake mushroom
shō·chū 焼酎 distilled spirit made from sweet potato, rice, millet or lees (sediment) from rice wine
shō·ga しょうが ginger
shō·ga·su しょうが酢 ginger vinegar

shō·ga·ya·ki しょうが焼き grilled meat or fish flavoured with ginger & shō·yu
shō·ga·yu しょうが湯 ginger & hot water – a traditional cure
shō·jin·a·ge 精進揚げ vegetarian tem·pu·ra
shō·jin·ryō·ri 精進料理 traditional vegetarian food
sho·ku·bu·tsu·yu 植物油 vegetable oil
sho·ku·pan 食パン square-shaped loaf of bread
sho·ku·ryō 食料 stock (food)
shop·pai しょっぱい salty
shot·tsu·ru しょっつる fermented fish sauce made from ha·ta·ha·ta (Akita Prefecture)
shō·yu しょう油 soy sauce made from fermented soy bean & wheat
shō·yu·ya·ki しょう油焼き grilled with shō·yu
shō·yu·zu·ke しょう油漬け vegetables pickled in shō·yu
shū·mai シュウマイ steamed, round Chinese dumplings
shun·gi·ku 春菊 crown daisy • garland chrysanthemum – eaten as o·hi·ta·shi, a·e·mo·no & na·be
shu·tō 酒盗 salted & fermented ka·tsu·o intestine – a good accompaniment for drinking sa·ke
skam·pi スカンピ scampi
skas·shu スカッシュ squash
skā·to スカート skirt (a cut of beef from the flank)
snak·ku スナック snacks
so·ba そば buckwheat • noodles made of buckwheat
so·ba·cha そば茶 buckwheat tea
so·ba·ga·ki そばがき dough made of buckwheat flour mixed with boiled water
sō·da ソーダ soda water
sō·men そうめん fine wheat noodles eaten cold & dipped in sauce
so·ra·ma·me そら豆 broad bean
sō·sē·ji ソーセージ sausage
sō·su ソース sauce • Worcester sauce
so·tē ソテー sauté
su 酢 vinegar
su·ga·ta·mu·shi 姿蒸し steamed whole fish
su·gu·ki 酢茎 turnip pickle (Kyoto Prefecture)
su·gu·ri スグリ currant • gooseberry
spair·ri·bu スペアリブ sparerib
spā·ku·rin·gu·wain スパークリングワイン sparkling wine
su·i·ka すいか watermelon
su·i·ku·chi 吸い口 topping for clear soup
su·i·mo·no 吸い物 clear Japanese soup made of fish stock (also called su·ma·shi or su·ma·shi·ji·ru)
su·ī·to·kōn スウィートコーン sweetcorn
su·ī·to·ba·ji·ru スウィートバジル sweet basil
su·i·ton すいとん balls made of wheat flour & boiled with vegetables in soup
su·ji スジ sinew • tendon of pork or beef (term used in ya·ki·to·ri restaurants)
su·ji·ko すじこ salted salmon roe
su·ki·ya·ki すき焼き beef, tō·fu, vegetables & shi·ra·ta·ki cooked in an iron pan with shō·yu, sugar & sa·ke & served with raw egg dip
su·ma·shi(·ji·ru) 澄まし(汁) see su·i·mo·no
su·me·shi 酢飯 vinegared rice used for su·shi
su·mi·bi·ya·ki 炭火焼き charcoal-grilled food
su·mi·so 酢味噌 sauce made of vinegar & mi·so
su·mo·mo スモモ plum
su·ne·ni·ku すね肉 shank
su·no·mo·no 酢の物 vinegared food
sup·pon スッポン snapping turtle
sup·pon·na·be スッポン鍋 hotpot of sup·pon

sup·pon·ryō·ri スッポン料理 snapping turtle served as na·be·mo·no, sa·shi·mi, or deep-fried
sū·pu スープ soup
su·ri·ba·chi すり鉢 mortar (as in mortar & pestle)
su·ri·go·ma すりごま ground sesame
su·ru·me スルメ dried squid
su·shi すし any food served on or rolled in vinegared rice
su·shi·da·ne すし種 su·shi topping
su·shi·me·shi すし飯 vinegared rice for su·shi
su·ya·ki 素焼き plainly grilled without salt
su·zu·ke 酢漬け vinegared pickles
su·zu·ki スズキ common sea bass • Japanese sea perch
su·zu·ki no hō·sho·ya·ki スズキの奉書焼 grilled sea bass served wrapped in traditional Japanese paper (city of Matsue & Shimane Prefecture)
su·zu·me すずめ sparrow – served at ya·ki·to·ri restaurants

T

ta·chi·u·o タチウオ cutlass fish • hairtail (fish)
tai タイ snapper • bream
tai·mu タイム thyme
tai·ra·gai タイラ貝 fan shell • sea pen (mollusc)
tai·ra·gi タイラギ see tai·ra·gai
tai·ryō·ri 鯛料理 sea bream cuisine
tai·shō·e·bi 大正エビ fleshy prawn
ta·ka·na 高菜 broad-leafed mustard
ta·ka·na·zu·ke 高菜漬け mustard leaf pickles
ta·ka no tsu·me 鷹の爪 red-hot peppers
ta·ke·no·ko タケノコ bamboo shoots
ta·ki·ko·mi·go·han 炊き込み御飯 rice cooked together with vegetables & seasonings
ta·ko タコ octopus
ta·ko·ya·ki タコ焼き balls made of batter with octopus inside, fried (Osaka)
ta·ku·an たくあん pickled dai·kon
ta·ma·go 卵 egg
ta·ma·go·to·ji 卵とじ cooked vegetables or meat covered with whisked egg
ta·ma·go·ya·ki 卵焼き Japanese-style fried egg • omelette
ta·ma·ne·gi たまねぎ onion
ta·ma·ne·gi no su·zu·ke たまねぎの酢漬け pickling onion
ta·ma·ri·dō·fu たまりどうふ tō·fu infused with egg
ta·ma·ri·jō·yu たまりじょう油 wheat-free shō·yu
tan タン tongue
ta·ra タラ cod • Pacific cod • grey cod
ta·ra·ba·ga·ni タラバガニ Alaskan crab • king crab
ta·ra·gon タラゴン tarragon
ta·ra·ko タラコ salted cod • collack roe
ta·ra·no·me タラノメ angelica tree sprout (available only in early spring)
ta·re たれ sauce – usually made from shō·yu, mi·rin & sugar
ta·ro·i·mo タロイモ taro
ta·ta·ki たたき minced raw fish flesh • meat or fish seared on the outside & served sliced, with the inside remaining rare
ta·tsu·ta·a·ge 竜田揚げ meat or fish dipped in shō·yu & seasoned flour, then deep-fried
te·kī·ra テキーラ tequila
tek·ka·don 鉄火丼 tuna sa·shi·mi on a large bowl of steamed rice
tek·ka·ma·ki 鉄火巻き tuna su·shi roll
te·ma·ki·zu·shi 手巻きずし do-it-yourself su·shi roll
tem·pu·ra てんぷら seafood, meat & vegetables deep-fried in light batter & eaten dipped in a light sauce with ginger & grated dai·kon

tem·pu·ra·so·ba てんぷらそば buckwheat noodles in broth with tem·pu·ra pieces on top
tem·pu·ra·u·don てんぷらうどん wheat flour noodles in broth with tem·pu·ra pieces on top
ten·don 天丼 battered prawn on rice
te·ri·ya·ki 照り焼き meat or fish, brushed with marinade made of shō·yu, mi·rin & sugar, then grilled
tē·sho·ku 定食 set menu
tes·sa てっさ fu·gu sa·shi·mi
te·u·chi·so·ba 手打ちそば traditional, handmade so·ba
to·bi·u·o トビウオ flying fish
tō·fu とうふ soy-bean curd (tofu)
tō·ga·ra·shi とうがらし red chilli pepper • cayenne
to·ki·shi·ra·zu ときしらず see a·ra·ma·ki·za·ke
to·ma·to トマト tomato
to·ma·to·sō·su トマトソース tomato sauce
tō·mo·ro·ko·shi トウモロコシ corn
ton·ko·tsu とんこつ pork broth
ton·ko·tsu·rā·men とんこつラーメン rā·men with white pork broth
ton·ka·tsu·sō·su とんかつソース sauce to go with ton·ka·tsu (pork cutlet)
to·nik·ku トニック tonic water
tō·nyū 豆乳 soy milk
top·pin·gu トッピング topping
to·ra·fu·gu トラフグ tiger fu·gu
to·rai·pu トライプ tripe
to·ra·ma·me とら豆 tiger beans
to·ri·ni·ku 鶏肉 chicken (meat)
to·ri·ni·ku 鳥肉 poultry
to·ro とろ the fattiest (and also considered the tastiest) meat of tuna fish ma·gu·ro
to·ro·ro とろろ grated yam
to·ro·ro·ji·ru とろろ汁 grated yam mixed with stock
to·ryu·fu トリュフ truffle
to·shō·shi·yu 杜松子油 juniper berry oil
tōs·to トースト toast
tsu·ba·me·u·o ツバメ魚 swallow fish • a type of batfish
tsu·bo·ya·ki つぼ焼き shellfish (normally whelks) grilled in its own shell
tsu·ke·mo·no 漬物 pickles
tsu·ki·mi·so·ba 月見そば buckwheat noodles in broth with a raw egg
tsu·ki·mi·u·don 月見うどん wheat flour noodles in broth with a raw egg
tsu·ku·da·ni 佃煮 seafood or vegetables simmered in a thick sauce made from salt, sugar & shō·yu until all moisture is reduced
tsu·ku·ne つくね minced fish or chicken balls eaten fried or boiled
tsu·ku·ri 造り slices of raw fish, another term for sa·shi·mi
tsu·ma つま garnish
tsu·me·mo·no 詰め物 stuffing
tsu·mi·re つみれ fish-cake balls – used in o·den & stew
tsu·no·ga·rē ツノガレイ plaice
tsu·yu つゆ dipping sauce
tu·ke·a·wa·se 付け合せ garnish • relish

U

u·ba·gai ウバ貝 hen clam
u·do ウド mountain vegetable eaten fresh, stewed or pickled
u·don うどん thick noodles made of wheat flour
u·kon ウコン turmeric
u·me 梅 Japanese plum
u·me·bo·shi 梅干 dried & pickled Japanese plum
u·me·zu 梅酢 sour-plum vinegar
u·mi·u·o 海魚 fish from the ocean
u·na·don うな丼 grilled eel on rice
u·na·gi うなぎ eel
u·na·gi no ka·ba·ya·ki うなぎの蒲焼 grilled eel flavoured with soy-based sauce
u·na·jū うな重 grilled eel served on rice in a lacquered box

u·ni ウニ sea urchin
u·no·ha·na 卯の花 see o·ka·ra
u·ro·ko うろこ fish scales
ū·ron·cha 烏龍茶 oolong tea
u·ru·chi·mai うるち米 non-glutinous rice
u·ru·ka ウルカ salted innards of a·yu
u·ru·me·i·wa·shi ウルメイワシ Japanese sardine
u·shi no o 牛の尾 oxtail
u·shi·o·ji·ru うしお汁 delicately flavoured clear soup made from fish & shellfish
u·su·a·ji 薄味 light-tasting or lightly seasoned
u·su·cha 薄茶 thinner tea than koy·cha
u·su·ku·chi·shō·yu 薄口しょう油 light shō·yu
u·su·tā·sō·su ウスターソース Worcester sauce
u·su·zu·ku·ri 薄作り raw, thinly sliced fu·gu flesh
u·zu·ra ウズラ quail
u·zu·ra no ta·ma·go ウズラの卵 quail egg

W

wa·ga·shi 和菓子 Japanese sweets
wa·gyū 和牛 Japanese beef
wai·ru·do·rai·su ワイルドライス wild rice
wa·ka·me ワカメ type of seaweed
wa·ka·sa·gi わかさぎ pond smelt (a freshwater fish)
wa·ke·gi ワケギ shallots
wa·ni ワニ shark meat (Chūgoku region) • crocodile
wan·tan·men ワンタン麺 rā·men noodles in broth, with meat dumplings
wa·ra·bi 蕨 a kind of fern of which the tender young shoots are eaten
wa·ra·ma·ki·bu·ri 藁巻きブリ salted & dried bu·ri, which is then rolled in straw (Toyama Prefecture)
wa·ri·shi·ta 割り下 sauce of shō·yu, mi·rin & sugar, used in su·ki·ya·ki
wa·sa·bi ワサビ very hot Japanese horseradish
wa·sa·bi·ma·ki ワサビ巻き su·shi roll containing wa·sa·bi
wa·sa·bi·zu·ke ワサビ漬け vegetables pickled in a wa·sa·bi base
wa·ta わた see ha·ra·wa·ta
wa·ta·ri·ga·ni ワタリガニ blue swimmer crab
wi·kyō ウイキョウ fennel
wi·kyō no mi ウイキョウの実 fennel seed
wi·rō ういろう a steamed sweet made of rice flour & arrowroot (Nagoya)

Y

...·ya …屋 ... shop • ... restaurant, eg su·shi·ya, sha·bu·sha·bu·ya
ya·e·na·ri ヤエナリ mung bean
...·ya·ki/ya·ki ... …焼き/焼き… food that is grilled, baked, barbecued or pan fried
ya·ki·dō·fu 焼き豆腐 grilled tō·fu used for hotpot
ya·ki·gyō·za 焼きギョウザ grilled gyō·za dumpling
ya·ki·me·shi 焼き飯 fried rice
ya·ki·mo·chi 焼きもち toasted rice cake
ya·ki·mo·no 焼きもの broiled, grilled or pan-fried dishes
ya·ki·na·su 焼きナス grilled eggplant
ya·ki·ni·ku 焼肉 cook-it-yourself, Korean-style barbecue
ya·ki·no·ri 焼き海苔 lightly toasted no·ri
ya·ki·o·ni·gi·ri 焼きおにぎり grilled rice ball
ya·ki·so·ba 焼きそば fried so·ba noodles with vegetables, meat & sauce
ya·ki·to·ri 焼きとり grilled meat on skewers served with ta·re or salt
ya·ki·za·ka·na 焼き魚 grilled fish
ya·ku·mi 薬味 condiment • relish • seasoning

ya·ma·i·mo 山芋 yam
ya·ma·ka·ke 山かけ grated yam with seasoning
ya·ma·ku·ji·ra 山鯨 'mountain whale' – the renamed i·no·shi·shi (wild boar)
ya·ma·me ヤマメ freshwater salmon
ya·ma no mo·no 山のもの mountain dishes
ya·na·ga·wa·na·be 柳川鍋 boiled loach or weatherfish with whisked eggs on top
ya·sai 野菜 vegetables
ya·sai·i·ta·me 野菜炒め fried vegetables
ya·sē 野生 wild
ya·sō 野草 wild greens
ya·tsu·ga·shi·ra 八ッ頭 most sought-after type of taro
ya·tsu·ha·shi 八橋 sweet cinnamon-flavoured hard crackers (Kyoto Prefecture)
yō·kan ようかん sweet jelly made of ground a·zu·ki beans
yo·mo·gi ヨモギ mugwort
yō·na·shi 洋ナシ pear
yo·se·na·be 寄せ鍋 hotpot with seafood, chicken & vegetables in a light stock
yō·sho·ku 洋食 Japanese versions of Western dishes
yu·ba ゆば thin layers of skin skimmed from boiled soy milk
yu·de·gyō·za ゆでギョウザ boiled gyō·za dumpling
yu·de·ta·ma·go ゆで卵 boiled eggs
yu·dō·fu 湯豆腐 tō·fu boiled in a weak kom·bu broth
yū·ga·o ユウガオ white-flower gourd • bottle gourd
yū·han 夕飯 dinner
yu·shi·dō·fu ゆし豆腐 a soft variety of tō·fu from Okinawa
yu·zu ゆず a type of citrus fruit

Z

zak·ko·ku 雑穀 millet
za·ku·ro ざくろ pomegranate
za·ru·gai ザルガイ cockle
za·ru·so·ba ざるそば cold buckwheat noodles served with no·ri, spring onion & wa·sa·bi
zem·mai ゼンマイ osmund • royal fern (mountain vegetable)
zen·ryū·ko·mu·gi 全粒小麦 whole-wheat
zen·ryū·ko·mu·gi·ko 全粒小麦粉 wholewheat flour
zen·zai ぜんざい sweet a·zu·ki bean soup with rice cakes
ze·ra·chin ゼラチン gelatine
ze·rī ゼリー jelly
zo·me·ki·ryō·ri ぞめき料理 cuisine of local vegetables & seafood from Tokushima Prefecture
zō·mo·tsu 臓物 offal • giblets
zō·ni 雑煮 rice cake in soup
zō·su·i 雑炊 rice gruel • soup with vegetables & seafood flavoured with mi·so or shō·yu
zu·i·ki ずいき taro stem
zu·wai·ga·ni ズワイガニ red crab • snow crab

DICTIONARY

English to Japanese

英語－日本語

Verbs in this dictionary are in their ·mas (ます) form (for more information on this, see **grammar**, p16). The symbols ⓝ, ⓐ and ⓥ (indicating noun, adjective and verb) have been added for clarity where an English term could be either. Basic food terms have been included – for a more extensive list of ingredients and dishes, see the **menu decoder** (p196).

A

aboard 乗って not·te
abortion 中絶 chū·ze·tsu
about だいたい dai·tai
above 上に u·e ni
abroad 海外 kai·gai
accident 事故 ji·ko
accommodation 宿泊 shu·ku·ha·ku
(bank) account 口座 kō·za
across 横切って yo·ko·git·te
actor 俳優 hai·yū
acupuncture 鍼 ha·ri
adaptor アダプター a·da·pu·tā
addiction 中毒 chū·do·ku
address 住所 jū·sho
administration 管理 kan·ri
admission (price) 入場料 nyū·jō·ryō
adult ⓝ 大人 o·to·na
adventure 冒険 bō·ken
advertisement 広告 kō·ko·ku
advice 意見 i·ken
aerobics エアロビクス air·ro·bi·kus
aeroplane 飛行機 hi·kō·ki
Africa アフリカ a·fu·ri·ka
after あと a·to
afternoon 午後 go·go
(this) afternoon (今日の)午後 (kyō no) go·go
aftershave アフターシェーブ af·tā·shē·bu
again また ma·ta
age ⓝ 年齢 nen·rē
(three days) ago (3日)前 (mik·ka) ma·e
aggressive 攻撃的な kō·ge·ki·te·ki na
agree 賛成します san·sē shi·mas
agriculture 農業 nō·gyō
ahead 向うに mu·kō ni
AIDS エイズ ē·zu
air 空気 kū·ki
air-conditioned エアコン付きの air·kon·tsu·ki no
air-conditioning エアコン air·kon
airline 航空 kō·kū
airmail 航空便 kō·kū·bin
airplane 飛行機 hi·kō·ki
airport 空港 kū·kō
airport tax 空港税 kū·kō·zē
aisle (eg on plane) 通路 tsū·ro

alarm clock 目覚し時計 me·za·ma·shi·do·kē
alcohol アルコール a·ru·kō·ru
alcove (in house) 床の間 to·ko·no·ma
all 全部 zem·bu
allergy アレルギー a·re·ru·gī
almond アーモンド ā·mon·do
almost ほとんど ho·ton·do
alone ひとりで hi·to·ri de
already もう mō
also また ma·ta
altar 祭壇 sai·dan
altitude 標高 hyō·kō
always いつも i·tsu·mo
ambassador 大使 tai·shi
ambulance 救急車 kyū·kyū·sha
America アメリカ a·me·ri·ka
amount (money) 総計 sō·kē
anaemia 貧血 hin·ke·tsu
anaesthetic 麻酔 ma·su·i
anchovy アンチョビ・カタクチイワシ an·cho·bi • ka·ta·ku·chi·i·wa·shi
ancient 大昔の ō·mu·ka·shi no
and そして so·shi·te
angry 怒ります o·ko·ri·mas
animal 動物 dō·bu·tsu
ankle 足首 a·shi·ku·bi
annual 年一回の nen·ik·kai no
another もう一つの mō·hi·to·tsu no
answer ⓝ 答え ko·ta·e
ant アリ a·ri
antibiotics 抗生剤 kō·sē·zai
antihistamines 抗ヒスタミン剤 kō·hi·su·ta·min·zai
antinuclear 反核の han·ka·ku no
antique ⓝ アンティーク an·tī·ku
antiseptic ⓝ 消毒剤 shō·do·ku·zai
any いくらか i·ku·ra·ka
apartment マンション・アパート man·shon • a·pā·to
apéritif 食前酒 sho·ku·zen·shu
appendix (organ) 盲腸 mō·chō
appetiser 前菜 zen·sai
apple りんご rin·go
appointment 予約 yo·ya·ku
apricot あんず an·zu
archaeological 考古学的な kō·ko·ga·ku·te·ki na
architect 建築家 ken·chi·ku·ka
architecture 建築 ken·chi·ku
argue 反論します han·ron shi·mas
arm 腕 u·de
aromatherapy アロマテラピー a·ro·ma·te·ra·pī
arrest ⓥ 逮捕します tai·ho shi·mas
arrivals 到着 tō·cha·ku
arrive 到着します tō·cha·ku shi·mas
art 美術 bi·ju·tsu
art gallery 美術館 bi·ju·tsu·kan
artist 芸術家 gē·ju·tsu·ka
ashtray 灰皿 hai·za·ra
Asia アジア a·jya
ask (a question) たずねます ta·zu·ne·mas
ask (for something) たのみます ta·no·mi·mas
asparagus アスパラガス as·pa·ra·gas
aspirin アスピリン as·pi·rin
assault 暴行 bō·kō
asthma 喘息 zen·so·ku
at で de
athletics 運動 un·dō
atmosphere 雰囲気 fun·i·ki
aubergine ナス na·su
aunt おばさん o·ba·san
Australia オーストラリア ō·sto·ra·rya
automatic ⓐ オートマチック ō·to·ma·chik·ku
ATM ATM ē·tī·e·mu
autumn 秋 a·ki
avenue 大通り ō·dō·ri
avocado アボガド a·bo·ga·do
awful ひどい hi·doy

B

B&W (film) 白黒（フィルム） shi·ro·ku·ro (fi·ru·mu)
baby 赤ちゃん a·ka·chan
baby food 離乳食 ri·nyū·sho·ku
baby powder ベビーパウダー be·bī·pow·dā
babysitter ベビーシッター be·bī·shit·tā

back (body part) 背中 se·na·ka
back (position) うしろ u·shi·ro
backpack バックパック bak·ku·pak·ku
bacon ベーコン bē·kon
bad 悪い wa·ru·i
bag (general) かばん ka·ban
bag (shopping) 袋 fu·ku·ro
baggage 手荷物 te·ni·mo·tsu
baggage allowance 手荷物許容量 te·ni·mo·tsu·kyo·yō·ryō
baggage claim バッゲージクレーム bag·gē·ji·ku·rē·mu
bakery パン屋 pan·ya
balance (account) 残高 zan·da·ka
balcony バルコニー ba·ru·ko·nī
ball (sport) ボール bō·ru
ballet バレエ ba·rē
banana バナナ ba·na·na
band (music) バンド ban·do
bandage 包帯 hō·tai
Band-Aids バンドエイド ban·do·ēdo
bank (money) 銀行 gin·kō
bank account 銀行口座 gin·kō·kō·za
banknote 紙幣 shi·hē
bar バー bā
bar fridge ミニバー mi·ni·bā
bar work バーテンダー bā·ten·dā
barber 床屋 to·ko·ya
baseball 野球 ya·kyū
basketball バスケット(ボール) bas·ket·to (bō·ru)
bath ⓝ お風呂 o·fu·ro
bath house 銭湯 sen·tō
bathing suit 水着 mi·zu·gi
bathroom 風呂場 fu·ro·ba
batter バター ba·tā
battery (general) 電池 den·chi
battery (for car) バッテリー bat·te·rī
be です des
beach ビーチ bī·chi
beach volleyball ビーチバレー bī·chi·ba·rē
beans 豆 ma·me
beansprouts もやし mo·ya·shi
bear ⓝ クマ ku·ma
beautiful 美しい u·tsu·ku·shī
beauty salon 美容室 bi·yō·shi·tsu
because だから da·ka·ra
bed ベッド bed·do
bed linen シーツ shī·tsu
bedding 寝具 shin·gu
bedroom 寝室 shin·shi·tsu
bee 蜂 ha·chi
beef 牛肉 gyū·ni·ku
beer ビール bī·ru
beetroot ビートルート bī·to·rū·to
before 前 ma·e
beggar 乞食 ko·ji·ki
behind うしろ u·shi·ro
Belgium ベルギー be·ru·gī
below 下 shi·ta
belt 帯 o·bi
berries 木の実・ベリー ki·no·mi • be·rī
beside 横 yo·ko
best 最高の sai·kō no
bet ⓝ 賭け ka·ke
better より良い yo·ri yoy
between あいだ ai·da
bicycle 自転車 ji·ten·sha
big 大きい ō·kī
bigger より大きい yo·ri ō·kī
biggest いちばん大きい i·chi·ban ō·kī
bike ⓝ 自転車 ji·ten·sha
bike chain 自転車のチェーン ji·ten·sha no chēn
bike lock 自転車の鍵 ji·ten·sha no ka·gi
bike path 自転車道 ji·ten·sha·dō
bike shop 自転車屋 ji·ten·sha·ya
bill (restaurant etc) ⓝ 勘定 kan·jō
binoculars 双眼鏡 sō·gan·kyō
bird 鳥 to·ri
birth certificate 出生証明書 shus·sē·shō·mē·sho
birthday 誕生日 tan·jō·bi
biscuit ビスケット bis·ket·to
bite (dog) ⓝ かみ傷 ka·mi·ki·zu
bite (insect) ⓝ 虫刺され mu·shi·sa·sa·re
bitter ⓐ 苦い ni·gai
black 黒い ku·roy
black (coffee) ブラック bu·rak·ku
bladder 膀胱 bō·kō

blanket 毛布 mō·fu
blind 目が見えない me ga mi·e·nai
blister 水疱 su·i·hō
blocked つまります tsu·ma·ri·mas
blood 血 chi
blood group 血液型 ke·tsu·e·ki·ga·ta
blood pressure 血圧 ke·tsu·a·tsu
blood test 血液検査 ke·tsu·e·ki·ken·sa
blue 青い a·oy
board (a plane, ship etc) ⓥ 乗ります no·ri·mas
boarding house 下宿屋 ge·shu·ku·ya
boarding pass 搭乗券 tō·jō·ken
boat ⓝ 船 fu·ne
boat trip ボートツアー bō·to·tsu·ā
bok choy チンゲンサイ chin·gen·sai
body 体 ka·ra·da
boil (in hot water) ゆでます yu·de·mas
boil (in stock) 煮ます ni·mas
bone 骨 ho·ne
book ⓝ 本 hon
book (make a booking) ⓥ 予約します yo·ya·ku shi·mas
booked out 満席 man·se·ki
bookshop 本屋 hon·ya
boots (footwear) ブーツ bū·tsu
border ⓝ 境界 kyō·kai
boring 退屈な tai·ku·tsu na
borrow 借ります ka·ri·mas
botanic garden 植物園 sho·ku·bu·tsu·en
both 両方 ryō·hō
bottle ビン bin
bottle opener 栓抜き sen·nu·ki
bottle shop 酒屋 sa·ka·ya
bottom (body) お尻 o·shi·ri
bottom (last) 最後 sai·go
bowl ⓝ ボール bō·ru
  rice bowl 茶碗 cha·wan
  soup bowl お椀 o·wan
box 箱 ha·ko
boxing ⓝ ボクシング bo·ku·shin·gu
boy 男の子 o·to·ko no ko
boyfriend ボーイフレンド bōy·fu·ren·do
bra ブラジャー bu·ra·jā
Braille ブレール式点字 bu·rē·ru·shi·ki·ten·ji
brakes ブレーキ bu·rē·ki
brandy ブランデー bu·ran·dē
brave 勇敢な yū·kan na
bread パン pan
bread rolls ロールパン rō·ru·pan
break (damage) ⓥ 壊します ko·wa·shi·mas
break down ⓥ 壊れます ko·wa·re·mas
breakfast 朝食・朝ごはん chō·sho·ku · a·sa·go·han
breast (body) 乳房 chi·bu·sa
breathe 息をします i·ki o shi·mas
bribe ⓝ わいろ wai·ro
bridge ⓝ 橋 ha·shi
briefcase ブリーフケース bu·rī·fu·kēs
bring 持ってきます mot·te·ki·mas
brochure パンフレット pan·fu·ret·to
broken 壊れた ko·wa·re·ta
broken down 故障した ko·shō·shi·ta
bronchitis 気管支炎 ki·kan·shi·en
broth だし汁 da·shi·ji·ru
brother 兄弟 kyō·dai
brown 茶色い chai·roy
brown rice 玄米 gem·mai
bruise あざ a·za
brush ⓝ ブラシ bu·ra·shi
bucket バケツ ba·ke·tsu
Buddhist ⓝ 仏教徒 buk·kyō·to
budget 予算 yo·san
buffet (meal) ビュッフェ byuf·fe
bug ⓝ 虫 mu·shi
building 建物 ta·te·mo·no
bullet train 新幹線 shin·kan·sen
bum (body) お尻 o·shi·ri
bumbag ウエストポーチ wes·to·pō·chi
burn ⓝ やけど ya·ke·do
burnt 焼けた ya·ke·ta
bus (city) （市）バス (shi) bas
bus (intercity) （長距離）バス (chō·kyo·ri) bas
bus station バスターミナル bas·tā·mi·na·ru
bus stop バス停 bas·tē
business ビジネス bi·ji·nes

business card 名刺 mē·shi
business class ビジネスクラス bi·ji·nes·ku·ras
business man サラリーマン sa·ra·rī·man
business person ビジネスマン bi·ji·nes·pā·son
business trip 出張 shut·chō
business woman ビジネスウーマン bi·ji·nes·ū·man
busker 大道芸人 dai·dō·gē·nin
busy 忙しい i·so·ga·shī
but しかし shi·ka·shi
butcher's shop 肉屋 ni·ku·ya
butter バター ba·tā
butterfly 蝶 chō
button ボタン bo·tan
buy ⓥ 買います kai·mas

C

cabbage キャベツ kya·be·tsu
cabin 船室 sen·shi·tsu
cable car ケーブルカー kē·bu·ru·kā
cafe カフェ ka·fe
cake ケーキ kē·ki
cake shop ケーキ屋 kē·ki·ya
calculator 計算機 kē·san·ki
calendar カレンダー ka·ren·dā
call ⓥ 呼びます yo·bi·mas
calligraphy 書道 sho·dō
camera カメラ ka·me·ra
camera shop カメラ屋 ka·me·ra·ya
camp site キャンプ場 kyam·pu·jō
camping store キャンプ用品店 kyam·pu·yō·hin·ten
can (be able) できます de·ki·mas
can (have permission) してもいいです shi·te·mo ī des
can (tin) 缶 kan
can opener 缶切 kan·ki·ri
Canada カナダ ka·na·da
cancel キャンセル kyan·se·ru
cancer (illness) 癌 gan
candle ろうそく rō·so·ku
candy キャンディー kyan·dī
cantaloupe メロン me·ron
capsicum ピーマン pī·man
capsule hotel カプセルホテル ka·pu·se·ru·ho·te·ru
car 自動車 ji·dō·sha
car deck 車両甲板 sha·ryō·kam·pan
car hire レンタカー ren·ta·kā
car lights ヘッドライト hed·do·rai·to
car owner's title 自動車所有権 ji·dō·sha·sho·yū·ken
car park 駐車場 chū·sha·jō
car registration 自動車登録 ji·dō·sha·tō·ro·ku
caravan キャンピングカー kyam·pin·gu·kā
cardiac arrest 心拍停止 shim·pa·ku·tē·shi
cards (playing) トランプ to·ram·pu
care (for someone) ⓥ 面倒を見ます men·dō o mi·mas
carpenter 大工 dai·ku
carrot ニンジン nin·jin
carry 運びます ha·ko·bi·mas
carry-on luggage 機内持込の手荷物 ki·nai·mo·chi·ko·mi no te·ni·mo·tsu
carton カートン kā·ton
cartoons 漫画 man·ga
cash ⓝ 現金 gen·kin
cash (a cheque) ⓥ 現金化します gen·kin·ka shi·mas
cash register レジ re·ji
cashew カシューナッツ ka·shū·nat·tsu
cashier レジ re·ji
casino カジノ ka·ji·no
cassette カセット ka·set·to
castle 城 shi·ro
casual work 臨時の仕事 rin·ji no shi·go·to
cat ネコ ne·ko
cathedral 大聖堂 dai·sē·dō
Catholic ⓝ カトリック ka·to·rik·ku
cauliflower カリフラワー ka·ri·fu·ra·wā
cave 洞窟 dō·ku·tsu
caviar キャビア kya·bya
CD CD shī·dī
celebration お祝い oy·wai
cell phone 携帯電話 kē·tai·den·wa

cemetery 墓地 bo·chi
centimetre センチ sen·chi
central 中央の chū·ō no
centre 中央 chū·ō
ceramics セラミックス se·ra·mik·ku·su
cereal シリアル shi·ri·a·ru
certificate 証明書 shō·mē·sho
chain ⓝ 鎖 ku·sa·ri
chair 椅子 i·su
chair (legless) 座椅子 za·i·su
chairlift (skiing) リフト ri·fu·to
champagne シャンペン sham·pen
championships 選手権 sen·shu·ken
change ⓝ 変化 hen·ka
change (coins) ⓝ 小銭 ko·ze·ni
change (money) ⓥ 換金します kan·kin shi·mas
changing room (in shop) 試着室 shi·cha·ku·shi·tsu
changing room (for sport) 更衣室 kōy·shi·tsu
charming チャーミングな chā·min·gu·na
cheap 安い ya·su·i
cheat ⓝ ずる zu·ru
check (banking) ⓝ 小切 ko·git·te
check (bill) ⓝ 勘定 kan·jō
check ⓥ 点検します ten·ken shi·mas
check-in (desk) ⓝ チェックイン chek·ku·in
checkpoint チェックポイント chek·ku·poyn·to
cheese チーズ chī·zu
chef シェフ she·fu
chemist (shop) 薬局 yak·kyo·ku
chemist (person) 薬剤師 ya·ku·zai·shi
cheque (banking) 小切 ko·git·te
cheque (bill) 手形 te·ga·ta
cherry さくらんぼ sa·ku·ram·bo
cherry blossom 桜 sa·ku·ra
chess (Japanese) 将棋 shō·gi
chess (Western) チェス ches
chest (body) 胸 mu·ne
chestnut 栗 ku·ri
chewing gum チューインガム chū·in·ga·mu
chicken (animal) にわとり ni·wa·to·ri
chicken (meat) 鶏肉 to·ri·ni·ku
chicken pox 水ぼうそう mi·zu·bō·sō
chickpeas ヒヨコマメ hi·yo·ko·ma·me
child 子供 ko·do·mo
child seat チャイルドシート chai·ru·do·shī·to
childminding 子守り ko·mo·ri
children 子供 ko·do·mo
chilli 唐辛子 tō·ga·ra·shi
chilli oil ラー油 rā·yu
chilli sauce チリソース chi·ri·sō·su
China 中国 chū·go·ku
Chinese ⓐ 中国の chū·go·ku no
Chinese cabbage 白菜 ha·ku·sai
Chinese food 中華料理 chū·ka·ryō·ri
Chinese radish 大根 dai·kon
Chinese tea 中国茶 chū·go·ku·cha
chips (crisps) チップ chip·pu
chiropractor カイロプラクター kai·ro·pu·ra·ku·tā
chocolate チョコレート cho·ko·rē·to
choose 選びます e·ra·bi·mas
chopping board まな板 ma·nai·ta
chopping knife 包丁 hō·chō
chopsticks はし ha·shi
chopsticks (disposable) 割り箸 wa·ri·ba·shi
chopstick rest はし置き ha·shi·o·ki
Christian ⓝ キリスト教徒 ki·ri·su·to·kyō·to
Christian name 洗礼名 sen·rē·mē
Christmas クリスマス ku·ri·su·mas
church 教会 kyō·kai
cider サイダー sai·dā
cigar 葉巻 ha·ma·ki
cigarette タバコ ta·ba·ko
cigarette lighter ライター rai·tā
cinema 映画館 ē·ga·kan
circus サーカス sā·kas
citizenship 市民権 shi·min·ken
city 市 shi
city centre 市の中心 shi no chū·shin
civil rights 公民権 kō·min·ken
class (category) 種類 shu·ru·i
class system 階級 kai·kyū

classical クラシックの ku·ra·shik·ku no
classical art 古典芸術 ko·ten·gē·ju·tsu
classical music クラシック音楽 ku·ra·shik·ku·on·ga·ku
classical theatre 古典演劇 ko·ten·en·ge·ki
clean ⓐ きれいな ki·rē na
clean ⓥ 掃除をします sō·ji o shi·mas
cleaning ⓝ クリーニング ku·rī·nin·gu
client 顧客 ko·kya·ku
cliff がけ ga·ke
climb ⓥ 登ります no·bo·ri·mas
cloakroom クローク ku·rō·ku
clock 時計 to·kē
close (nearby) 近く chi·ka·ku
close ⓥ 閉めます shi·me·mas
closed ⓐ 閉店した hē·ten·shi·ta
cloth フキン fu·kin
clothes 衣類 i·ru·i
clothesline 物干し mo·no·ho·shi
clothing 衣類 i·ru·i
clothing store 衣料店 i·ryō·ten
cloud 雲 ku·mo
cloudy 曇りの ku·mo·ri·no
clutch (car) クラッチ ku·rat·chi
coach (bus) バス bas
coach (sport) コーチ kō·chi
coast 海岸 kai·gan
coat コート kō·to
cocaine コカイン ko·kain
cockroach ゴキブリ go·ki·bu·ri
cocktail カクテル ka·ku·te·ru
cocoa ココア ko·ko·a
coconut ココナツ ko·ko·na·tsu
coffee コーヒー kō·hī
coins コイン ko·in
cold ⓝ 風邪 ka·ze
have a cold 風邪を引いています ka·ze o hī·te i·mas
cold (atmosphere) ⓐ 寒い sa·m·u·i
cold (to the touch) ⓐ 冷たい tsu·me·ta·i
colleague 同僚 dō·ryō
college カレッジ ka·rej·ji
colour 色 i·ro
comb くし ku·shi
come 来ます ki·mas
comedy コメディー ko·me·dī
comfortable 心地よい ko·ko·chi·yoy
comics 漫画 man·ga
commission 手数料 te·sū·ryō
communist ⓝ 共産主義者 kyō·san·shu·gi·sha
companion コンパニオン kom·pa·ni·on
company (firm) 会社 kai·sha
compass 方位磁石 hōy·ji·sha·ku
complaint 苦情 ku·jō
complimentary (free) 無料の mu·ryō no
computer コンピュータ kom·pyū·ta
computer game コンピュータゲーム kom·pyū·ta·gē·mu
concert コンサート kon·sā·to
concussion 脳しんとう nō·shin·tō
conditioner (hair) コンディショナー kon·di·sho·nā
condom コンドーム kon·dō·mu
conference (big) コンファレンス kon·fa·ren·su
conference (small) ミーティング mī·tin·gu
confirm (a booking) コンファーム kon·fā·mu
conjunctivitis 結膜炎 ke·tsu·ma·ku·en
connection 接続 se·tsu·zo·ku
conservative ⓝ 保守 ho·shu
constipation 便秘 bem·pi
consulate 領事館 ryō·ji·kan
contact lens solution コンタクトレンズの洗浄液 kon·ta·ku·to·ren·zu no sen·jō·e·ki
contact lenses コンタクトレンズ kon·ta·ku·to·ren·zu
contraceptives (devices) 避妊具 hi·nin·gu
contraceptives (medicine) 避妊薬 hi·nin·ya·ku
contract 契約 kē·ya·ku
convenience store コンビニ kom·bi·ni

cook ⓝ コック kok·ku
cook ⓥ 料理します ryō·ri shi·mas
cooked 火が通った hi ga tōt·ta
cookie クッキー kuk·kī
cooking ⓝ 料理 ryō·ri
cool (temperature) 涼しい su·zu·shī
corkscrew コークスクリュー kō·ku·sku·ryū
corn とうもろこし tō·mo·ro·ko·shi
corner 角 ka·do
cornflakes コーンフレーク kōn·fu·rē·ku
corrupt 腐敗した fu·hai shi·ta
cost ⓥ 費用がかかります hi·yō ga ka·ka·ri·mas
cotton 綿 men
cotton balls 脱脂綿 das·shi·men
cotton buds 綿棒 mem·bō
cough ⓥ せきが出ます se·ki ga de·mas
cough medicine せき止め se·ki·do·me
count ⓥ かぞえます ka·zo·e·mas
counter (at bar) カウンター ka·un·tā
country (nation) 国 ku·ni
countryside 田舎 i·na·ka
coupon クーポン kū·pon
courgette クルゼット ku·ru·zet·to
course (class) コース kōs
court (legal) 裁判所 sai·ban·sho
court (tennis) コート kō·to
cover charge カバーチャージ ka·bā·chā·ji
cow 牛 u·shi
crab カニ ka·ni
cracker クラッカー ku·rak·kā
crafts 工芸品 kō·gē·hin
crash ⓝ 衝突 shō·to·tsu
crazy きちがいの ki·chi·gai no
cream クリーム ku·rī·mu
crèche 託児所 ta·ku·ji·sho
credit 預金 yo·kin
credit card クレジットカード ku·re·jit·to·kā·do
cricket (sport) クリケット ku·ri·ket·to
crime 犯罪 han·zai
crowded 混雑している kon·za·tsu shi·te i·ru
cucumber キュウリ kyū·ri
cup カップ kap·pu
cupboard 食器棚 shok·ki·da·na
currency exchange 為替 ka·wa·se
current (electricity) 電流 den·ryū
current affairs 時事問題 ji·ji·mon·dai
curry カレー ka·rē
cushion 座布団 za·bu·ton
custom 習慣 shū·kan
customs 税関 zē·kan
cut (wound) ⓝ 切り傷 ki·ri·ki·zu
cut ⓥ 切りま ki·ri·mas
cutlery ナイフとフォーク nai·fu to fō·ku
CV 履歴書 ri·re·ki·sho
cycling ⓝ サイクリング sai·ku·rin·gu
cyclist サイクリスト sai·ku·ris·to
cystitis ぼうこう炎 bō·kō·en

D

dad お父さん o·tō·san
daily 毎日 mai·ni·chi
dairy 乳製品 nyū·sē·hin
damage 被害 hi·gai
dance ⓥ 踊ります o·do·ri·mas
dancing ⓝ ダンス dan·su
dangerous 危ない a·bu·nai
dark 暗い ku·rai
date (a person) ⓥ デートします dē·to shi·mas
date (appointment) 予約 yo·ya·ku
date (day) ⓝ 日付 hi·zu·ke
date (fruit) ⓝ ナツメヤシ na·tsu·me·ya·shi
date (with a person) ⓝ デート dē·to
date of birth 誕生日 tan·jō·bi
daughter 娘 mu·su·me
dawn 夜明け yo·a·ke
day 日中 nit·chū
(the) day after tomorrow あさって a·sat·te
(the) day before yesterday おととい o·to·toy

day trip 1日観光 i·chi·ni·chi kan·kō
dead 死んでいる shin·de iru
deaf 耳が聞こえない mi·mi ga ki·ko·e·nai
decaffeinated デカフェ de·ka·fe
deck (ship) 甲板 kam·pan
decide 決めます ki·me·mas
deep 深い fu·kai
deep-fried 揚げて a·ge·te
deforestation 森林伐採 shin·rin·bas·sai
degrees (temperature) 度 do
delay 遅れ o·ku·re
delicatessen デリカテッセン de·ri·ka·tes·sen
deliver 配達します hai·ta·tsu shi·mas
democracy 民主主義 min·shu·shu·gi
demonstration (protest) デモ de·mo
Denmark デンマーク dem·mā·ku
dental floss デンタルフロス den·ta·ru·fu·ros
dentist 歯医者 ha·i·sha
deodorant 消臭剤 shō·shū·zai
depart (leave) 出発します shup·pa·tsu shi·mas
department store デパート de·pā·to
departure 出発 shup·pa·tsu
departure gate 出発ゲート shup·pa·tsu·gē·to
deposit (bank) 預金 yo·kin
deposit (refundable) 預かり金 a·zu·ka·ri·kin
desert ⓝ 砂漠 sa·ba·ku
design ⓝ デザイン de·za·in
dessert デザート de·zā·to
destination 目的地 mo·ku·te·ki·chi
details 詳細 shō·sai
diabetes 糖尿病 tō·nyō·byō
dial tone ダイアルトーン dai·a·ru·tōn
diaper オムツ o·mu·tsu
diaphragm 腹膜 fu·ku·ma·ku
diarrhoea 下痢 ge·ri
diary 日記 nik·ki
dictionary 辞書 ji·sho
die ⓥ 死にます shi·ni·mas
diesel ディーゼル dī·ze·ru
diet ダイエット dai·et·to
different 違う chi·ga·u
difficult 難しい mu·zu·ka·shī
digital デジタルの de·ji·ta·ru no
dining car 食堂車 sho·ku·dō·sha
dinner 夕食・晩ごはん yū·sho·ku · ban·go·han
direct 直接に cho·ku·se·tsu ni
direct-dial ⓝ 直通 cho·ku·tsū
direction 方向 hō·kō
director ディレクター di·re·ku·tā
dirty 汚い ki·ta·nai
disabled ⓐ 障害をもつ shō·gai o mo·tsu
discount ⓝ 割引 wa·ri·bi·ki
discrimination 差別 sa·be·tsu
disease 病気 byō·ki
dish (food) 皿 sa·ra
disposable 使い捨ての tsu·kai·su·te no
disposable chopsticks 割り箸 wa·ri·ba·shi
diving ダイビング dai·bin·gu
diving equipment ダイビング用具 dai·bin·gu·yō·gu
divorced 離婚した ri·kon shi·ta
dizzy めまいがする me·mai ga su·ru
do します shi·mas
doctor 医者 i·sha
documentary ドキュメンタリー do·kyu·men·ta·rī
dog 犬 i·nu
dole (allowance) 失業手当 shi·tsu·gyō·te·a·te
doll 人形 nin·gyō
dollar ドル do·ru
domestic 国内 ko·ku·nai
door ドア do·a
door (Japanese-style) ふすま fu·su·ma
dope (drugs) マリファナ ma·ri·fa·na
double 2倍の ni·bai no
double bed ダブルベッド da·bu·ru·bed·do
double room ダブルルーム da·bu·ru·rū·mu
down 下へ shi·ta e

downhill 下り坂の ku·da·ri·za·ka no
dozen ダース dās
drama ドラマ do·ra·ma
dream ⓝ 夢 yu·me
dress ⓝ ドレス do·res
dried 乾いた ka·wai·ta
dried fruit ドライフルーツ do·rai·fu·rū·tsu
drink ⓝ 飲み物 no·mi·mo·no
drink (alcoholic) ⓝ 酒・アルコール sa·ke • a·ru·kō·ru
drink ⓥ 飲みます no·mi·mas
drive ⓥ 運転します un·ten shi·mas
driver 運転手 un·ten·shu
drivers licence 運転免許証 un·ten·men·kyo·shō
drug (medicine) 薬 ku·su·ri
drug (narcotic) 麻薬 ma·ya·ku
drug addiction 麻薬中毒 ma·ya·ku·chū·do·ku
drug dealer 麻薬の密売人 ma·ya·ku no mi·tsu·bai·nin
drug trafficking 麻薬の輸送 ma·ya·ku no yu·sō
drug user 麻薬使用者 ma·ya·ku·shi·yō·sha
drum (music) ⓝ ドラム do·ra·mu
drunk ⓐ 酔った yot·ta
dry ⓐ 乾いた ka·wai·ta
dry ⓥ 乾きます ka·wa·ki·mas
dry (clothes) ⓥ 乾かします ka·wa·ka·shi·mas
duck アヒル a·hi·ru
dummy (pacifier) おしゃぶり o·sha·bu·ri
dumplings ギョウザ gyō·za
during あいだ ai·da
duty-free 免税店 men·zē·ten
DVD DVD dī·bī·dī

E

each それぞれ so·re·zo·re
ear 耳 mi·mi
early 早く ha·ya·ku
earn 稼ぎます ka·se·gi·mas
earplugs 耳栓 mi·mi·sen
earrings イヤリング i·ya·rin·gu
earthquake 地 ji·shin
east 東 hi·ga·shi
Easter イースター ī·stā
easy 簡単な kan·tan na
eat 食べます ta·be·mas
economy class エコノミークラス e·ko·no·mī·ku·ras
ecstacy (drug) エクスタシー e·kus·ta·shī
eczema 湿疹 shis·shin
education 教育 kyō·y·ku
eel うなぎ u·na·gi
egg 卵 ta·ma·go
  boiled egg ゆで卵 yu·de·ta·ma·go
  fried egg 目玉焼き me·da·ma·ya·ki
  hard-boiled egg 固ゆで卵 ka·ta·yu·de·ta·ma·go
  poached egg ポーチドエッグ pō·chi·do·eg·gu
  scrambled egg 卵焼き ta·ma·go·ya·ki
  raw egg 生卵 na·ma·ta·ma·go
eggplant ナス na·su
election 選挙 sen·kyo
electrical store 電化製品店 den·ka·sē·hin
electrician 電気技師 den·ki·gi·shi
electricity 電気 den·ki
elevator エレベーター e·re·bē·tā
email Eメール ī·mē·ru
embarrassed 恥ずかしい ha·zu·ka·shī
embassy 大使館 tai·shi·kan
emergency 救急 kyū·kyū
emotional 感情的な kan·jō·te·ki na
Emperor (Japanese) 天皇 ten·nō
Emperor (non-Japanese) 皇帝 kō·tē
Empress 皇后 kō·gō
employee 従業員 jū·gyō·in
employer 雇用者 ko·yō·sha
empty 空の ka·ra no
end ⓝ おわり o·wa·ri
endangered species 絶滅に瀕した生物 ze·tsu·me·tsu ni hin shi·ta sē·bu·tsu

engaged (phone) お話中 o·ha·na·shi·chū
engaged (to be married) 婚約した kon·ya·ku shi·ta
entrée アントレー an·to·rē
engine エンジン en·jin
engineer 技術者 gi·ju·tsu·sha
engineering 工学 kō·ga·ku
England イギリス i·gi·ri·su
English (language) 英語 ē·go
enjoy (oneself) 楽しみます ta·no·shi·mi·mas
enough 充分な jū·bun na
enter 入ります hai·ri·mas
entertainment guide エンターテイメントガイド en·tā·tē·men·to·gai·do
entry 入場 nyū·jō
envelope 封筒 fū·tō
environment 環境 kan·kyō
epilepsy てんかん ten·kan
equality 平等 byō·dō
equipment 道具 dō·gu
escalator エスカレータ es·ka·rē·ta
estate agency 不動産屋 fu·dō·san·ya
euro ユーロ yū·ro
Europe ヨーロッパ yō·rop·pa
euthanasia 安楽死 an·ra·ku·shi
evening 晩 ban
every 毎 mai
everyone みんな min·na
everything 全部 zem·bu
exactly ちょうど chō·do
example 例 rē
excellent 素晴らしい su·ba·ra·shī
excess (baggage) 超過 chō·ka
exchange ⓝ 交換 kō·kan
exchange ⓥ 交換します kō·kan shi·mas
exchange rate 為替レート ka·wa·se·rē·to
excluded 抜きで nu·ki de
exhaust (car) 排気 hai·ki
exhibition 展覧会 ten·ran·kai
exit ⓝ 出口 de·gu·chi
expensive 高い ta·kai
experience 経験 kē·ken
exploitation 開発 kai·ha·tsu
express ⓐ 明白な mē·ha·ku na
express (mail) 速達 so·ku·ta·tsu
express train 急行 kyū·kō
extension (visa) 延長 en·chō
eye 目 me
eye drops 目薬 me·gu·su·ri

F

fabric 布 nu·no
face ⓝ 顔 ka·o
face cloth 洗面タオル sen·men·tow·ru
factory 工場 kō·jō
factory worker 工員 kō·in
fall (autumn) ⓝ 秋 a·ki
fall (down) ⓥ 倒れます tow·re·mas
family 家族 ka·zo·ku
family name 名字 myō·ji
family ticket 家族チケット ka·zo·ku·chi·ket·to
famous 有名な yū·mē na
fan (machine) 扇風機 sem·pū·ki
fan (made of paper) 扇子 sen·su
fan (sport etc) ファン fan
fanbelt ファンベルト fan·be·ru·to
far 遠い tōy
fare 料金 ryō·kin
farm 農場 nō·jō
farmer 農民 nō·min
fashion ファッション fas·shon
fast ⓐ 速い ha·yai
fat ⓐ 太った fu·tot·ta
father お父さん o·tō·san
father-in-law 義理のお父さん gi·ri no o·tō·san
faucet 蛇口 ja·gu·chi
fault (someone's) 間違い ma·chi·gai
faulty 欠点のある ket·ten no a·ru
favourite 好きな su·ki na
fax ⓝ ファックス fak·kus
fee 料金 ryō·kin
feed (an animal) ⓥ 餌をやります e·sa o ya·ri·mas
feeling (physical) 感触 kan·sho·ku
feelings 感情 kan·jō

female 女性 jo·sē
fence フェンス fen·su
fencing (sport) ⓝ フェンシング fen·sin·gu
ferry ⓝ フェリー fe·rī
festival 祭 ma·tsu·ri
fever 熱 ne·tsu
few (2 or 3) 2、3の ni, san no
few (more than 2 or 3) いくつかの i·ku·tsu·ka no
fiancé(e) 婚約者 kon·ya·ku·sha
fiction フィクション fik·shon
fig イチジク i·chi·ji·ku
fight ⓝ 戦い ta·ta·kai
fill いっぱいにします ip·pai ni shi·mas
fillet ⓝ フィレ fi·re
film (cinema) ⓝ 映画 ē·ga
film (for camera) ⓝ フィルム fi·ru·mu
film speed フィルムの感度 fi·ru·mu no kan·do
filtered フィルターを通した fi·ru·tā o tō·shi·ta
find ⓥ 見つけます mi·tsu·ke·mas
fine (penalty) ⓝ 罰金 bak·kin
fine ⓐ 元気な gen·ki na
finger 指 yu·bi
finish ⓝ 終わり o·wa·ri
finish ⓥ 終わります o·wa·ri·mas
Finland フィンランド fin·ran·do
fire 火 hi
firewood 薪 ma·ki
first 最初の sai·sho no
first-aid kit 救急箱 kyū·kyū·ba·ko
first class ⓝ ファーストクラス fā·sto·ku·ras
first name 名前 na·ma·e
first name 洗礼名 sen·rē·mē
fish ⓝ 魚 sa·ka·na
fish paste 魚のペースト sa·ka·na no pē·sto
fish sauce 魚醤 gyo·shō
fish shop 魚屋 sa·ka·na·ya
fishing ⓝ 釣り tsu·ri
flag ⓝ 旗 ha·ta
flannel フランネル fu·ran·ne·ru
flashlight (torch) 懐中電灯 kai·chū·den·tō
flat (apartment) フラット fu·rat·to
flat ⓐ 平らな tai·ra na
flea 蚤 no·mi
fleamarket フリーマーケット fu·rī·mā·ket·to
flight 航空便 kō·kū·bin
flood ⓝ 洪水 kō·zu·i
floor (ground) 床 yu·ka
floor (storey) 階 kai
florist 花屋 ha·na·ya
flour 小麦粉 ko·mu·gi·ko
flower 花 ha·na
flower arranging 生け花 i·ke·ba·na
flu インフルエンザ in·fu·ru·en·za
fly ⓝ ハエ ha·e
fly ⓥ 飛びます to·bi·mas
foggy 霧がかかった ki·ri ga ka·kat·ta
follow ついていきます tsu·i·te i·ki·mas
food 食べ物 ta·be·mo·no
food poisoning 食中毒 sho·ku·chū·do·ku
food supplies 食料 sho·ku·ryō
foot 足 a·shi
football (soccer) サッカー sak·kā
footpath 歩道 ho·dō
foreign 外国の gai·ko·ku no
forest 森 mo·ri
forever 永遠に ēn ni
forget 忘れます wa·su·re·mas
forgive 許します yu·ru·shi·mas
fork フォーク fō·ku
fortnight 2週間 ni·shū·kan
foul ⓝ ファウル fow·ru
foyer ロビー ro·bī
fragile (item etc) 壊れやすい ko·wa·re·ya·su·i
France フランス fu·ran·su
free (gratis) 無料の mu·ryō no
free (not bound) 自由に ji·yū ni
freeze 凍ります kō·ri·mas
fresh 新鮮な shin·sen na
fridge 冷蔵庫 rē·zō·ko
fried 揚げた a·ge·ta
fried noodles 焼きそば ya·ki·so·ba

fried rice チャーハン・焼き飯 chā·han • ya·ki·me·shi
fried vegetables 野菜炒め ya·sai·i·ta·me
friend 友達 to·mo·da·chi
fries チップ chip·pu
frog カエル ka·e·ru
from から ka·ra
frost 霜 shi·mo
frozen 凍った kōt·ta
fruit 果物 ku·da·mo·no
fruit juice フルーツジュース fu·rū·tsu·jū·su
fry 揚げます a·ge·mas
frying pan フライパン fu·rai·pan
full いっぱいの ip·pai no
full-time work 正社員の仕事 sē·shain no shi·go·to
fun ⓐ 楽しい ta·no·shī
have fun 楽しみます ta·no·shi·mi·mas
funeral 葬式 sō·shi·ki
funny おかしい o·ka·shī
furniture 家具 ka·gu
futon ふとん fu·ton
future ⓝ 未来 mi·rai

G

game (computer) ゲーム gē·mu
game (sport) 試合 shi·ai
garage ガレージ ga·rē·ji
garbage ごみ go·mi
garbage can ごみ箱 go·mi·ba·ko
garden 庭 ni·wa
gardening ⓝ 庭仕事 ni·wa·shi·go·to
garlic ニンニク nin·ni·ku
gas (for cooking) ガス gas
gas (petrol) ガソリン ga·so·rin
gas cartridge ガスカートリッジ gas·kā·to·rij·ji
gastroenteritis 胃腸炎 i·chō·en
gate (airport etc) ゲート gē·to
gauze ガーゼ gā·ze
gay (homosexual) ⓐ ゲイの gē no
gears (bicycle) ギア gya
geisha 芸者 gē·sha
Germany ドイツ doy·tsu
get 手に入れます te ni i·re·mas
get off (a train etc) 降ります o·ri·mas
geyser 間欠泉 kan·kets·sen
gift 贈物 o·ku·ri·mo·no
gig ギグ gi·gu
gin ジン jin
ginger しょうが・ジンジャー shō·ga • jin·jā
girl 女の子 on·na no ko
girlfriend ガールフレンド gā·ru·fu·ren·do
give あげます a·ge·mas
given name 名前 na·ma·e
given name 洗礼名 sen·rē·mē
glandular fever 腺熱 sen·ne·tsu
glass (drinking) グラス gu·ra·su
glasses (spectacles) 眼鏡 me·ga·ne
gloves 手袋 te·bu·ku·ro
glue 糊 no·ri
go 行きます i·ki·mas
go out 出かけます de·ka·ke·mas
go out with 付き合います tsu·ki·ai·mas
goal ゴール gō·ru
goalkeeper ゴールキーパー gō·ru·kī·pā
goat ヤギ ya·gi
god (general) 神 ka·mi
goggles (skiing) ゴーグル gō·gu·ru
goggles (swimming) 水中眼鏡 su·i·chū·me·ga·ne
gold 金 kin
golf ball ゴルフボール go·ru·fu·bō·ru
golf course ゴルフコース go·ru·fu·kō·su
good いい ī
government 政府 sē·fu
gram グラム gu·ra·mu
grandchild 孫 ma·go
grandfather おじいさん o·jī·san
grandmother おばあさん o·bā·san
grapefruit グレープフルーツ gu·rē·pu·fu·rū·tsu
grapes ブドウ bu·dō
grass 草 ku·sa

grateful 感謝している kan·sha shi·te i·ru
grave 墓 ha·ka
gray 灰色の haī·ro no
great (fantastic) 素晴らしい su·ba·ra·shī
green 緑の mi·do·ri no
greengrocer 八百屋 ya·o·ya
greens (vegetables) 野菜 ya·sai
grey 灰色の haī·ro no
grilled グリルして gu·ri·ru shi·te
grocery 食料品 sho·ku·ryō·hin
groundnut ピーナツ pī·na·tsu
group グループ gu·rū·pu
grow 育ちます so·da·chi·mas
guaranteed 保証された ho·shō sa·re·ta
guess ⓥ 言い当てます ī·a·te·mas
guesthouse ゲストハウス ges·to·how·su
guide (audio) ⓝ 案内 an·nai
guide (person) ⓝ ガイド gai·do
guidebook ガイドブック gai·do·buk·ku
guide dog 盲導犬 mō·dō·ken
guided tour ガイド付きツアー gai·do·tsu·ki·tsu·ā
guilty 有罪の yū·zai no
guitar ギター gi·tā
gum (chewing) ガム ga·mu
gums (of mouth) 歯茎 ha·gu·ki
gun 銃 jū
gym (place) ジム ji·mu
gymnastics 体操 tai·sō
gynaecologist 婦人科医 fu·jin·ka·i

H

hair 毛 ke
hairbrush ヘアブラシ hair·bu·ra·shi
haircut ヘアカット hair·kat·to
hairdresser 美容師 bi·yō·shi
halal ハラルの ha·ra·ru no
half ⓝ 半分 ham·bun
hallucination 幻覚 gen·ka·ku
ham ハム ha·mu
hammer ハンマー ham·mā
hammock ハンモック ham·mok·ku
hand 手 te
handbag ハンドバッグ han·do·bag·gu
handball ハンドボール han·do·bō·ru
handicrafts 手芸品 shu·gē·hin
handkerchief ハンカチ han·ka·chi
handlebars ハンドル han·do·ru
handmade 手作りの te·zu·ku·ri no
handsome ハンサムな han·sa·mu na
happy 幸せな shi·a·wa·se na
harassment いやがらせ i·ya·ga·ra·se
harbour 港 mi·na·to
hard (not soft) かたい ka·tai
hard (not easy) たいへんな tai·hen na
hard-boiled 固ゆでの ka·ta·yu·de no
hardware store ホームセンター hō·mu·sen·tā
hash (meat) こま切れ肉 ko·ma·gi·re·ni·ku
hat 帽子 bō·shi
have 持っています mot·te i·mas
have a cold 風邪を引いています ka·ze o hī·te i·mas
have fun 楽しみます ta·no·shi·mi·mas
hay fever 花粉症 ka·fun·shō
hazelnut ヘーゼルナッツ hē·ze·ru·nat·tsu
he 彼は ka·re wa
head 頭 a·ta·ma
headache 頭痛 zu·tsū
headlights ヘッドライト hed·do·rai·to
health 健康 ken·kō
hear 聞きます ki·ki·mas
hearing aid 補聴器 ho·chō·ki
heart 心臓 shin·zō
heart attack 心臓麻痺 shin·zō·ma·hi
heart condition 心臓病 shin·zō·byō
heat 熱 ne·tsu
heated 熱くなった a·tsu·ku nat·ta
heater ヒーター hī·tā
heavy 重い o·moy
helmet ヘルメット he·ru·met·to
help ⓝ たすけ tas·ke
help ⓥ たすけます tas·ke·mas
hepatitis 肝炎 kan·en
her (ownership) 彼女の ka·no·jo no

her (object of sentence) 彼女を ka·no·jo o
herb ハーブ hā·bu
herbalist ハーバリスト hā·ba·ris·to
here ここで ko·ko de
heroin ヘロイン he·royn
high 高い ta·kai
high school 高校 kō·kō
highchair ベビーチェア be·bī·che·a
highway 幹線道路 kan·sen·dō·ro
hike ⓥ ハイキングをします hai·kin·gu o shi·mas
hiking ⓝ ハイキング hai·kin·gu
hiking boots ハイキングブーツ hai·kin·gu·bū·tsu
hiking route ハイキングルート hai·kin·gu·rū·to
hill 丘 o·ka
him 彼を ka·re o
Hindu ⓝ ヒンズー教 hin·zū·kyō
hire ⓥ 賃貸します chin·tai shi·mas
his 彼の ka·re no
historical 歴史的な re·ki·shi·te·ki na
history 歴史 re·ki·shi
hitchhike ヒッチハイク hit·chi·hai·ku
HIV HIV et·chi·ai·vī
hobby 趣味 shu·mi
hockey ホッケー hok·kē
holiday 休日 kyū·ji·tsu
holidays 休暇 kyū·ka
home ⓝ うち u·chi
homeless ホームレス hō·mu·res
homemaker (female) 主婦 shu·fu
homemaker (male) 主夫 shu·fu
homeopathy ホメオパシー ho·me·o·pa·shī
honey 蜂蜜 ha·chi·mi·tsu
honeymoon ハネムーン ha·ne·mūn
horoscope 星占い ho·shi·u·ra·nai
horse 馬 u·ma
horseradish わさび wa·sa·bi
horse riding 乗馬 jō·ba
hospital 病院 byō·in
hospitality もてなし mo·te·na·shi
hot 熱い a·tsu·i
hot water お湯 o·yu
hotel ホテル ho·te·ru
hotpot 鍋・鍋もの na·be・na·be·mo·no
hour 時間 ji·kan
house 家 i·e
housework 家事 ka·ji
how どのように do·no yō ni
how much どのくらい do·no ku·rai
how much (money) いくら i·ku·ra
hug ⓥ 抱きます da·ki·mas
huge 巨大な kyo·dai na
human resources 人的資源 jin·te·ki·shi·gen
human rights 人権 jin·ken
humanities 人文科学 jim·bun·ka·ga·ku
hundred 百 hya·ku
hungry (to be) ⓐ お腹がすいた o·na·ka ga su·i·ta
hunting ⓝ 猟 ryō
hurt ⓥ 傷つけます ki·zu·tsu·ke·mas
(to be in a) hurry ⓥ 急ぎます i·so·gi·mas
husband 夫 ot·to

I

I 私は wa·ta·shi wa
ice 氷 kō·ri
ice axe ピッケル pik·ke·ru
ice cream アイスクリーム ais·ku·rī·mu
ice hockey アイスホッケー ais·hok·kē
identification 身分証明 mi·bun·shō·mē
identification card (ID) 身分証明書 mi·bun·shō·mē·sho
idiot ばか ba·ka
if もし mo·shi
ill 病気の byō·ki no
illegal 違法の i·hō no
immigration 移民 i·min
important 大切 tai·se·tsu na
impossible 不可能な fu·ka·nō na
in なか na·ka
in a hurry 急いで i·soy de
in front of 前 ma·e
incense 香 kō
included 含んで fu·kun·de

income tax 所得税 sho·to·ku·zē
India インド in·do
indicator 標識 hyō·shi·ki
indigestion 消化不良 shō·ka·fu·ryō
indoor 室内の shi·tsu·nai no
industry 産業 san·gyō
infection 感染 kan·sen
inflammation 発火 hak·ka
influenza インフルエンザ in·fu·ru·en·za
information 情報 jō·hō
information office 案内所 an·nai·jo
ingredient 成分 sē·bun
inhaler 吸入器 kyū·nyū·ki
injection 注射 chū·sha
injury けが ke·ga
inn (traditional Japanese) 旅館 ryo·kan
inner tube チューブ chū·bu
innocent 潔白な kep·pa·ku na
insect 虫 mu·shi
inside 内部 nai·bu
instructor インストラクター in·sto·rak·tā
insurance 保険 ho·ken
interesting おもしろい o·mo·shi·roy
intermission 中止 chū·shi
international 国際的な ko·ku·sai·te·ki na
internet インターネット in·tā·net·to
interpreter 通訳 tsū·ya·ku
intersection 交差点 kō·sa·ten
interview 面接 men·se·tsu
invite ⓥ 招待します shō·tai shi·mas
Ireland アイルランド ai·ru·ran·do
iron (for clothes) ⓝ アイロン ai·ron
island 島 shi·ma
Israel イスラエル i·su·ra·e·ru
it それ so·re
IT IT ai·tī
Italy イタリア i·ta·rya
itch かゆみ ka·yu·mi
itemised 箇条書きの ka·jō·ga·ki no
itinerary 旅行日程 ryo·kō·nit·tē

J

jacket ジャケット ja·ket·to
jail 牢屋 rō·ya
jam ジャム ja·mu
Japan 日本 ni·hon • nip·pon
Japanese ⓐ 日本の ni·hon no
Japanese doll 日本人形 ni·hon·nin·gyō
Japanese food 和食 wa·sho·ku
Japanese garden 日本庭園 ni·hon·tēn
jar ジャー jā
jaw あご a·go
jealous 嫉妬深い shit·to·bu·kai
jeans ジーンズ jīn·zu
jeep ジープ jī·pu
jet lag 時差ぼけ ji·sa·bo·ke
jewellery 宝石 hō·se·ki
Jewish ユダヤ教の yu·da·ya·kyō no
job 仕事 shi·go·to
jogging ⓝ ジョギング jo·gin·gu
joke 冗談 jō·dan
journalist ジャーナリスト jā·na·ris·to
journey 旅 ta·bi
judge ⓝ 裁判官 sai·ban·kan
judo 柔道 jū·dō
juice ジュース jū·su
jumper (sweater) セーター sē·tā
jumper leads ブースターケーブル bū·stā·kē·bu·ru

K

kelp 昆布 kom·bu
ketchup ケチャップ ke·chap·pu
key 鍵 ka·gi
keyboard キーボード kī·bō·do
kick ⓥ けります ke·ri·mas
kill 殺します ko·ro·shi·mas
kidney 腎臓 jin·zō
kilo(gram) キロ(グラム) ki·ro(·gu·ra·mu)
kilometre キロメートル ki·ro·mē·to·ru
kimono (bath robe) 浴衣 yu·ka·ta
kind (nice) 親切な shin·se·tsu na
kindergarten 幼稚園 yō·chi·en
king 王 ō
kiosk キヨスク ki·yos·ku
kiss ⓝ キス kis

kiss ⓥ キスします kis·shi·mas
kitchen 台所 dai·do·ko·ro
kiwifruit キウィ ki·wi
knee ひざ hi·za
knife ナイフ nai·fu
know 知っています shit·te i·mas
kosher コーシャー kō·shā

L

labourer 労働者 rō·dō·sha
lake 湖 mi·zū·mi
lamb 子羊 ko·hi·tsu·ji
land 陸 ri·ku
landlady 女主人 on·na·shu·jin
landlord 地主 ji·nu·shi
language 言語 gen·go
laptop ラップトップ rap·pu·top·pu
laquerware 漆器 shik·ki
large 大きい ō·kī
last (final) 最後の sai·go no
last (previous) 前の ma·e no
last (week) 先（週） sen(·shū)
late 遅い o·soy
later あとで a·to de
laugh ⓥ 笑います wa·rai·mas
launderette コインランドリー ko·in·ran·do·rī
laundry (clothes) 洗濯物 sen·ta·ku·mo·no
laundry (place) 洗濯場 sen·ta·ku·ba
laundry (room) 洗濯室 sen·ta·ku·shi·tsu
law 法律 hō·ri·tsu
law (study, professsion) 法学 hō·ga·ku
lawyer 弁護士 ben·go·shi
laxative 下剤 ge·zai
lazy 怠け者の na·ma·ke·mo·no no
leader リーダー rī·dā
leaf 葉 ha
learn 習います na·rai·mas
leather 皮 ka·wa
ledge 岩礁 gan·shō
leek リーキ rī·ki
left (direction) ⓐ 左 hi·da·ri
left luggage (office) 手荷物預かり所 te·ni·mo·tsu·a·zu·ka·ri·sho
left-wing 左翼の sa·yo·ku no
leg (body part) 脚 a·shi
legal 法的な hō·te·ki na
legume 豆類 ma·me·ru·i
lemon レモン re·mon
lemonade レモネード re·mo·nē·do
lens レンズ ren·zu
lentil レンズマメ ren·zu·ma·me
lesbian ⓝ レズビアン re·zu·bi·an
less 少ない su·ku·nai
letter (mail) 手紙 te·ga·mi
lettuce レタス re·tas
liar うそつき u·so·tsu·ki
library 図書館 to·sho·kan
lice 虱 shi·ra·mi
licence ライセンス rai·sen·su
licence plate number ナンバープレート nam·bā·pu·rē·to
lie (not stand) 横になります yo·ko ni na·ri·mas
life 命 i·no·chi
life boat 救命艇 kyū·mē·tē
life jacket 救命胴衣 kyū·mē·dōy
lift (elevator) エレベータ e·re·bē·ta
light ⓝ 電気 den·ki
light (not heavy) 軽い ka·ru·i
light (of colour) 明るい a·ka·ru·i
light bulb 電球 den·kyū
light meter 照度計 shō·do·kē
lighter (cigarette) ライター rai·tā
lights (on car) ヘッドライト hed·do·rai·to
like ⓥ 好きです su·ki des
lime ライム rai·mu
linen (material) リンネル rin·ne·ru
linen (sheets etc) リネン ri·nen
lip balm リップクリーム rip·pu·ku·rī·mu
lips 唇 ku·chi·bi·ru
lipstick 口紅 ku·chi·be·ni
liquor store 酒屋 sa·ka·ya
list ⓝ リスト ris·to
listen (to) 聴きます ki·ki·mas
litre リットル rit·to·ru
little (not much) ⓝ 少し su·ko·shi
little ⓐ 小さい chī·sai
live (somewhere) 住みます su·mi·mas

liver 肝臓 kan·zō
lizard トカゲ to·ka·ge
lobster ロブスター ro·bus·tā
local ⓐ 地元 ji·mo·to
local train 各駅停車 ka·ku·e·ki·tē·sha
lock ⓝ 錠 jō
lock ⓥ 鍵をかけます ka·gi o ka·ke·mas
locked 鍵をかけた ka·gi o ka·ke·ta
lollies キャンデー kyan·dē
long 長い na·gai
look ⓥ 見ます mi·mas
look after 面倒を見ます men·dō o mi·mas
look for 探します sa·ga·shi·mas
lookout 見晴台 mi·ha·ra·shi·dai
loose ⓐ 緩んだ yu·run·da
loose change 小銭 ko·ze·ni
lost (item) なくした na·ku·shi·ta
lost property office 遺失物取扱所 i·shi·tsu·bu·tsu·to·ri·a·tsu·kai·jo
(a) lot たくさん tak·san
loud うるさい u·ru·sai
love ⓝ 愛 ai
love ⓥ 愛します ai shi·mas
love hotel ラブホテル ra·bu·ho·te·ru
lover 恋人 koy·bi·to
low 低い hi·ku·i
lubricant 潤滑油 jun·ka·tsu·yu
lucky 幸運な kō·un na
luggage 手荷物 te·ni·mo·tsu
luggage lockers ロッカー rok·kā
luggage tag 手荷物札 te·ni·mo·tsu·fu·da
lump こぶ ko·bu
lunch 昼食・昼ごはん chū·sho·ku・hi·ru·go·han
lung 肺 hai
luxury ⓐ 豪華な gō·ka na
lychee レイシ rē·shi

M

machine ⓝ 機械 ki·kai
made of (cotton) (コットン)製の (kot·ton)·sē no
Mafia (Japanese) ヤクザ ya·ku·za
magazine 雑誌 zas·shi
mail (letters) 郵送 yū·sō
mail (postal system) 郵便 yū·bin
mailbox 郵便ポスト yū·bin·pos·to
main 主な o·mo na
main course メインコース mēn·kō·su
main road 幹線道路 kan·sen·dō·ro
make ⓥ 作ります tsu·ku·ri·mas
make-up メーキャップ mē·kyap·pu
mammogram マンモグラム mam·mo·gu·ra·mu
man (human) 人 hi·to
man (male) 男の人 o·to·ko no hi·to
manager (company) 支配人 shi·hai·nin
manager (restaurant, hotel) マネージャー ma·nē·jā
mandarin マンダリン man·da·rin
mango マンゴー man·gō
monorail モノレール mo·no·rē·ru
manual (instructions) マニュアル ma·nyu·a·ru
manual worker 肉体労働者 ni·ku·tai·rō·dō·sha
many たくさんの ta·ku·san no
map 地図 chi·zu
marble 大理石 dai·ri·se·ki
margarine マーガリン mā·ga·rin
marijuana マリファナ ma·ri·fa·na
marital status 配偶関係 hai·gū·kan·kē
market ⓝ 市場 i·chi·ba
marmalade マーマレード mā·ma·rē·do
married 既婚 ki·kon
marry 結婚します kek·kon shi·mas
martial arts 武道 bu·dō
mass (Catholic) ミサ mi·sa
massage マッサージ mas·sā·ji
masseur マッサージ師 mas·sā·ji·shi
masseuse マッサージ師 mas·sā·ji·shi
mat マット mat·to
mat (reed) たたみ ta·ta·mi
match (sports) 試合 shi·ai
matches (for lighting) マッチ mat·chi

mattress マットレス mat·to·res
maybe たぶん ta·bun
mayonnaise マヨネーズ ma·yo·nē·zu
me 私を wa·ta·shi o
meal 食事 sho·ku·ji
measles はしか ha·shi·ka
meat 肉 ni·ku
mechanic 機械工 ki·kai·kō
media メディア me·dya
medicine (medication) 薬 ku·su·ri
medicine (study, profession) 医学 i·ga·ku
meditation 瞑想 mē·sō
meet 会います ai·mas
meeting ミーティング mī·tin·gu
melon メロン me·ron
member メンバー mem·bā
menstruation 月経 gek·kē
menu メニュー me·nyū
message 伝言 den·gon
metal ⓝ 金属 kin·zo·ku
metre メートル mē·to·ru
meter (in taxi) メーター mē·tā
metro (train) 地下鉄 chi·ka·te·tsu
metro station 地下鉄の駅 chi·ka·te·tsu no eki
microwave (oven) 電子レンジ den·shi·ren·ji
midday 正午 shō·go
midnight 真夜中 ma·yo·na·ka
migraine 偏頭痛 hen·zu·tsū
military ⓝ 軍 gun
military service 軍役 gun·e·ki
milk ミルク mi·ru·ku
millimetre ミリ（メートル） mi·ri(·mē·to·ru)
million 百 hya·ku·man
mince ⓝ ひき肉 hi·ki·ni·ku
mineral hot-spring spa 温泉 on·sen
mineral water ミネラルウォーター mi·ne·ra·ru·wō·tā
mini-bar ミニバー mi·ni·bā
minute 分 fun
mirror ⓝ 鏡 ka·ga·mi
miscarriage 流産 ryū·zan
miso-soup 味噌汁 mi·so·shi·ru
miso-soup bowl お椀 o·wan
miss (feel absence of) ⓥ 懐かしがります na·tsu·ka·shi·ga·ri·mas
mistake 間違い ma·chi·gai
mix ⓥ 混ぜます ma·ze·mas
mobile phone 携帯電話 kē·tai·den·wa
modem モデム mo·de·mu
modern モダンな mo·dan na
moisturiser 保湿剤 ho·shi·tsu·zai
monastery 修道院 shū·dō·in
money お金 o·ka·ne
monk 僧 sō
month 月 ga·tsu
monument 記念碑 ki·nen·hi
moon 月 tsu·ki
more もっと mot·to
morning 朝 a·sa
morning sickness つわり tsu·wa·ri
mosque モスク mos·ku
mosquito 蚊 ka
mosquito coil 蚊取り線香 ka·to·ri·sen·kō
mosquito net 蚊帳 ka·ya
motel モーテル mō·te·ru
mother お母さん o·kā·san
mother-in-law 義理のお母さん gi·ri no o·kā·san
motorbike オートバイ ō·to·bai
motorboat モーターボート mō·tā·bō·to
motorcycle オートバイ ō·to·bai
motorway (tollway) 高速道路 kō·so·ku·dō·ro
mountain 山 ya·ma
mountain bike マウンテンバイク ma·un·ten·bai·ku
mountain path 登山道 to·zan·dō
mountain range 山脈 sam·mya·ku
mountaineering 登山 to·zan
mouse ネズミ ne·zu·mi
mouth 口 ku·chi
movie 映画 ē·ga
Mr/Mrs/Ms/Miss さん ·san
MSG グルタミン酸ソーダ gu·ru·ta·min·san·sō·da
mud 泥 do·ro

muesli ミューズリー myū·zu·rī
mum お母さん o·kā·san
mumps おたふく風邪 o·ta·fu·ku·ka·ze
murder ⓝ 殺人 sa·tsu·jin
muscle 筋肉 kin·ni·ku
museum 博物館 ha·ku·bu·tsu·kan
mushroom キノコ ki·no·ko
music 音楽 on·ga·ku
music shop レコード店 re·kō·do·ten
musician 音楽家 on·gak·ka
Muslim ⓝ イスラム教徒 i·su·ra·mu·kyō·to
mussel ムール貝 mū·ru·gai
mustard マスタード mas·tā·do
my 私の wa·ta·shi no

N

nail clippers 爪切 tsu·me·ki·ri
name 名前 na·ma·e
napkin ナプキン na·pu·kin
nappy オムツ o·mu·tsu
nappy rash オムツかぶれ o·mu·tsu·ka·bu·re
national 国の ku·ni no
national park 国立公園 ko·ku·ri·tsu·kō·en
nationality 国籍 ko·ku·se·ki
nature 自然 shi·zen
naturopathy 自然療法 shi·zen·ryō·hō
nausea 吐き気 ha·ki·ke
near 近く chi·ka·ku
nearby 近くの chi·ka·ku no
nearest いちばん近くの i·chi·ban chi·ka·ku no
necessary 必要な hi·tsu·yō na
neck 首 ku·bi
nectarine ネクタリン ne·ku·ta·rin
need ⓥ 必要があります hi·tsu·yō ga a·ri·mas
needle (sewing) 針 ha·ri
needle (syringe) 注射針 chū·sha·ba·ri
negative 否定的な hi·tē·te·ki na
net 網 a·mi
Netherlands オランダ o·ran·da
never 決してない kes·shi·te nai
new 新しい a·ta·ra·shī
New Year's Day 元旦 gan·tan
New Year's Eve 大晦日 ō·mi·so·ka
New Zealand ニュージーランド nyū·jī·ran·do
news ニュース nyū·su
news stand 新聞販売店 shim·bun·ham·bai·ten
newsagency 通信社 tsū·shin·sha
newspaper 新聞 shim·bun
next つぎ tsu·gi
next (month) 来(月) rai(·ge·tsu)
next to となり to·na·ri
nice いい ī
nickname あだ名 a·da·na
night 夜 yo·ru
night out 夜遊び yo·a·so·bi
nightclub ナイトクラブ nai·to·ku·ra·bu
no いいえ ī·e
no vacancy 満室 man·shi·tsu
noisy うるさい u·ru·sai
none なにもない na·ni·mo nai
nonsmoking 禁煙の kin·en no
noodles 麺類 men·ru·i
noon (lunchtime) 昼 hi·ru
noon (midday) 正午 shō·go
north 北 ki·ta
Norway ノルウェー no·ru·wē
nose 鼻 ha·na
not ない nai
notebook (paper) ノート nō·to
nothing 何もない na·ni·mo nai
not yet まだ ma·da
now 今 i·ma
nuclear energy 核エネルギー ka·ku·e·ne·ru·gī
nuclear testing 核実験 ka·ku·jik·ken
nuclear waste 核廃棄物 ka·ku·hai·ki·bu·tsu
number 数字 sū·ji
numberplate ナンバープレート nam·bā·pu·rē·to
nun 修道女 shū·dō·jo
nurse 看護婦 kan·go·fu
nut ナッツ nat·tsu

O

oats オート麦 ō·to·mu·gi
occupation (work) 職業 sho·ku·gyō
ocean 海 u·mi
octopus タコ ta·ko
off (spoiled) いたんだ i·tan·da
office 事務所 ji·mu·sho
office worker 事務員 ji·mu·in
often しばしば shi·ba·shi·ba
oil (food) 油 a·bu·ra
oil (petrol) 石油 se·ki·yu
old 古い fu·ru·i
olive オリーブ o·rī·bu
olive oil オリーブオイル o·rī·bu·oy·ru
Olympic Games オリンピック o·rim·pik·ku
omelette オムレツ o·mu·re·tsu
on (top of) 上に u·e ni
on time 時間どおり ji·kan·dō·ri
once 1度 i·chi·do
one 1 i·chi
one-way (ticket) 片道(切符) ka·ta·mi·chi(·kip·pu)
onion タマネギ ta·ma·ne·gi
only たったの tat·ta no
open ⓐ 開いている hi·rai·te i·ru
open ⓥ 開きます hi·ra·ki·mas
open-air baths 露天風呂 ro·tem·bu·ro
opening hours 開店時間 kai·ten·ji·kan
opera オペラ o·pe·ra
opera house オペラ劇場 o·pe·ra·ge·ki·jō
operation (medical) 手術 shu·ju·tsu
operator オペレーター o·pe·rē·tā
opinion 意見 i·ken
opposite 反対の han·tai no
optometrist 検眼医 ken·gan·i
or または ma·ta wa
orange (colour) オレンジ o·ren·ji
orange (fruit) オレンジ o·ren·ji
orange juice オレンジジュース o·ren·ji·jū·su
orchestra オーケストラ ō·kes·to·ra
order ⓝ 命令 mē·rē
order ⓥ 命令します mē·rē shi·mas
ordinary 普通の fu·tsū no
orgasm オーガズム ō·ga·zu·mu
original オリジナルの o·ri·ji·na·ru no
other ほかの ho·ka no
our 私たちの wa·ta·shi·ta·chi no
out of order 故障中 ko·shō·chū
outside 外側の so·to·ga·wa no
ovarian cyst 卵巣のう腫 ran·sō·nō·shu
ovary 卵巣 ran·sō
oven オーブン ō·bun
overcoat オーバー ō·bā
overdose 薬の飲みすぎ ku·su·ri no no·mi·su·gi
overnight 一晩 hi·to·ban
overseas 海外 kai·gai
owe 借りがあります ka·ri ga a·ri·mas
owner 所持者 sho·ji·sha
oxygen 酸素 san·so
oyster カキ ka·ki
ozone layer オゾン層 o·zon·sō

P

pacemaker ペースメーカー pēs·mē·kā
pacifier (dummy) おしゃぶり o·sha·bu·ri
package 包み tsu·tsu·mi
packet (general) 小包 ko·zu·tsu·mi
padlock 南京錠 nan·kin·jō
page ページ pē·ji
pain 痛み i·ta·mi
painkiller 鎮痛剤 chin·tsū·zai
painter 画家 ga·ka
painting (a work) ⓝ 絵 e
painting (the art) ⓝ 絵画 kai·ga
pair ⓝ ペア pair
pair of chopsticks 箸 ha·shi
palace 宮殿 kyū·den
pan 鍋 na·be
pants (trousers) ズボン zu·bon
panty liners 生理用ナプキン sē·ri·yō·na·pu·kin
pantyhose パンティーストッキング pan·tī·stok·kin·gu
pap smear 子宮癌塗抹検査 shi·kyū·gan·to·ma·tsu·ken·sa

P ENGLISH TO JAPANESE

paper 紙 ka·mi
papers (documents) 書類 sho·ru·i
paperwork 事務処理 ji·mu·sho·ri
paraplegic ⓝ 下半身不随 ka·han·shin·fu·zu·i
parcel 小包 ko·zu·tsu·mi
parents 両親 ryō·shin
park ⓝ 公園 kō·en
park (a car) ⓥ 駐車します chū·sha shi·mas
parliament 国会 kok·kai
part (component) 部分 bu·bun
partner (intimate) パートナー pā·to·nā
part-time job アルバイト a·ru·bai·to
party (night out) ⓝ パーティー pā·tī
party (politics) ⓝ 党 tō
pass (document) ⓝ 許可証 kyo·ka·shō
pass (mountain) ⓝ 山道 ya·ma·mi·chi
pass (sport) ⓝ パス pas
pass ⓥ 通過します tsū·ka shi·mas
passenger 乗客 jō·kya·ku
passionfruit パッションフルーツ pas·shon·fu·rū·tsu
passport パスポート pas·pō·to
passport number パスポート番号 pas·pō·to·ban·gō
past ⓝ 過去 ka·ko
pasta パスタ pas·ta
pastry ペストリー pes·to·rī
path 小道 ko·mi·chi
pay ⓥ 支払います shi·a·rai·mas
payment 支払い shi·ha·rai
pea 豆 ma·me
peace 平和 hē·wa
peach 桃 mo·mo
peak (mountain) ⓝ 峰 mi·ne
peanut ピーナツ pī·na·tsu
pear 洋ナシ yō·na·shi
pedal ⓝ ペダル pe·da·ru
pedestrian 歩行者 ho·kō·sha
pedestrian crossing 横断歩道 ō·dan·ho·dō
pegs (camping) ペグ pe·gu
pen (ballpoint) ペン pen
pencil エンピツ em·pi·tsu
penis ペニス pe·nis
penicillin ペニシリン pe·ni·shi·rin
penknife ペンナイフ pen·nai·fu
pensioner 年金者 nen·kin·sha
people 人びと hi·to·bi·to
pepper コショウ koshō
pepper (bell) ピーマン pī·man
per (eg day) 毎 mai
per cent パーセント pā·sen·to
perfect 完璧な kam·pe·ki na
performance パフォーマンス pa·fō·man·su
perfume 香水 kō·su·i
period 時代 ji·dai
period (menstruation) 月経 gek·kē
period pain 生理痛 sē·ri·tsū
permanent 永久の ē·kyū no
permission 許可 kyo·ka
permit 許可証 kyo·ka·shō
persimmon 柿 ka·ki
person 人 hi·to
personal 個人的な ko·jin·te·ki na
petition 嘆願書 tan·gan·sho
petrol ガソリン ga·so·rin
petrol station ガソリンスタンド ga·so·rin·stan·do
pharmacy 薬局 yak·kyo·ku
phone box 電話ボックス den·wa·bok·kus
phone call 電話 den·wa
phone card テレフォンカード te·re·fon·kā·do
phone number 電話番号 den·wa·ban·gō
photo 写真 sha·shin
photographer 写真家 sha·shin·ka
photography 写真 sha·shin
phrasebook フレーズブック fu·rē·zu·buk·ku
pickaxe つるはし tsu·ru·ha·shi
picnic ピクニック pi·ku·nik·ku
pie パイ pai
piece かけら ka·ke·ra
pig 豚 bu·ta
pigeon 鳩 ha·to
pill 錠剤 jō·zai
the Pill ピル pi·ru

pillow 枕 ma·ku·ra
pillowcase 枕カバー ma·ku·ra·ka·bā
pinball ピンボール pin·bō·ru
pineapple パイナップル pai·nap·pu·ru
pink ピンクの pin·ku no
pistachio ピスタチオ pis·ta·chi·o
place 場所 ba·sho
place of birth 出身地 shus·shin·chi
plane ⓝ 飛行機 hi·kō·ki
planet 惑星 wa·ku·sē
plant ⓝ 植物 sho·ku·bu·tsu
plastic ⓐ プラスチックの pu·ras·chik·ku no
plate (big) 皿 sa·ra
plate (small) 小皿 ko·za·ra
plateau 高原 kō·gen
platform プラットフォーム pu·rat·to·fō·mu
play (cards, game) ⓥ します shi·mas
play (instrument) ⓥ 弾きます hi·ki·mas
play (theatre) ⓝ 劇 ge·ki
playground 遊び場 a·so·bi·ba
plug (bath) 栓 sen
plug (electricity) プラグ pu·ra·gu
plum スモモ su·mo·mo
poached ポーチした pō·chi shi·ta
pocket ポケット po·ket·to
pocket knife ポケットナイフ po·ket·to·nai·fu
poetry 詩 shi
point ⓝ 点 ten
point ⓥ 示します shi·me·shi·mas
poisonous 毒の do·ku no
police 警察 kē·sa·tsu
police box 交番 kō·ban
police officer 警官 kē·kan
police station 警察署 kē·sa·tsu·sho
policy 方針 hō·shin
politician 政治家 sē·ji·ka
politics 政治 sē·ji
pollen 花粉 ka·fun
pollution 公害 kō·gai
pool (game) ビリヤード bi·ri·yā·do
pool (swimming) プール pū·ru
poor 貧しい ma·zu·shī
popular 人気がある nin·ki ga a·ru
pork 豚肉 bu·ta·ni·ku
porridge おかゆ o·ka·yu
port (sea) 港 mi·na·to
positive 積極的な sek·kyo·ku·te·ki na
portion 部分 bu·bun
possible 可能な ka·nō na
postcode 郵便番号 yū·bin·ban·gō
post office 郵便局 yū·bin·kyo·ku
poste restante 局留め kyo·ku·do·me
postage 郵送料 yū·sō·ryō
postcard はがき ha·ga·ki
poster ポスター pos·tā
pot (ceramics) つぼ tsu·bo
pot (dope) マリファナ ma·ri·fa·na
potato ジャガイモ ja·ga·i·mo
pottery 陶器 tō·ki
poultry 鳥肉 to·ri·ni·ku
pound (money, weight) ポンド pon·do
poverty 貧困 hin·kon
powder 粉 ko·na
power 力 chi·ka·ra
prawn エビ e·bi
prayer 祈り i·no·ri
prefer ... …のほうがすきです ... no hō ga su·ki·des
pregnancy test kit 妊娠テストキット nin·shin·tes·to·kit·to
pregnant 妊娠している nin·shin shi·te i·ru
premenstrual tension 月経前緊張症 gek·kē·zen·kin·chō·shō
prepare 準備します jum·bi shi·mas
prescription 処方箋 sho·hō·sen
present (gift) ⓝ プレゼント pu·re·zen·to
present (time) ⓝ 現在 gen·zai
president 大統領 dai·tō·ryō
pretty かわいい ka·wa·ī
previous 前の ma·e no
price 値段 ne·dan
priest (Christian) 牧師 bo·ku·shi
priest (Shinto) 神主 kan·nu·shi
prime minister 総理大臣 sō·ri·dai·jin
prince 王子 ō·ji
princess 姫 hi·me

printer (computer) プリンタ prin·ta
prison 牢屋 rō·ya
prisoner 囚人 shū·jin
private ⓐ 個人的な ko·jin·te·ki na
produce ⓥ 生産します sē·san shi·mas
profit ⓝ 利益 ri·e·ki
program ⓝ プログラム pu·ro·gu·ra·mu
projector 映写機 ē·sha·ki
promise ⓥ 約束します ya·ku·so·ku shi·mas
prostitution 売春 bai·shun
protect 保護します ho·go shi·mas
protected (species) 保護された (生物) ho·go sa·re·ta (sē·bu·tsu)
protest ⓝ 反対 han·tai
provisions 食料 sho·ku·ryō
prune プルーン pu·rūn
pub (bar) パブ pa·bu
public baths 銭湯 sen·tō
public gardens 公園 kō·en
public holiday 祭日 sai·ji·tsu
public telephone 公衆電話 kō·shū·den·wa
public toilet 公衆トイレ kō·shū·toy·re
pufferfish フグ fu·gu
pull 引きます hi·ki·mas
pump ⓝ ポンプ pom·pu
pumpkin カボチャ ka·bo·cha
puncture パンク pan·ku
puppet 人形 nin·gyō
puppet theatre 人形劇 nin·gyō·ge·ki
pure 純粋な jun·su·i na
purple 紫の mu·ra·sa·ki no
purse 財布 sai·fu
push ⓥ 押します o·shi·mas
put 置きます o·ki·mas

Q

quadriplegic ⓝ 四肢麻痺 shi·shi·ma·hi
qualifications 資格 shi·ka·ku
quality 品質 hin·shi·tsu
quarantine ⓝ 検疫 ken·e·ki
quarter ⓝ 4分の1 yon·bun no i·chi
queen 女王 jō
question ⓝ 質問 shi·tsu·mon
queue ⓝ 列 re·tsu
quick すばやい su·ba·yai
quiet 静かな shi·zu·ka na
quilt 掛け布団 ka·ke·bu·ton
quit 辞めます ya·me·mas

R

rabbit ウサギ u·sa·gi
race (sport) レース rē·su
racetrack 競走場 kyō·gi·jō
racing bike レーシングバイク rē·shin·gu·bai·ku
racism 人種差別 jin·shu·sa·be·tsu
racquet ラケット ra·ket·to
radiator ラジエーター ra·ji·ē·tā
radio ラジオ ra·ji·o
radish ラディッシュ ra·dis·shu
railway station 駅 e·ki
rain ⓝ 雨 a·me
raincoat レインコート re·in·kō·to
raisin レーズン rē·zun
rally ⓝ 集会 shū·kai
rape ⓝ レイプ rē·pu
rapid train 快速 kai·so·ku
rare (food) レアの rair no
rare (uncommon) 珍しい me·zu·ra·shī
rash 発疹 has·shin
raspberry ラズベリー ra·zu·be·rī
rat ネズミ ne·zu·mi
rave ⓝ レイブ rē·bu
raw 生の na·ma no
razor 剃刀 ka·mi·so·ri
razor blade 剃刀の刃 ka·mi·so·ri no ha
read 読みます yo·mi·mas
ready 準備ができた jum·bi ga de·ki·ta
real estate agent 不動産屋 fu·dō·san·ya
rear (seat etc) ⓐ 後ろの u·shi·ro no
reason ⓝ 理由 ri·yū
receipt レシート re·shī·to
recently 最近 sai·kin
recommend 勧めます su·su·me·mas
record ⓥ 記録します ki·ro·ku shi·mas

recording ⓝ レコーディング re·kō·din·gu
recyclable リサイクルできる ri·sai·ku·ru de·ki·ru
recycle リサイクルします ri·sai·ku·ru shi·mas
red 赤い a·kai
red wine 赤ワイン a·ka·wain
referee 審判 shim·pan
reference 参照 san·shō
reflexology リフレクソロジー ri·fu·re·ku·so·ro·jī
refrigerator 冷蔵庫 rē·zō·ko
refugee 難民 nam·min
refund ⓝ 払い戻し ha·rai·mo·do·shi
refuse ⓥ 拒絶します kyo·ze·tsu shi·mas
regional 地方の chi·hō no
registered mail/post 書留 ka·ki·to·me
regular ⓐ 通常の tsū·jō no
rehydration salts 経口補水塩 kē·kō·ho·su·i·en
relationship 関係 kan·kē
relax リラックスします ri·rak·ku·su shi·mas
relic 遺物 i·bu·tsu
religion 宗教 shū·kyō
religious 宗教的な shū·kyō·te·ki na
remote 遠い tōy
remote control リモコン ri·mo·kon
rent 貸します ka·shi·mas
repair 修理します shū·ri shi·mas
republic 共和国 kyō·wa·ko·ku
reservation (booking) 予約 yo·ya·ku
rest ⓥ 休みます ya·su·mi·mas
restaurant レストラン res·to·ran
résumé (CV) ⓝ 履歴書 ri·re·ki·sho
retired 退職した tai·sho·ku shi·ta
return (come back) ⓥ もどります mo·do·ri·mas
return ticket 往復切符 ō·fu·ku·kip·pu
review ⓝ 評論 hyō·ron
rhythm リズム ri·zu·mu
rib 肋骨 rok·ko·tsu
rice (cooked) ごはん go·han
rice (uncooked) 米 ko·me
rice bowl 茶碗 cha·wan
rice cake もち mo·chi
rice cooker 炊飯器 su·i·han·ki
rice cracker せんべい sen·bē
rich (wealthy) お金持ちの o·ka·ne·mo·chi no
ride ⓝ 乗ること no·ru ko·to
ride (horse) ⓥ 乗ります no·ri·mas
right (correct) 正しい ta·da·shī
right (direction) 右 mi·gi
right-wing 右翼 u·yo·ku
ring (on finger) ⓝ 指輪 yu·bi·wa
ring (by phone) ⓥ 電話します den·wa shi·mas
rip-off ⓝ ぼられること bo·ra·re·ru ko·to
risk ⓝ リスク ris·ku
river 川 ka·wa
road 道 mi·chi
road map ロードマップ rō·do·map·pu
rob 強盗します gō·tō shi·mas
robbery 強奪 gō·da·tsu
rock ⓝ 岩 i·wa
rock (music) ⓝ ロック rok·ku
rock climbing ロッククライミング rok·ku·ku·rai·min·gu
rock group ロックバンド rok·ku·ban·do
rockmelon メロン me·ron
roll (bread) ⓝ ロール rō·ru
rollerblading ⓝ ローラーブレード rō·rā·bu·rē·do
romantic ロマンチックな ro·man·chik·ku na
room 部屋 he·ya
room number ルームナンバー rū·mu·nam·bā
rope ロープ rō·pu
round (shape) まるい ma·ru·i
roundabout ロータリー rō·ta·rī
route ルート rū·to
rowing ⓝ ローイング rō·in·gu
rubbish ごみ go·mi
rubella 風疹 fū·shin
rug じゅうたん jū·tan

rugby ラグビー ra·gu·bī
ruins 廃墟 hai·kyo
rum ラム ra·mu
run ⓥ 走ります ha·shi·ri·mas
running (sport) ランニング ran·nin·gu

S

sad 悲しい ka·na·shī
saddle サドル sa·do·ru
safe ⓝ 金庫 kin·ko
safe ⓐ 安全な an·zen na
safe sex セーフセックス sē·fu·sek·kus
saint 聖人 sē·jin
salad サラダ sa·ra·da
salary サラリー sa·ra·rī
sale セール sē·ru
sales tax 消費税 shō·hi·zē
salmon サケ sa·ke
salt 塩 shi·o
same 同じ o·na·ji
sand 砂 su·na
sandal サンダル san·da·ru
sandwich サンドイッチ san·do·it·chi
sanitary napkin 生理用ナプキン sē·ri·yō·na·pu·kin
sardine イワシ i·wa·shi
sauce ソース sō·su
saucepan 鍋 na·be
sauna サウナ sow·na
sausage ソーセージ sō·sē·ji
say ⓥ 言います ī·mas
scallop ホタテ ho·ta·te
scalp 頭皮 tō·hi
scampi スカンピ・クルマエビ skam·pi • ku·ru·ma·e·bi
scarf スカーフ skā·fu
school 学校 gak·kō
science 科学 ka·ga·ku
scientist 科学者 ka·ga·ku·sha
scissors ハサミ ha·sa·mi
scooter スクーター skū·tā
score ⓥ 得点します to·ku·ten shi·mas
scoreboard スコアボード sko·a·bō·do
Scotland スコットランド skot·to·ran·do
scrambled かき混ぜた ka·ki·ma·ze·ta
screen (room) ついたて tsu·i·ta·te
screen (sliding) 障子 shō·ji
sculpture 彫刻 chō·ko·ku
sea 海 u·mi
seafood 海産物・シーフード kai·sam·bu·tsu • shī·fū·do
seasick 船酔い fu·na·yoy
seaside 海辺 u·mi·be
season 季節 ki·se·tsu
seat (place) 席 se·ki
seatbelt シートベルト shī·to·be·ru·to
sea urchin ウニ u·ni
sea vegetables 海藻 kai·sō
seaweed 海藻 kai·sō
second ⓝ 秒 byō
second ⓐ 2番目の ni·bam·me no
secondhand 中古の chū·ko no
secondhand shop 中古品店 chū·ko·hin·ten
second class ⓝ セカンドクラス se·kan·do·ku·ras
secretary 秘書 hi·sho
see 見ます mi·mas
self service ⓐ セルフサービスの se·ru·fu·sā·bis no
self-employed 自営業 ji·ē·gyō
sell 売ります u·ri·mas
send 送ります o·ku·ri·mas
sensible 分別のある fum·be·tsu no a·ru
sensual 官能的な kan·nō·te·ki na
separate 別々の be·tsu·be·tsu no
serious まじめな ma·ji·me na
service ⓝ サービス sā·bis
service charge サービス料 sā·bis·ryō
service station ガソリンスタンド ga·so·rin·stan·do
serviette ナプキン na·pu·kin
sesame oil ごま油 go·ma·a·bu·ra
sesame seed ごま go·ma
several いくつかの i·ku·tsu·ka no
sew 縫います nu·i·mas
sex セックス sek·kus
sexism 性差別 sē·sa·be·tsu
sexy セクシーな sek·shī na
shade 日陰 hi·ka·ge

shadow 影 ka·ge
shallot (onion) ワケギ wa·ke·gi
shampoo ⓝ シャンプー sham·pū
shape ⓝ 形 ka·ta·chi
share (a dorm etc) ⓥ シェアします she·a shi·mas
share (with) ⓥ 分け合います wa·ke·ai·mas
shave ⓝ シェービング shē·bin·gu
shaving cream シェービングクリーム shē·bin·gu·ku·rī·mu
she 彼女は ka·no·jo wa
sheep 羊 hi·tsu·ji
sheet (bed) シーツ shī·tsu
shelf 棚 ta·na
shellfish 貝 kai
shingles (illness) 帯状疱疹 tai·jō·hō·shin
ship ⓝ 船 fu·ne
shirt シャツ sha·tsu
shoe 靴 ku·tsu
shoe shop 靴屋 ku·tsu·ya
shoot 撃ちます u·chi·mas
shop ⓝ 店 mi·se
shop ⓥ 買い物をします kai·mo·no o shi·mas
shopping ⓝ 買い物 kai·mo·no
shopping centre ショッピングセンター shop·pin·gu·sen·tā
short (height) 低い hi·ku·i
short (length) 短い mi·ji·kai
shortage 不足 fu·so·ku
short-grain rice ジャポニカ米 ja·po·ni·ka·mai
shorts 半ズボン han·zu·bon
shoulder 肩 ka·ta
shout ⓥ 怒鳴ります do·na·ri·mas
show ⓝ ショー shō
show ⓥ 見せます mi·se·mas
shower シャワー sha·wā
shrine 神社 jin·ja
shrimp 小エビ ko·e·bi
shut ⓐ 閉まった shi·mat·ta
shy 恥ずかしがり屋の ha·zu·ka·shi·ga·ri·ya no
sick 病気の byō·ki no
sick bag 乗り物酔いの袋 no·ri·mo·no·yoy no fu·ku·ro
side 側 ga·wa
sign ⓝ 標識 hyō·shi·ki
side plate 小皿 ko·za·ra
signature サイン sain
silk ⓝ 絹 ki·nu
silver ⓝ 銀 gin
SIM card SIMカード shi·mu·kā·do
similar よく似た yo·ku ni·ta
simple 単純な tan·jun na
since ... (time) …から ... ka·ra
sing 歌います u·tai·mas
singer 歌手 ka·shu
single (for person) ⓐ 独身 do·ku·shin
single room シングルルーム shin·gu·ru·rū·mu
singlet アンダーシャツ an·dā·sha·tsu
sister 姉妹 shi·mai
sit 座ります su·wa·ri·mas
size (general) サイズ sai·zu
skate ⓥ スケート skē·to
skateboarding ⓝ スケートボード skē·to·bō·do
ski ⓝ スキー skī
ski ⓥ スキーをします skī o shi·mas
skiing ⓝ スキー skī
skim milk スキムミルク ski·mu·mi·ru·ku
skin 皮膚 hi·fu
skirt スカート skā·to
skull 頭蓋骨 zu·gai·ko·tsu
sky 空 ka·ra
sleep ⓥ 眠ります ne·mu·ri·mas
sleeping bag 寝袋 ne·bu·ku·ro
sleeping berth 寝台 shin·dai
sleeping car 寝台車 shin·dai·sha
sleeping pills 睡眠薬 su·i·min·ya·ku
sleepy 眠い ne·mu·i
slice ⓝ スライス su·rai·su
slide (film) ⓝ スライド su·rai·do
sliding screen 障子 shō·ji
slow 遅い o·soy
slowly ゆっくり yuk·ku·ri
small 小さい chī·sai
smaller より小さい yo·ri chī·sai

smallest いちばん小さい i·chi·ban chī·sai
smell ⓝ におい ni·oy
smile ⓥ 笑顔 e·ga·o
smoke ⓥ タバコを吸います ta·ba·ko o su·i·mas
smoked (food) ⓐ 燻製 kun·sē
smoking ⓐ 喫煙 ki·tsu·en
snack 軽食 kē·sho·ku
snail カタツムリ ka·ta·tsu·mu·ri
snake ヘビ he·bi
snorkelling ⓝ シュノーケリング shu·nō·ke·rin·gu
snow 雪 yu·ki
snowboarding ⓝ スノーボード su·nō·bō·do
snow pea サヤエンドウ sa·ya·en·dō
soap 石鹸 sek·ken
soap opera メロドラマ me·ro·do·ra·ma
soccer サッカー sak·kā
social welfare 社会福祉 sha·kai·fu·ku·shi
socialist 社会主義者 sha·kai·shu·gi·sha
socks 靴下 ku·tsu·shi·ta
soft やわらかい ya·wa·ra·kai
soft drink ソフトドリンク so·fu·to·do·rin·ku
soft-boiled 半熟の han·ju·ku no
soldier 兵士 hē·shi
some いくらかの i·ku·ra ka no
someone 誰か da·re ka
something 何か na·ni ka
sometimes ときどき to·ki·do·ki
son 息子 mu·su·ko
song 歌 u·ta
soon すぐに su·gu ni
sore ⓐ 痛い i·tai
soup スープ sū·pu
soup bowl お椀 o·wan
sour cream サワークリーム sa·wā·ku·rī·mu
south 南 mi·na·mi
souvenir お土産 o·mi·ya·ge
souvenir shop お土産屋 o·mi·ya·ge·ya
soy bean 大豆 dai·zu
soy milk 豆乳 tō·nyū
soy sauce しょう油 shō·yu
space スペース spēs
Spain スペイン spe·in
sparkling wine スパークリングワイン spā·ku·rin·gu·wain
speak 話します ha·na·shi·mas
special ⓐ 特別な to·ku·be·tsu na
specialist 専門家 sem·mon·ka
speed (velocity) ⓝ スピード spī·do
speed limit 制限速度 sē·gen·so·ku·do
spicy スパイシー spai·shī
spider クモ ku·mo
spinach ホウレンソウ hō·ren·sō
spoiled 悪くなった wa·ru·ku nat·ta
spoke スポーク spō·ku
spoon スプーン spūn
sport スポーツ spō·tsu
sports store/shop スポーツ用品店 spō·tsu·yō·hin·ten
sportsperson アスリート a·su·rī·to
sprain ⓝ 捻挫 nen·za
spring (coil) スプリング sprin·gu
spring (season) 春 ha·ru
spring onion ねぎ ne·gi
square (town) 広場 hi·ro·ba
squid イカ i·ka
stadium スタジアム sta·ji·a·mu
stairway 階段 kai·dan
stale 新鮮じゃない shin·sen ja nai
stamp ⓝ 切 kit·te
stand-by ticket スタンドバイチケット stan·do·bai·chi·ket·to
star 星 ho·shi
(three-/four-)star (3つ/4つ)星 (mi·tsu/yo·tsu)·bo·shi
start ⓝ スタート stā·to
start ⓥ 始めます ha·ji·me·mas
station 駅 e·ki
stationer's (shop) 文房具(店) bum·bō·gu(·ten)
statue 像 zō
stay (at a hotel) ⓥ 泊まります to·ma·ri·mas
stay (in one place) ⓥ 滞在します tai·zai shi·mas

steak (beef) ステーキ stē·ki
steal 盗みます nu·su·mi·mas
steamed 蒸して mu·shi·te
steep 急な kyū na
step ⓝ 段 dan
stereo ステレオ ste·re·o
still water 静かな水 shi·zu·ka na mi·zu
stock (food) 食料 sho·ku·ryō
stockings ストッキング stok·kin·gu
stolen 盗まれた nu·su·ma·re·ta
stomach 胃 i
stomachache 腹痛 fu·ku·tsū
stone 石 i·shi
stoned (drugged) ラリった ra·rit·ta
stop (bus, tram etc) ⓝ 停留所 tē·ryū·jo
stop (cease) ⓥ 止まります to·ma·ri·mas
stop (prevent) ⓥ 止めさせます ya·me·sa·se·mas
storm 嵐 a·ra·shi
story 話 ha·na·shi
stove ストーブ stō·bu
straight まっすぐな mas·su·gu na
strange 変な hen na
stranger よそ者 yo·so·mo·no
strawberry イチゴ i·chi·go
stream 流れ na·ga·re
street 道 mi·chi
street market 青空市場 a·o·zo·ra·i·chi·ba
strike ⓝ ストライキ sto·rai·ki
string ひも hi·mo
stroke (health) ⓝ 発作 hos·sa
stroller ベビーカー be·bī·kā
strong 強い tsu·yoy
stubborn 頑固な gan·ko na
student 生徒 sē·to
studio スタジオ sta·ji·o
stupid ばかな ba·ka na
style スタイル stai·ru
subtitles 字幕 ji·ma·ku
suburb 郊外 kō·gai
subway (underpass) 地下道 chi·ka·dō
subway (train) 地下鉄 chi·ka·te·tsu
sugar 砂糖 sa·tō
suitcase スーツケース sūts·kēs
sultana レーズン rē·zun
summer 夏 na·tsu
sun 太陽 tai·yō
sunblock 日焼け止め hi·ya·ke·do·me
sunburn 日焼け hi·ya·ke
sunglasses サングラス san·gu·ras
sunny 晴れた ha·re·ta
sunrise 日の出 hi·no·de
sunscreen 日焼け止め hi·ya·ke·do·me
sunset 日の入り hi·no·i·ri
sunstroke 日射病 nis·sha·byō
supermarket スーパー sū·pā
superstition 迷信 mē·shin
supporter (politics) 支持者 shi·ji·sha
supporter (sport) ファン fan
surf ⓥ サーフィンをします sā·fin o shi·mas
surface mail (land) 普通便 fu·tsū·bin
surface mail (sea) 船便 fu·na·bin
surfboard サーフボード sā·fu·bō·do
surfing ⓝ サーフィン sā·fin
surname 名字 myō·ji
surprise ⓝ 驚き o·do·ro·ki
sushi bar すし屋 su·shi·ya
sweater セーター sē·tā
Sweden スウェーデン swē·den
sweet ⓐ 甘い a·mai
sweets お菓子 o·ka·shi
swelling 腫れ ha·re
swim ⓥ 泳ぎます o·yo·gi·mas
swimming (sport) ⓝ 水泳 su·i·ē
swimming pool プール pū·ru
swimsuit 水着 mi·zu·gi
Switzerland スイス su·i·su
sword 刀 ka·ta·na
synagogue シナゴーグ shi·na·gō·gu
synthetic 合成の gō·sē no
syringe 注射器 chū·sha·ki

T

table テーブル tē·bu·ru
table (low) ちゃぶ台 cha·bu·dai
table tennis 卓球 tak·kyū
tablecloth テーブルクロス tē·bu·ru·ku·ros

tail 尻尾 ship·po
tailor テーラー tē·rā
take 取ります to·ri·mas
take a photo 写真を撮ります sha·shin o to·ri·mas
talk 話します ha·na·shi·mas
tall 高い ta·kai
tampon タンポン tam·pon
tanning lotion 日焼けローション hi·ya·ke·rō·shon
tap 蛇口 ja·gu·chi
tape (music, video) ⓝ テープ tē·pu
tap water 水道水 su·i·dō·su·i
tasty おいしい oy·shī
tattoo 刺青 i·re·zu·mi
tattooing ⓝ 刺青 i·re·zu·mi
tax ⓝ 税金 zē·kin
taxi タクシー tak·shī
taxi stand タクシー乗り場 tak·shī·no·ri·ba
tea (Japanese) お茶 o·cha
tea (Western) 紅茶 kō·cha
tea ceremony 茶道 sa·dō
tea cup 湯飲み茶碗 yu·no·mi·ja·wan
tea garden 茶畑 cha·ba·ta·ke
teacher 教師 kyō·shi
team チーム chī·mu
teapot ティーポット・急須 tī·pot·to · kyū·su
teaspoon ティースプーン tī·spūn
technique 技術 gi·ju·tsu
teeth 歯 ha
telephone ⓝ 電話 den·wa
telephone ⓥ 電話します den·wa shi·mas
telephone box 電話ボックス den·wa·bok·kus
telescope 望遠鏡 bō·en·kyō
television テレビ te·re·bi
tell 言います ī·mas
temperature (fever) 体温 tai·on
temperature (weather) 気温 ki·on
temple 寺 te·ra
tennis テニス te·nis
tennis court テニスコート te·nis kō·to
tent テント ten·to
tent peg ペグ pe·gu
terrible ひどい hi·doy
test ⓝ テスト tes·to
thank 感謝します kan·sha shi·mas
that (one) あれ a·re
theatre 劇場 ge·ki·jō
their 彼らの ka·re·ra no
there そこに so·ko ni
thermometer 体温計 tai·on·kē
they 彼らは ka·re·ra wa
thick 厚い a·tsu·i
thief どろぼう do·ro·bō
thin 薄い u·su·i
think 思います o·moy·mas
third 3番の sam·ban no
(to be) thirsty ⓐ のどが渇い no·do ga ka·wai·ta
this (one) これ ko·re
this month 今月 kon·ge·tsu
this week 今週 kon·shū
this year 今年 ko·to·shi
thread 糸 i·to
throat のど no·do
thrush (health) 口腔カンジダ症 kō·kū·kan·ji·da·shō
thunderstorm 嵐 a·ra·shi
ticket 切 kip·pu
ticket collector 切符回収 kip·pu·kai·shū·ga·ka·ri
ticket machine 切符販売 kip·pu·ham·bai·ki
ticket office 切符売り場 kip·pu·u·ri·ba
tide 潮 shi·o
tight きつい ki·tsu·i
time 時間 ji·kan
time difference 時差 ji·sa
timetable 時刻表 ji·ko·ku·hyō
tin (can) 缶 kan
tin opener 缶切 kan·ki·ri
tiny とても小さい to·te·mo chī·sai
tip (gratuity) ⓝ チップ chip·pu
tire ⓝ タイヤ tai·ya
tired 疲れた tsu·ka·re·ta
tissues ティッシュ tis·shu
to へ e

toast ⓝ トースト tōs·to
toaster トースター tōs·tā
tobacco タバコ tabako
tobacconist タバコ屋 ta·ba·ko·ya
tobogganing ⓝ そり so·ri
today 今日 kyō
toe つま先 tsu·ma·sa·ki
tofu 豆腐 tō·fu
together いっしょに is·sho ni
toilet トイレ toy·re
toilet paper トイレットペーパー toy·ret·to·pē·pā
token トークン tō·kun
toll ⓝ 通行料 tsū·kō·ryō
tomato トマト to·ma·to
tomato sauce トマトソース to·ma·to·sō·su
tomorrow 明日 a·shi·ta
tomorrow afternoon 明日の午後 a·shi·ta no go·go
tomorrow evening 明日の夜 a·shi·ta no yo·ru
tomorrow morning 明日の朝 a·shi·ta no a·sa
tonight 今夜 kon·ya
too (expensive etc) すぎる su·gi·ru
too many/much 多すぎます ō·su·gi·mas
tooth 歯 ha
toothache 歯痛 hai·ta
toothbrush 歯ブラシ ha·bu·ra·shi
toothpaste 練り歯磨き ne·ri·ha·mi·ga·ki
toothpick 楊枝 yō·ji
torch (flashlight) 懐中電灯 kai·chū·den·tō
touch ⓥ 触ります sa·wa·ri·mas
tour ⓝ ツアー tsu·ā
tourist 旅行者 ryo·kō·sha
tourist office 観光案内所 kan·kō·an·nai·jo
towel タオル tow·ru
tower 搭 tō
toxic waste 有害廃棄物 yū·gai·hai·ki·bu·tsu
toy shop おもちゃ屋 o·mo·cha·ya
track (path) ⓝ 通路 tsū·ro
track (sport) ⓝ トラック競技 to·rak·ku·kyō·gi
trade 貿易 bō·e·ki
tradesperson 貿易商 bō·e·ki·shō
traffic 交通 kō·tsū
traffic jam 渋滞 jū·tai
traffic light 信号 shin·gō
trail ⓝ 足跡 a·shi·a·to
train 電車 den·sha
train station 駅 e·ki
tram 市電 shi·den
transfer (trains) ⓝ 乗り換え no·ri·ka·e
transit lounge 待合室 ma·chi·ai·shi·tsu
translate 翻訳します hon·ya·ku shi·mas
transport ⓝ 輸送 yu·sō
travel ⓥ 旅行します ryo·kō shi·mas
travel agency 旅行代理店 ryo·kō·dai·ri·ten
travel sickness 乗り物酔い no·ri·mo·no·yoy
travellers cheque トラベラーズチェック to·ra·be·rāz·chek·ku
tree 木 ki
trip (journey) 旅 ta·bi
trolley トロリー to·ro·rī
trousers ズボン zu·bon
truck トラック to·rak·ku
true 本当の hon·tō no
try (attempt) ⓥ 試します ta·me·shi·mas
T-shirt Tシャツ tī·sha·tsu
tube (tyre) チューブ chū·bu
tumour 腫瘍 shu·yō
tuna マグロ ma·gu·ro
tune チューン chūn
turkey 七面鳥 shi·chi·men·chō
turn ⓥ 曲がります ma·ga·ri·mas
TV テレビ te·re·bi
tweezers 毛抜き ke·nu·ki
twice 2倍に ni·bai ni
twin beds ツインベッド tsu·in·bed·do
twins 双子 fu·ta·go

two 2 ni
type ⓝ タイプ tai·pu
typical 典型的な ten·kē·te·ki na
typhoon 台風 tai·fū
tyre タイヤ tai·ya

U

ugly みにくい mi·ni·ku·i
ultrasound 超音波 chōm·pa
umbrella かさ ka·sa
uncomfortable 不安な fu·an na
understand 理解します ri·kai shi·mas
underwear 下着 shi·ta·gi
unemployed 失業した shi·tsu·gyō shi·ta
unfair 不公平な fu·kō·hē na
uniform ⓝ 制服 sē·fu·ku
universe 宇宙 u·chū
university 大学 dai·ga·ku
unsafe 安全じゃない an·zen ja nai
until (time) まで ma·de
unusual 珍しい me·zu·ra·shī
up 上に u·e ni
uphill 上り坂の no·bo·ri·za·ka no
urgent 緊急の kin·kyū no
urinary infection 尿道炎 nyō·dō·en
USA アメリカ a·me·ri·ka
useful 便利な ben·ri na

V

vacancy 空室の kū·shi·tsu no
no vacancy 満室 man·shi·tsu
vacant 空いている ai·te i·ru
vacation 休暇 kyū·ka
vaccination 予防注射 yo·bō·chū·sha
vagina ヴァギナ va·gi·na
validate 有効にします yū·kō ni shi·mas
valley 谷 ta·ni
valuable ⓐ 高価な kō·ka na
valuables ⓝ 貴重品 ki·chō·hin
value (price) ⓝ 価値 ka·chi
van バン ban
veal 子牛 ko·u·shi
vegan 厳格な菜食主義者 gen·ka·ku na sai·sho·ku·shu·gi·sha
vegetable(s) 野菜 ya·sai
vegetables (fried) 野菜炒め ya·sai·i·ta·me
vegetarian ベジタリアン be·ji·ta·ri·an
vein 静脈 jō·mya·ku
vending machine 自動販売機 ji·dō·ham·bai·ki
venereal disease 性病 sē·byō
venue 現場 gem·ba
very とても to·te·mo
view ⓝ 眺め na·ga·me
village 村 mu·ra
vinegar 酢 su
vineyard ブドウ畑 bu·dō·ba·ta·ke
virus ウィルス wi·ru·su
visa ビザ bi·za
visit ⓥ 訪問します hō·mon shi·mas
vitamins ビタミン bi·ta·min
vodka ウォッカ wok·ka
voice ⓝ 声 ko·e
volcano 火山 ka·zan
volleyball バレーボール ba·rē·bō·ru
volume 量 ryō
vote ⓥ 投票します tō·hyō shi·mas

W

wage 賃金 chin·gin
wait (for) ⓥ 待ちます ma·chi·mas
waiter ウェイター wē·tā
waiting room 待合室 ma·chi·ai·shi·tsu
wake (someone) up 起こします o·ko·shi·mas
Wales ウェールズ wē·ru·zu
walk ⓥ 歩きます a·ru·ki·mas
wallet 財布 sai·fu
wall 壁 ka·be
want ⓥ 欲しいです ho·shī des
war 戦争 sen·sō
wardrobe たんす tan·su
warm あたたかい a·ta·ta·kai
warn 警告します kē·ko·ku shi·mas

wash (oneself/something) 洗います a·rai·mas
wash cloth (flannel, eg face) 洗顔タオル sen·gan·tow·ru
washing machine 洗濯機 sen·tak·ki
watch ⓝ 腕時計 u·de·do·kē
watch ⓥ 見ます mi·mas
water 水 mi·zu
water bottle 水筒 su·i·tō
water bottle (hot) ポット pot·to
waterfall 滝 ta·ki
watermelon スイカ su·i·ka
waterproof 防水 bō·su·i
water-skiing ⓝ 水上スキー su·i·jō·skī
wave ⓝ 波 na·mi
way 道 mi·chi
we 私たちは wa·ta·shi·ta·chi wa
weak 弱い yo·wai
wealthy 裕福な yū·fu·ku na
wear 着ます ki·mas
weather 天気 ten·ki
wedding 結婚式 kek·kon·shi·ki
week 週 shū
weekend 週末 shū·ma·tsu
weekly 1週間 is·shū·kan
weight 重さ o·mo·sa
welfare 福祉 fu·ku·shi
well よく yo·ku
west 西 ni·shi
wet ⓐ 濡れている nu·re·te i·ru
whale くじら ku·ji·ra
what なに na·ni
wheel 車輪 sha·rin
wheelchair 車椅子 ku·ru·ma·i·su
when いつ i·tsu
where どこ do·ko
which どちら do·chi·ra
whisky ウィスキー wis·kī
white 白い shi·roy
white (coffee) ホワイト ho·wai·to
white wine 白ワイン shi·ro·wain
who だれ da·re
wholemeal bread ホールミールのパン hō·ru·mī·ru no pan
why なぜ na·ze
wide 広く hi·ro·ku
wife 妻 tsu·ma
wild 野生 ya·sē
wild rice ワイルドライス wai·ru·do·rai·su
win ⓥ 勝ちます ka·chi·mas
wind 風 ka·ze
wineglass ワイングラス wain·gu·ra·su
window 窓 ma·do
windscreen フロントガラス fu·ron·to·ga·ra·su
windsurfing ⓝ ウィンドサーフィン win·do·sā·fin
wine ワイン wain
wing 翼 tsu·ba·sa
winner 受賞者 ju·shō·sha
winter 冬 fu·yu
with いっしょに is·sho ni
within (an hour) (1時間)内に (i·chi·ji·kan) nai ni
without なしで na·shi de
wok 中華鍋 chū·ka·na·be
woman 女性 jo·sē
wonderful 素晴らしい su·ba·ra·shī
wood 木 ki
wood-block prints 浮世絵 u·ki·yo·e
wool ウール ū·ru
word 言葉 ko·to·ba
work ⓝ 仕事 shi·go·to
work ⓥ 働きます ha·ta·ra·ki·mas
work experience 職歴 sho·ku·re·ki
work permit 就労許可 shū·rō·kyo·ka
workout ⓝ 練習 ren·shū
world 世界 se·kai
World Cup ワールドカップ wā·ru·do·kap·pu
worms イモムシ i·mo·mu·shi
worried 心配な shim·pai na
wrist 手首 te·ku·bi
write 書きます ka·ki·mas
writer 作家 sak·ka
wrong 間違った ma·chi·gat·ta

Y

year 年 nen
yellow 黄色い kī·roy
yes はい hai
yesterday きのう ki·nō
yoga ヨガ yo·ga
yogurt ヨーグルト yō·gu·ru·to
you sg あなた a·na·ta
you pl あなたたち a·na·ta·ta·chi
young 若い wa·kai
your あなたの a·na·ta no
youth hostel ユースホステル yū·su·ho·su·te·ru

Z

zip(per) ジッパー jip·pā
zodiac 12宮 jū·ni·gū
zoo 動物園 dō·bu·tsu·en
zucchini ズッキーニ zuk·kī·ni

DICTIONARY

Japanese to English

日本語–英語

The entries in this Japanese–English dictionary are ordered according to the gojūon (or aiueo) system, which is widely used in Japan. The order is: **a**-i-u-e-o-**ka**-ga-ki-gi-kya-gya-kyu-gyu-kyo-gyo-ku-gu-ke-ge-ko-go-**sa**-za-shi-ji-sha-ja-shu-ju-sho-jo-su-zu-se-ze-so-zo-**ta**-da-chi-(ji)-cha-chu-cho-tsu-(zu)-te-de-to-do-**na**-ni-nya-nyu-nyo-nu-ne-no-**ha**-ba-pa-hi-bi-pi-hya-bya-pya-hyu-byu-pyu-hyo-byo-pyo-fu-bu-pu-he-be-pe-ho-bo-po-**ma**-mi-mya-myu-myo-mu-me-mo-**ya**-yu-yo-ra-ri-rya-ryu-ryo-ru-re-ro-**wa**-n

Verbs in the dictionary are given in their ·mas (ます) form (for more information on this, see **grammar**, p16). The symbols ⓝ, ⓐ and ⓥ (indicating noun, adjective and verb) have been added for clarity where an English term could be either.

あ A

愛 ai love ⓝ
愛します ai shi·mas love ⓥ
アイスクリーム ais·ku·rī·mu ice cream
空いている ai·te i·ru vacant
アイルランド ai·ru·ran·do Ireland
アイロン ai·ron iron (for clothes) ⓝ
青い a·oy blue
青空市場 a·o·zo·ra·i·chi·ba street market
赤い a·kai red
赤ちゃん a·ka·chan baby
明るい a·ka·ru·i light (of colour) ⓐ
赤ワイン a·ka·wain red wine
秋 a·ki autumn • fall
揚げます a·ge·mas fry
朝 a·sa morning
朝ごはん a·sa·go·han breakfast
あさって a·sat·te (the) day after tomorrow
足 a·shi foot
脚 a·shi leg (body part)
足首 a·shi·ku·bi ankle
明日 a·shi·ta tomorrow
明日の朝 a·shi·ta no a·sa tomorrow morning
明日の午後 a·shi·ta no go·go tomorrow afternoon
明日の夜 a·shi·ta no yo·ru tomorrow evening
アスピリン as·pi·rin aspirin
あたたかい a·ta·ta·kai warm
頭 a·ta·ma head ⓝ
新しい a·ta·ra·shī new
熱い a·tsu·i hot
熱くなった a·tsu·ku nat·ta heated
あと a·to after

あとで a·to de later
あなた a·na·ta you sg
あなたたち a·na·ta·ta·chi you pl
危ない a·bu·nai dangerous
油 a·bu·ra oil (food)
甘い a·mai sweet ⓐ
雨 a·me rain
アメリカ a·me·ri·ka USA
歩きます a·ru·ki·mas walk ⓥ
アルコール a·ru·kō·ru alcohol
あれ a·re that (one)
アレルギー a·re·ru·gī allergy
アントレー an·to·rē entrée
案内所 an·nai·jo information office
胃 i stomach
いい ī good
いいえ ī·e no
Eメール ī·mē·ru email ⓝ
医学 i·ga·ku medicine (study, profession)
行きます i·ki·mas go ⓥ
イギリス i·gi·ri·su England
遺失物取扱所 i·shi·tsu·bu·tsu·to·ri·a·tsu·kai·jo lost property office
医者 i·sha doctor
椅子 i·su chair
忙しい i·so·ga·shī busy
痛み i·ta·mi pain
いたんだ i·tan·da off (spoiled)
1 i·chi one
市場 i·chi·ba market
いちばん大きい i·chi·ban ō·kī biggest
いちばん小さい i·chi·ban chī·sai smallest
いちばん近くの i·chi·ban chi·ka·ku no nearest
胃腸炎 i·chō·en gastroenteritis
いつ i·tsu when
いっしょに is·sho ni together
いっぱいの ip·pai no full
田舎 i·na·ka countryside
犬 i·nu dog
今 i·ma now
妹 i·mō·to younger sister
衣料店 i·ryō·ten clothing store
衣類 i·ru·i clothing
刺青 i·re·zu·mi tattoo • tattooing
色 i·ro colour
インターネット in·tā·net·to internet
インターネットカフェ in·tā·net·to·ka·fe internet cafe
インフルエンザ in·fu·ru·en·za flu • influenza
ウール ū·ru wool
ウェイター wē·tā waiter
ウェールズ wē·ru·zu Wales
上に u·e ni on • up
うしろ u·shi·ro behind
後ろの u·shi·ro no rear (seat etc) ⓐ
美しい u·tsu·ku·shī beautiful
腕 u·de arm
腕時計 u·de·do·kē watch ⓝ
海 u·mi sea
うるさい u·ru·sai loud • noisy
運転します un·ten shi·mas drive
運転手 un·ten·shu driver
運転免許証 un·ten·men·kyo·shō drivers licence
絵 e painting (a work)
エアコン付きの air·kon·tsu·ki no air-conditioned
映画 ē·ga film (cinema) • movie
映画館 ē·ga·kan cinema
英語 ē·go English (language)
ATM ē·tī·e·mu ATM
駅 e·ki (train) station
エコノミークラス e·ko·no·mī·ku·ras economy class
エスカレータ es·ka·rē·ta escalator
エレベーター e·re·bē·tā elevator • lift
エンジン en·jin engine
エンターテイメントガイド en·tā·tē·men·to·gai·do entertainment guide
エンピツ em·pi·tsu pencil
おいしい oy·shī tasty
往復切符 ō·fu·ku·kip·pu return ticket
OL ō·e·ru female office worker
大きい ō·kī big
オーストラリア ō·sto·ra·rya Australia
オートバイ ō·to·bai motorcycle
オートマチック ō·to·ma·chik·ku automatic ⓐ
大晦日 ō·mi·so·ka New Year's Eve

お母さん o·kā·san mother
おかしい o·ka·shī funny
お金 o·ka·ne money
贈物 o·ku·ri·mo·no gift
遅れ o·ku·re delay ⓝ
起こします o·ko·shi·mas wake (someone) up
おじいさん o·jī·san grandfather
おしゃぶり o·sha·bu·ri dummy • pacifier
遅い o·soy late
お茶 o·cha tea (Japanese)
夫 ot·to husband
お父さん o·tō·san father
弟 o·tō·to younger brother
男の子 o·to·ko no ko boy
おととい o·to·toy (the) day before yesterday
踊ります o·do·ri·mas dance ⓥ
お腹がすいた o·na·ka ga su·i·ta (to be) hungry
お兄さん o·nī·san older brother
お姉さん o·nē·san older sister
おばあさん o·bā·san grandmother
おばさん o·ba·san aunt
お話中 o·ha·na·shi·chū engaged (phone)
お風呂 o·fu·ro bath ⓝ
お土産 o·mi·ya·ge souvenir
お土産屋 o·mi·ya·ge·ya souvenir shop
オムツ o·mu·tsu diaper • nappy
おめでとう o·me·de·tō congratulations
重い o·moy heavy
泳ぎます o·yo·gi·mas swim
オランダ o·ran·da Netherlands
降ります o·ri·mas get off (a train etc)
オレンジ o·ren·ji orange (colour) • orange (fruit)
おわり o·wa·ri end ⓝ
お椀 o·wan miso-soup bowl • soup bowl
音楽 on·ga·ku music
温泉 on·sen mineral hot-spring spa
女の子 on·na no ko girl

か KA

ガールフレンド gā·ru·fu·ren·do girlfriend
階 kai floor (storey)
絵画 kai·ga painting (the art)
海外 kai·gai abroad • overseas
外国の gai·ko·ku no foreign
会社 kai·sha company (firm)
快速 kai·so·ku rapid train
階段 kai·dan stairway
懐中電灯 kai·chū·den·tō torch (flashlight)
開店時間 kai·ten·ji·kan opening hours
ガイド gai·do guide (person)
ガイド付きツアー gai·do·tsu·ki·tsu·ā guided tour
ガイドブック gai·do·buk·ku guidebook
買います kai·mas buy
買い物をします kai·mo·no o shi·mas shop ⓥ
顔 ka·o face
画家 ga·ka painter
科学 ka·ga·ku science
鏡 ka·ga·mi mirror
鍵 ka·gi key
書留 ka·ki·to·me registered mail
書きます ka·ki·mas write
鍵をかけた ka·gi o ka·ke·ta locked
鍵をかけます ka·gi o ka·ke·mas lock ⓥ
家具 ka·gu furniture
カクテル ka·ku·te·ru cocktail
かさ ka·sa umbrella
貸します ka·shi·mas rent ⓥ
ガス gas gas (for cooking)
カセット ka·set·to cassette
家族 ka·zo·ku family
ガソリン ga·so·rin gas • petrol
ガソリンスタンド ga·so·rin·stan·do petrol station • service station
肩 ka·ta shoulder
かたい ka·tai hard (not soft)
片道切 ka·ta·mi·chi·kip·pu one-way ticket
月 ga·tsu month
カップ kap·pu cup

カナダ ka·na·da Canada
彼女の ka·no·jo no her (ownership)
彼女は ka·no·jo wa she
彼女を ka·no·jo o her (as object of sentence)
カバーチャージ ka·bā·chā·ji cover charge
かばん ka·ban bag
カフェ ka·fe cafe
カプセルホテル ka·pu·se·ru·ho·te·ru capsule hotel
花粉症 ka·fun·shō hay fever
紙 ka·mi paper
剃刀 ka·mi·so·ri razor
剃刀の刃 ka·mi·so·ri no ha razor blade
カメラ ka·me·ra camera
かゆみ ka·yu·mi itch ⓝ
から ka·ra from
空の ka·ra no empty
軽い ka·ru·i light (not heavy) ⓐ
彼の ka·re no his
彼は ka·re wa he
彼を kare o him
皮 ka·wa leather ⓝ
川 ka·wa river
乾いた ka·wai·ta dry ⓐ
乾かします ka·wa·ka·shi·mas dry (clothes) ⓥ
為替 ka·wa·se currency exchange
為替レート ka·wa·se·rē·to exchange rate
缶 kan can • tin
缶切 kan·ki·ri can opener • tin opener
換金します kan·kin shi·mas change (money) ⓥ
間欠泉 kan·kets·sen geyser
観光案内所 kan·kō·an·nai·jo tourist office
看護婦 kan·go·fu nurse
感謝している kan·sha shi·te i·ru grateful
勘定 kan·jō bill (restaurant etc) ⓝ
感触 kan·sho·ku feeling (physical)
感染 kan·sen infection
幹線道路 kan·sen·dō·ro highway
元旦 gan·tan New Year's Day
黄色い kī·roy yellow
気温 ki·on temperature (weather)
聴きます ki·ki·mas listen (to)
既婚 ki·kon married
技術者 gi·ju·tsu·sha engineer
季節 ki·se·tsu season
北 ki·ta north
汚い ki·ta·nai dirty
喫煙 ki·tsu·en smoking ⓐ
切 kit·te stamp ⓝ
切 kip·pu ticket
切符売り kip·pu·u·ri·ba ticket office
切符販売 kip·pu·ham·bai·ki ticket machine
絹 ki·nu silk ⓝ
きのう ki·nō yesterday
キャンセル kyan·se·ru cancel ⓥ
キャンプ場 kyam·pu·jō camping ground
休暇 kyū·ka holidays • vacation
救急 kyū·kyū emergency
救急車 kyū·kyū·sha ambulance
救急箱 kyū·kyū·ba·ko first-aid kit
宮殿 kyū·den palace
救命胴衣 kyū·mē·dōy life jacket
今日 kyō today
境界 kyō·kai border
教会 kyō·kai church
教師 kyō·shi teacher
兄弟 kyō·dai brother
キヨスク ki·yos·ku kiosk
義理のお母さん gi·ri no o·kā·san mother-in-law
義理のお父さん gi·ri no o·tō·san father-in-law
切ります ki·ri·mas cut ⓥ
きれいな ki·rē na clean ⓐ
キロ(グラム) ki·ro(·gu·ra·mu) kilo(gram)
キロメートル ki·ro·mē·to·ru kilometre
金 kin gold ⓝ
銀 gin silver ⓝ
禁煙の kin·en no nonsmoking
緊急の kin·kyu no urgent
金庫 kin·ko safe ⓝ
銀行 gin·kō bank (money) ⓝ
銀行口座 gin·kō·kō·za bank account
航空 kō·kū airline

空港 kū·kō airport
空港税 kū·kō·zē airport tax
航空便 kō·kū·bin airmail
空室 kū·shi·tsu vacancy
くし ku·shi comb
苦情 ku·jō complaint
薬 ku·su·ri drug (medicine) • medication
果物 ku·da·mo·no fruit
口 ku·chi mouth
口紅 ku·chi·be·ni lipstick
靴 ku·tsu shoe
靴下 ku·tsu·shi·ta socks
靴屋 ku·tsu·ya shoe shop
首 ku·bi neck
暗い ku·rai dark
クラシックの ku·ra·shik·ku no classical
グラス gu·ra·su glass (for drinking)
グラム gu·ra·mu gram
クリーニング ku·rī·nin·gu cleaning ⓝ
クリーム ku·rī·mu cream
クリスマス ku·ri·su·mas Christmas
車椅子 ku·ru·ma·i·su wheelchair
クレジットカード ku·re·jit·to·kā·do credit card
黒い ku·roy black
クローク ku·rō·ku cloakroom
警官 kē·kan police officer
警察 kē·sa·tsu police
警察署 kē·sa·tsu·sho police station
計算機 kē·san·ki calculator
芸術家 gē·ju·tsu·ka artist
軽食 kē·sho·ku snack
携帯電話 kē·tai·den·wa mobile phone
ゲイの gē no gay ⓐ
けが ke·ga injury ⓝ
劇 ge·ki play (theatre) ⓝ
劇場 ge·ki·jō theatre
下剤 ge·zai laxative ⓝ
下宿屋 ge·shu·ku·ya boarding house
ゲストハウス ges·to·how·su guesthouse
血液型 ke·tsu·e·ki·ga·ta blood group
欠点のある ket·ten no a·ru faulty
毛抜き ke·nu·ki tweezers
下痢 ge·ri diarrhoea
現金 gen·kin cash ⓝ
現金化します gen·kin·ka shi·mas cash (a cheque) ⓥ
言語 gen·go language
建築 ken·chi·ku architecture
建築家 ken·chi·ku·ka architect
コイン ko·in coins
コインランドリー ko·in·ran·do·rī launderette
更衣室 kōy·shi·tsu changing room (for sport)
公園 kō·en park ⓝ
工学 kō·ga·ku engineering
高価な kō·ka na valuable ⓝ
豪華な gō·ka na luxury ⓐ
交換 kō·kan exchange ⓝ
交換します kō·kan shi·mas exchange ⓥ
航空便 kō·kū·bin flight
工芸品 kō·gē·hin crafts
公衆電話 kō·shū·den·wa public telephone
公衆トイレ kō·shū·toy·re public toilet
香水 kō·su·i perfume
抗生剤 kō·sē·zai antibiotics
高速道路 kō·so·ku·dō·ro motorway (tollway)
紅茶 kō·cha tea (Western)
交番 kō·ban police box
コークスクリュー kō·ku·sku·ryū corkscrew
凍った kōt·ta frozen
コート kō·to coat • court (tennis)
コーヒー kō·hī coffee
氷 kō·ri ice
小切 ko·git·te check (banking) ⓝ
顧客 ko·kya·ku client
午後 go·go afternoon
心地よい ko·ko·chi·yoy comfortable
ここで ko·ko de here
小皿 ko·za·ra plate (small)
故障した ko·shō·shi·ta broken down
故障中 ko·shō·chū out of order
個人的な ko·jin·te·ki na private
小銭 ko·ze·ni change (coins) ⓝ
コック kok·ku cook ⓝ
小包 ko·zu·tsu·mi packet (general) • parcel
子供 ko·do·mo child • children
ごはん go·han rice (cooked)

小道 ko·mi·chi path
ごみ箱 go·mi·ba·ko garbage can
米 ko·me rice (uncooked)
子守り ko·mo·ri childminding ⓝ
ゴルフ go·ru·fu golf
ゴルフコース go·ru·fu·kō·su golf course
これ ko·re this (one)
壊れた ko·wa·re·ta broken
壊れやすい ko·wa·re·ya·su·i fragile (item etc)
コンサート kon·sā·to concert
コンタクトレンズ kon·ta·ku·to·ren·zu contact lenses
コンドーム kon·dō·mu condom
コンパニオン kom·pa·ni·on companion
コンビニ kom·bi·ni convenience store
コンピュータ kom·pyū·ta computer
コンファーム kon·fā·mu confirm (a booking)
コンファレンス kon·fa·ren·su conference (big)
今夜 kon·ya tonight
婚約者 kon·ya·ku·sha fiancé(e)

さ SA

サーカス sā·kas circus
サービス sā·bis service
サービス料 sā·bis·ryō service charge
最高の sai·kō no best
最後の sai·go no last (final)
祭日 sai·ji·tsu public holiday
(厳格な)菜食主義者 (gen·ka·ku na) sai·sho·ku·shu·gi·sha vegan
サイズ sai·zu size (general)
財布 sai·fu purse • wallet
魚 sa·ka·na fish
魚屋 sa·ka·na·ya fish shop
酒屋 sa·ka·ya liquor store
酒 sa·ke alcoholic drink • sake
サッカー sak·kā football (soccer)
茶道 sa·dō tea ceremony
寒い sa·mu·i cold (atmosphere)
皿 sa·ra dish • plate (big)
サラリーマン sa·ra·rī·man business man
さん ·san Mr • Mrs • Ms • Miss
サングラス san·gu·ras sunglasses
市 shi city
試合 shi·ai game (sport) • match
幸せな shi·a·wa·se na happy
シーツ shī·tsu bed linen • sheet (bed)
シートベルト shī·to·be·ru·to seatbelt
ジーンズ jīn·zu jeans
シェアします she·a shi·mas share (a dorm etc) ⓥ
シェービングクリーム shē·bin·gu·ku·rī·mu shaving cream
シェフ she·fu chef
時間 ji·kan hour
時間どおり ji·kan·dō·ri on time
事故 ji·ko accident
時刻表 ji·ko·ku·hyō timetable
仕事 shi·go·to job
時差 ji·sa time difference
時差ぼけ ji·sa·bo·ke jet lag
辞書 ji·sho dictionary
静かな shi·zu·ka na quiet
下着 shi·ta·gi underwear
下へ shi·ta e down
試着室 shi·cha·ku·shi·tsu changing room (in shop)
失業した shi·tsu·gyō shi·ta unemployed
ジッパー jip·pā zip • zipper
自転車 ji·ten·sha bicycle
自動車 ji·dō·sha car
自動車所有権 ji·dō·sha·sho·yū·ken car owner's title
自動車登録 ji·dō·sha·tō·ro·ku car registration
自動販売機 ji·dō·ham·bai·ki vending machine
市の中心 shi no chū·shin city centre
支払い shi·ha·rai payment
紙幣 shi·hē banknote
島 shi·ma island
姉妹 shi·mai sister
字幕 ji·ma·ku subtitles
閉まった shi·mat·ta shut ⓐ
ジム ji·mu gym (place)
事務処理 ji·mu·sho·ri paperwork
閉めます shi·me·mas close ⓥ

地元 ji·mo·to local ⓐ
ジャーナリスト jā·na·ris·to journalist
蛇口 ja·gu·chi faucet • tap
ジャケット ja·ket·to jacket
写真 sha·shin photo • photography
写真家 sha·shin·ka photographer
シャツ sha·tsu shirt
シャワー sha·wā shower
シャンペン sham·pen champagne
週 shū week
習慣 shū·kan custom
住所 jū·sho address
充分な jū·bun na enough
週末 shū·ma·tsu weekend
修理します shū·ri shi·mas repair ⓥ
手芸品 shu·gē·hin handicrafts
出張 shut·chō business trip
出発 shup·pa·tsu departure
潤滑油 jun·ka·tsu·yu lubricant
障害をもつ shō·gai o mo·tsu disabled ⓐ
消化不良 shō·ka·fu·ryō indigestion
乗客 jō·kya·ku passenger
正午 shō·go midday • noon
錠剤 jō·zai pill
消臭剤 shō·shū·zai deodorant
消毒剤 shō·do·ku·zai antiseptic ⓝ
乗馬 jō·ba horse riding
情報 jō·hō information
ショー shō show ⓝ
食事 sho·ku·ji meal
食前酒 sho·ku·zen·shu apéritif
食中毒 sho·ku·chū·do·ku food poisoning
食堂車 sho·ku·dō·sha dining car
食料 sho·ku·ryō food supplies
食料品 sho·ku·ryō·hin grocery
女性 jo·sē female • woman
ショッピングセンター shop·pin·gu·sen·tā shopping centre
処方箋 sho·hō·sen prescription
書類 sho·ru·i papers (documents)
城 shi·ro castle
白い shi·roy white
白黒（フィルム）shi·ro·ku·ro (fi·ru·mu) B&W (film)
白ワイン shi·ro·wain white wine
新幹線 shin·kan·sen bullet train
シングルルーム shin·gu·ru·rū·mu single room
寝室 shin·shi·tsu bedroom
親切な shin·se·tsu na kind (nice)
新鮮な shin·sen na fresh
心臓 shin·zō heart
心臓病 shin·zō·byō heart condition
寝台車 shin·dai·sha sleeping car
新聞 shim·bun newspaper
水筒 su·i·tō water bottle
炊飯器 su·i·han·ki rice cooker
水疱 su·i·hō blister
数字 sū·ji number
スーツケース sūts·kēs suitcase
スーパー sū·pā supermarket
スカート skā·to skirt
スカーフ skā·fu scarf
スキー skī skiing ⓝ
好きです su·ki des like ⓥ
すぎる su·gi·ru too (expensive etc)
少ない su·ku·nai less
すぐに su·gu ni soon
スコットランド skot·to·ran·do Scotland
涼しい su·zu·shī cool (temperature)
勧めます su·su·me·mas recommend ⓥ
スタンドバイチケット stan·do·bai·chi·ket·to stand-by ticket
頭痛 zu·tsū headache
ストッキング stok·kin·gu stockings
ストライキ sto·rai·ki strike ⓝ
素晴らしい su·ba·ra·shī great (fantastic)
スプーン spūn spoon
スポーツ用品店 spō·tsu·yō·hin·ten sports shop • sports store
ズボン zu·bon pants • trousers
スライス su·rai·su slice ⓝ
スライド su·rai·do slide (film) ⓝ
税関 zē·kan customs
税金 zē·kin tax
制限速度 sē·gen·so·ku·do speed limit
生徒 sē·to student

生理用ナプキン sē·ri·yō·na·pu·kin panty liners • sanitary napkins
セーター sē·tā jumper • sweater
セーフセックス sē·fu·sek·kus safe sex
セカンドクラス se·kan·do·ku·ras second class ⓝ
席 se·ki seat (place)
せきが出ます se·ki ga de·mas cough ⓥ
せき止め se·ki·do·me cough medicine ⓝ
石油 se·ki·yu oil (petrol)
セックス sek·kus sex
石鹸 sek·ken soap
接続 se·tsu·zo·ku connection (transport)
背中 se·na·ka back (body part)
セルフサービスの se·ru·fu·sā·bis no self service ⓐ
栓 sen plug (bath)
前菜 zen·sai appetiser
洗濯場 sen·ta·ku·ba laundry (place)
洗濯物 sen·ta·ku·mo·no laundry (clothes)
洗濯機 sen·tak·ki washing machine
センチ sen·chi centimetre
銭湯 sen·tō bath house • public baths
栓抜き sen·nu·ki bottle opener
全部 zem·bu all • everything
掃除をします sō·ji o shi·mas clean ⓥ
速達 so·ku·ta·tsu express (mail) ⓝ
そこに so·ko ni there
そして so·shi·te and
外側の so·to·ga·wa no outside
剃ります so·ri·mas shave ⓥ
それぞれ so·re·zo·re each

た TA

ダイアルトーン dai·a·ru·tōn dial tone
大学 dai·ga·ku university
退屈な tai·ku·tsu na boring
大使館 tai·shi·kan embassy
大聖堂 dai·sē·dō cathedral
大切 tai·se·tsu na important
台所 dai·do·ko·ro kitchen
たいへんな tai·hen na hard (not easy)
タイヤ tai·ya tire • tyre
太陽 tai·yō sun
タオル tow·ru towel
高い ta·kai expensive • high
タクシー tak·shī taxi
タクシー乗り場 tak·shī·no·ri·ba taxi stand
たすけ tas·ke help ⓝ
たすけます tas·ke·mas help ⓥ
脱脂綿 das·shi·men cotton balls
建物 ta·te·mo·no building
タバコ ta·ba·ko cigarette
タバコを吸います ta·ba·ko o su·i·mas smoke ⓥ
旅 ta·bi journey
ダブルベッド da·bu·ru·bed·do double bed
ダブルルーム da·bu·ru·rū·mu double room
食べます ta·be·mas eat
食べ物 ta·be·mo·no food
だれ da·re who
誕生日 tan·jō·bi birthday • date of birth
ダンス dan·su dancing ⓝ
タンポン tam·pon tampon
血 chi blood
小さい chī·sai small
チーズ chī·zu cheese
チーム chī·mu team
チェックイン chek·ku·in check-in (desk) ⓝ
違う chi·ga·u different
近く chi·ka·ku close • near • nearby
地下鉄の駅 chi·ka·te·tsu no eki subway/metro station
地下道 chi·ka·dō subway (underpass)
地図 chi·zu map
チップ chip·pu tip (gratuity) ⓝ
チャイルドシート chai·ru·do·shī·to child seat
茶色い chai·roy brown ⓐ
茶畑 cha·ba·ta·ke tea garden
茶碗 cha·wan rice bowl
中央 chū ō centre
中止 chū·shi intermission
注射 chū·sha injection
駐車します chū·sha shi·mas park (a car) ⓥ

駐車場 chū·sha·jō car park
注射針 chū·sha·ba·ri needle (syringe)
昼食 chū·sho·ku lunch
超過 chō·ka excess (baggage)
彫刻 chō·ko·ku sculpture
朝食 chō·sho·ku breakfast
ちょうど chō·do exactly
直接に cho·ku·se·tsu ni direct
直通 cho·ku·tsū direct-dial
チョコレート cho·ko·rē·to chocolate
賃貸します chin·tai shi·mas hire
鎮痛剤 chin·tsū·zai painkiller
ツアー tsu·ā tour
ツインベッド tsu·in·bed·do twin beds
通信社 tsū·shin·sha newsagency
通訳 tsū·ya·ku interpreter
通路 tsū·ro aisle (eg on plane)
疲れた tsu·ka·re·ta tired
つぎ tsu·gi next
包み tsu·tsu·mi package
妻 tsu·ma wife
つまります tsu·ma·ri·mas blocked
爪切 tsu·me·ki·ri nail clippers
冷たい tsu·me·tai cold (to the touch) ⓐ
釣り tsu·ri fishing ⓝ
手 te hand
で de at
Tシャツ tī·sha·tsu T-shirt
ティースプーン tī·spūn teaspoon
ティーポット tī·pot·to teapot
ティッシュ tis·shu tissues
テーラー tē·rā tailor
手形 te·ga·ta check (bill)
出かけます de·ka·ke·mas go out
手紙 te·ga·mi letter (mail)
出口 de·gu·chi exit ⓝ
デザート de·zā·to dessert
手数料 te·sū·ryō commission
手作りの te·zu·ku·ri no handmade
テニス te·nis tennis
テニスコート te·nis kō·to tennis court
手荷物 te·ni·mo·tsu baggage • luggage
手荷物預かり所 te·ni·mo·tsu·a·zu·ka·ri·sho left luggage (office)
手荷物許容量 te·ni·mo·tsu·kyo·yō·ryō baggage allowance
デパート de·pā·to department store
手袋 te·bu·ku·ro gloves
寺 te·ra temple
デリカテッセン de·ri·ka·tes·sen delicatessen
テレビ te·re·bi television
テレフォンカード te·re·fon·kā·do phone card
電化製品店 den·ka·sē·hin electrical store
電気 den·ki electricity • light
電気技師 den·ki·gi·shi electrician
伝言 den·gon message
電車 den·sha train
電子レンジ den·shi·ren·ji microwave (oven)
電池 den·chi battery (general)
電報 dem·pō telegram
展覧会 ten·ran·kai exhibition
電流 den·ryū current (electricity)
電話 den·wa telephone • phone call ⓝ
電話します den·wa shi·mas telephone ⓥ
電話番号 den·wa·ban·gō phone number
電話ボックス den·wa·bok·kus phone box
ドイツ doy·tsu Germany
トイレ toy·re toilet
トイレットペーパー toy·ret·to·pē·pā toilet paper
搭乗券 tō·jō·ken boarding pass
到着 tō·cha·ku arrivals
糖尿病 tō·nyō·byō diabetes
動物園 dō·bu·tsu·en zoo
同僚 dō·ryō colleague
遠い tōy far
トースター tōs·tā toaster
トースト tōs·to toast
独身 do·ku·shin single (person)
毒の do·ku no poisonous
どこ do·ko where
図書館 to·sho·kan library
どちら do·chi·ra which

飛びます to·bi·mas fly ⓥ
友達 to·mo·da·chi friend
トラベラーズチェック to·ra·be·rāz·chek·ku travellers cheque
鶏肉 to·ri·ni·ku chicken (meat)
努力します do·ryo·ku shi·mas try (make an effort) ⓥ
ドル do·ru dollar
ドレス do·res dress
トロリー to·ro·rī trolley

な NA

ナイトクラブ nai·to·ku·ra·bu nightclub
ナイフ nai·fu knife
ナイフとフォーク nai·fu to fō·ku cutlery (lit: knife and fork)
なか na·ka in
長い na·gai long
眺め na·ga·me view
なくした na·ku·shi·ta lost (item)
なしで na·shi de without
なぜ na·ze why
夏 na·tsu summer
なに na·ni what
何もない na·ni·mo nai nothing
ナプキン na·pu·kin napkin
名前 na·ma·e name ⓝ
南京錠 nan·kin·jō padlock
2 ni two
におい ni·oy smell ⓝ
肉 ni·ku meat
肉屋 ni·ku·ya butcher's shop
西 ni·shi west
2週間 ni·shū·kan fortnight
日記 nik·ki diary
日中 nit·chū day
ニュージーランド nyū·jī·ran·do New Zealand
入場 nyū·jō entry
入場料 nyū·jō·ryō admission (price)
ニュース nyū·su news
庭 ni·wa garden
妊娠している nin·shin shi·te i·ru pregnant
盗まれた nu·su·ma·re·ta stolen
値段 ne·dan price
熱 ne·tsu heat • fever
寝袋 ne·bu·ku·ro sleeping bag
眠ります ne·mu·ri·mas sleep ⓥ
練り歯磨き ne·ri·ha·mi·ga·ki toothpaste
年 nen year
年金者 nen·kin·sha pensioner
捻挫 nen·za sprain ⓝ
脳しんとう nō·shin·tō concussion
ノート nō·to notebook (paper)
乗って not·te aboard
のど no·do throat
のどが渇いた no·do ga ka·wai·ta (to be) thirsty
飲みます no·mi·mas drink ⓥ
飲み物 no·mi·mo·no drink ⓝ
乗り換え no·ri·ka·e transfer (trains etc) ⓝ
乗ります no·ri·mas board (a plane, ship etc)
乗り物酔い no·ri·mo·no·yoy travel sickness

は HA

バー bā bar
パーティー pā·tī party (night out)
パートナー pā·to·nā partner (intimate)
はい hai yes
灰色の haī·ro no grey
廃墟 hai·kyo ruins
ハイキング hai·kin·gu hiking ⓝ
灰皿 hai·za·ra ashtray
歯医者 ha·i·sha dentist
売春 bai·shun prostitution
歯痛 hai·ta toothache
配達します hai·ta·tsu shi·mas deliver
俳優 hai·yū actor
入ります hai·ri·mas enter
はがき ha·ga·ki postcard
吐き気 ha·ki·ke nausea
博物館 ha·ku·bu·tsu·kan museum
箱 ha·ko box
ハサミ ha·sa·mi scissors
橋 ha·shi bridge
箸 ha·shi (pair of) chopsticks
はしけ ha·shi·ke lighter

(市)バス (shi·)bas bus (city)
(長距離)バス (chō·kyo·ri·)bas bus (intercity)
バスターミナル bas·tā·mi·na·ru bus station
バス停 bas·tē bus stop
パスポート pas·pō·to passport
パスポート番号 pas·pō·to·ban·gō passport number
罰金 bak·kin fine (penalty)
バックパック bak·ku·pak·ku backpack
バッゲージクレーム bag·gē·ji·ku·rē·mu baggage claim
鼻 ha·na nose
話します ha·na·shi·mas speak
花屋 ha·na·ya florist
ハネムーン ha·ne·mūn honeymoon
パブ pa·bu pub (bar)
歯ブラシ ha·bu·ra·shi toothbrush
葉巻 ha·ma·ki cigar
速い ha·yai fast
早く ha·ya·ku early
払い戻し ha·rai·mo·do·shi refund ⓝ
針 ha·ri needle (sewing)
春 ha·ru spring (season)
晩 ban evening
パン pan bread
ハンカチ han·ka·chi handkerchief
晩ごはん ban·go·han dinner
半ズボン han·zu·bon shorts
バンド ban·do band (music)
バンドエイド ban·do·ēdo Band-Aids
ハンドバッグ han·do·bag·gu handbag
パンフレット pan·fu·ret·to brochure
半分 ham·bun half
パン屋 pan·ya bakery
ヒーター hī·tā heater
ビーチ bī·chi beach
ビール bī·ru beer
日陰 hi·ka·ge shade
東 hi·ga·shi east
低い hi·ku·i short (height)
ピクニック pi·ku·nik·ku picnic
飛行機 hi·kō·ki aeroplane • airplane
ひざ hi·za knee
ビザ bi·za visa
ビジネス bi·ji·nes business
ビジネスクラス bi·ji·nes·ku·ras business class
美術 bi·ju·tsu art
美術館 bi·ju·tsu·kan art gallery
左 hi·da·ri left (direction)
日付 hi·zu·ke date (day)
ヒッチハイク hit·chi·hai·ku hitchhike
人 hi·to person • human being
ひどい hi·doy awful
一晩 hi·to·ban overnight
ひとりで hi·to·ri de alone
日の入り hi·no·i·ri sunset
日の出 hi·no·de sunrise
日焼け hi·ya·ke sunburn
日焼け止め hi·ya·ke·do·me sunblock
日焼けローション hi·ya·ke·rō·shon tanning lotion
ビュッフェ byuf·fe buffet
病院 byō·in hospital
費用がかかります hi·yō ga ka·ka·ri·mas cost ⓥ
病気の byō·ki no ill • sick
美容師 bi·yō·shi hairdresser
昼ごはん hi·ru·go·han lunch
広場 hi·ro·ba square (town) ⓝ
ビン bin bottle
ピンクの pin·ku no pink
ピンボール pin·bō·ru pinball
ファーストクラス fā·sto·ku·ras first class ⓝ
ファックス fak·kus fax • fax machine
不安な fu·an na uncomfortable
フィルム fi·ru·mu film (for camera)
フィルムの感度 fi·ru·mu no kan·do film speed
封筒 fū·tō envelope
プール pū·ru swimming pool
フェリー fe·rī ferry ⓝ
フォーク fō·ku fork
不可能な fu·ka·nō na impossible
腹痛 fu·ku·tsū stomachache
含んで fu·kun·de included
普通便 fu·tsū·bin surface mail (land)
不動産屋 fu·dō·san·ya estate agency
太った fu·tot·ta fat ⓐ

ふとん fu·ton futon
船便 fu·na·bin surface mail (sea)
船 fu·ne boat
冬 fu·yu winter
フライパン fu·rai·pan frying pan
プラグ pu·ra·gu plug (electricity)
ブラシ bu·ra·shi brush ⓝ
ブラジャー bu·ra·jā bra
プラットフォーム pu·rat·to·fō·mu platform
ブリーフケース bu·rī·fu·kēs briefcase
フリーマーケット fu·rī·mā·ket·to fleamarket
プリンタ pu·rin·ta printer (computer)
古い fu·ru·i old
ブレーキ bu·rē·ki brakes
フレーズブック fu·rē·zu·buk·ku phrasebook
プレゼント pu·re·zen·to present (gift) ⓝ
風呂場 fu·ro·ba bathroom
分 fun minute
文房具(店) bum·bō·gu(·ten) stationer's (shop)
へ e to
ヘアカット hair·kat·to haircut
閉店した hē·ten·shi·ta closed
ベジタリアン be·ji·ta·ri·an vegetarian ⓝ
ベッド bed·do bed
ヘッドライト hed·do·rai·to headlights
ペニシリン pe·ni·shi·rin penicillin
ペニス pe·nis penis
ベビーカー be·bī·kā stroller
ベビーシッター be·bī·shit·tā babysitter
部屋 he·ya room
ペン pen pen (ballpoint)
変化 hen·ka change ⓝ
弁護士 ben·go·shi lawyer
ペンナイフ pen·nai·fu penknife
法学 hō·ga·ku law (study, professsion)
方向 hō·kō direction
帽子 bō·shi hat
宝石 hō·sē·ki jewellery
包帯 hō·tai bandage
ボーイフレンド bōy·fu·ren·do boyfriend
ボール bō·ru bowl
ほかの ho·ka no other
保険 ho·ken insurance
保証された ho·shō sa·re·ta guaranteed
墓地 bo·chi cemetery
ポット pot·to water bottle (hot)
ホテル ho·te·ru hotel
歩道 ho·dō footpath
本 hon book ⓝ
ポンド pon·do pound (money, weight)
本屋 hon·ya bookshop
翻訳します hon·ya·ku shi·mas translate

ま MA

毎 mai every
毎 mai per (eg day)
毎日 mai·ni·chi daily
前 ma·e before
前の ma·e no last (previous)
枕 ma·ku·ra pillow
枕カバー ma·ku·ra·ka·bā pillowcase
孫 ma·go grandchild
また ma·ta again
待合室 ma·chi·ai·shi·tsu transit lounge • waiting room
待ちます ma·chi·mas wait (for) ⓥ
マッサージ mas·sā·ji massage
マッチ mat·chi matches (for lighting)
マットレス mat·to·res mattress
まで ma·de until (time)
窓 ma·do window
マネージャー ma·nē·jā manager (restaurant, hotel)
麻薬 ma·ya·ku drug (narcotic)
真夜中 ma·yo·na·ka midnight
マリファナ ma·ri·fa·na dope (drugs)
漫画 man·ga comics
満室 man·shi·tsu no vacancy
マンション man·shon apartment
ミーティング mī·tin·gu conference (small)
右 mi·gi right (direction) ⓐ
短い mi·ji·kai short (length)

水 mi·zu water
湖 mi·zū·mi lake
水着 mi·zu·gi swimsuit
店 mi·se shop ⓝ
見せます mi·se·mas show ⓥ
味噌汁 mi·so·shi·ru miso-soup
道 mi·chi street • road
緑の mi·do·ri no green
南 mi·na·mi south
ミネラルウォーター mi·ne·ra·ru·wō·tā mineral water
身分証明 mi·bun·shō·mē identification
身分証明書 mi·bun·shō·mē·sho identification card (ID)
耳 mi·mi ear
ミリ(メートル) mi·ri(·mē·to·ru) millimetre
ミルク mi·ru·ku milk
みんな min·na everyone
息子 mu·su·ko son
娘 mu·su·me daughter
胸 mu·ne chest (body part)
無料の mu·ryō no free (gratis) • complimentary (free)
目 me eye
名刺 mē·shi business card
メインコース mēn·kō·su main course
メーキャップ mē·kyap·pu make-up
メートル mē·to·ru metre
眼鏡 me·ga·ne glasses (spectacles)
目覚し時計 me·za·ma·shi·do·kē alarm clock
珍しい me·zu·ra·shī rare (uncommon)
メニュー me·nyū menu
綿 men cotton
もう一つの mō·hi·to·tsu no another
毛布 mō·fu blanket
モーテル mō·te·ru motel
目的地 mo·ku·te·ki·chi destination
モダンな mo·dan na modern
持っています mot·te i·mas have
もっと mot·to more
モデム mo·de·mu modem
もどります mo·do·ri·mas return (come back) ⓥ
森 mo·ri forest

や YA

薬剤師 ya·ku·zai·shi chemist (person)
野菜 ya·sai vegetable
安い ya·su·i cheap
薬局 yak·kyo·ku chemist (shop) • pharmacy
山 ya·ma mountain
有効にします yū·kō ni shi·mas validate
夕食 yū·sho·ku dinner
ユースホステル yū·su·ho·su·te·ru youth hostel
郵送 yū·sō mail (letters)
郵便 yū·bin mail (postal system)
郵便局 yū·bin·kyo·ku post office
郵便番号 yū·bin·ban·gō postcode
郵便ポスト yū·bin·pos·to mailbox
ユーロ yū·ro euro
雪 yu·ki snow
ゆっくり yuk·ku·ri slowly
湯飲み茶碗 yu·no·mi·ja·wan tea cup
指 yu·bi finger
指輪 yu·bi·wa ring (on finger) ⓝ
夜明け yo·a·ke dawn
夜遊び yo·a·so·bi night out
ヨーロッパ yō·rop·pa Europe
預金 yo·kin credit • deposit (bank)
横 yo·ko beside
予算 yo·san budget
酔った yot·ta drunk ⓐ
呼びます yo·bi·mas call ⓥ
予防注射 yo·bō·chū·sha vaccination
予約 yo·ya·ku appointment • reservation (booking)
予約します yo·ya·ku shi·mas book (make a booking) ⓥ
より大きい yo·ri ō·kī bigger
より小さい yo·ri chī·sai smaller
より良い yo·ri yoy better
夜 yo·ru night

ら RA

来(月) rai(·ge·tsu) next (month)
ライター rai·tā cigarette lighter
ラジオ ra·ji·o radio
ラップトップ rap·pu·top·pu laptop

離婚した ri·kon shi·ta divorced
離乳食 ri·nyū·sho·ku baby food
リネン ri·nen linen (sheets etc)
リフト ri·fu·to chairlift (skiing)
リモコン ri·mo·kon remote control
料金 ryō·kin fare • toll
領事館 ryō·ji·kan consulate
両親 ryō·shin parents
両方 ryō·hō both
料理します ryō·ri shi·mas cook ⓥ
旅館 ryo·kan traditional Japanese inn
旅行代理店 ryo·kō·dai·ri·ten travel agency
旅行日程 ryo·kō·nit·tē itinerary
リンネル rin·ne·ru linen (material)
ルームナンバー rū·mu·nam·bā room number
冷蔵庫 rē·zō·ko fridge • refrigerator
レインコート re·in·kō·to raincoat
レコード店 re·kō·do·ten music shop
レジ re·ji cashier • cash register
レシート re·shī·to receipt
レズビアン re·zu ·bi·an lesbian ⓝ
レストラン res·to·ran restaurant
レンズ ren·zu lens
レンタカー ren·ta·kā car hire
ローカル線 rō·ka·ru·sen local train (country)
ロッカー rok·kā luggage lockers
ロック rok·ku rock (music) ⓝ
露天風呂 ro·tem·bu·ro open-air baths
ロマンチックな ro·man·chik·ku na romantic
ワイン wain wine

わ WA

分け合います wa·ke·ai·mas share (with)
私たちの wa·ta·shi·ta·chi no our
私の wa·ta·shi no my
私は wa·ta·shi wa I
私を wa·ta·shi o me
割引 wa·ri·bi·ki discount
悪い wa·ru·i bad

INDEX

For topics that are covered in several sections of this book, we've indicated the most relevant page number in bold.

A

abbreviations ... 3
accommodation ... 68
activities (social) ... 132
addresses ... 64, **67**
addressing people ... 115
adjectives (grammar) ... **16**, 21
adverbs (grammar) ... 16
age ... 117
airports ... 52
allergies ... 167, 193
alphabet ... see *writing Japanese*
amounts ... **36**, 39
apologies ... **113**, 143
appointments ... 100, 135
art ... 104
articles (grammar) ... 17
asking someone out ... 138
automated teller machines ... 96

B

babies (travelling with) ... 109
baggage ... 51
banking ... 96
bar (drinking) ... 186
bargaining ... 82
baseball ... 149
basic language ... 112
beach ... 155
beliefs ... 142
be (verb) ... 17
bicycle ... 60
bills (accommodation) ... **69**, 95
bills (restaurant) ... 95, 175, **181**
boat ... 46, **54**
body parts (diagram) ... 168
booking (accommodation) ... 69
booking (restaurant) ... 173
booking (transport) ... 48
books ... 84
border crossing ... 62
bowing ... 113
breakfast ... 172
bullet train ... 46, 53
bus ... 46, 52
business ... 98
buying food ... 189
buying stuff ... **80**, 83, 95
buying tickets ... 48

C

calendar ... 42
calls (phone) ... 90
camping ... 68, **76**
cancelling tickets ... 50
car ... 56
car parts (diagram) ... 57
CDs (shopping) ... 85
cell phone ... 92
changing money ... 96
chatting ... 115
checking in (accommodation) ... 69
checking out (accommodation) ... 75
chemist ... 162, **170**
children ... **109**, 120
cinema ... 124
classifiers (grammar) ... 37
clothes ... 84
coach (bus) ... 52
commission (banking) ... 95
communication problems ... 34

compass points 66
complaints (accommodation) 74
compliments (accommodation) 76
compliments (food) 179
compliments (language) 128
computers **92**, 100
concerts 133, 134
conditions (medical) 164
confirming tickets 50
consonant sounds 11
contact details 99, 120
conversation 115
cooking 178, **191**
counters (grammar) 37
countries of origin 117
credit cards 95
cultural differences 142
cultural tips 79, 84, 99, 100, 113, 116, 128, 131, 141, 184, 187
customs (border crossing) 63
customs (cultural) 143
cycling 60

D

dates (time) 42
days of the week 42
debit cards 95
declarations (customs) 63
delays (transport) 47, 51
demonstratives (grammar) 19
dentist 169
dialects 6
dictionary English–Japanese 219
dictionary Japanese–English 253
diets (special) 193
differences (cultural & religious) 143
digital photography 86
dining tips 184
dinner 172
directions 64
disabled travellers 107
discounts 82, 104
dishes (menu decoder) 196
diving 156
doctor 162
drinks 181, 184, 186
drugs (illegal) 137
drugs (medical) 163, 165, 166, **170**
duty-free 52, 63
DVDs (shopping) 85

E

eating out **172**, 175
eateries 183
elevator 72, 108
email 94
emergencies 158
entertainment 124, 132
environment 130
etiquette (business) 99, 100
etiquette (eating & drinking) 184, 187
etiquette (general) 79, 113, 115, 116, 128, 131
etiquette (photography) 103
exchange (money) 96, 97

F

facilities (camping) 76
facilities (for children) 109
facilities (for older & disabled people) 107
facilities (sport) 148
families with children 109
family (kinship terms) 119
farewells 120
feelings 126
ferry 54
film (cinema) 124
film (photography) 86
flights (plane) 52
food-related allergies 193
food (general) 171
food (buying) 189
food (menu decoder) 196
football (soccer) 152
formal (grammar) 24
fractions (numbers) 39
future (grammar) 31
future (time) 44

G

gas (petrol) 57, 58, 59
gay venues 132
gender (grammar) 21
going out 132
golf 148
goodbyes 113
grammar 16
greetings 113
guides (hiking) 154
guides (sightseeing) 102

H

halal food 193
handshakes 113
have (verb) 20
health 162
health (special diets) 193
hiking 153
hiragana (script) 13, 15
hire (sporting equipment) 149, 150
hiring (car & motorbike) 56
hiring (bicycle) 60
hobbies 122
homestays 78
hotel **68**, 71
hugging 113

I

illnesses 164
immigration 62
ingredients (menu decoder) 196
injuries 158, **165**, 169
interests 122
internet 92
intersection (diagram) 66
intimacy 140
introduction (Japanese) 6
introductions (meeting people) 112
invitations 101, **133**

J

Japanese food (menu decoder) 196

K

kanji (script) 13
karaoke 136
katakana (script) 14, 15
kinship terms 119
kissing 113, 140
kosher food 193

L

language difficulties 34
laundry 72
legal assistance 161
lift (elevator) 72, 108
locals (staying with) 78
lockers (luggage) 51
loss of valuables 161
love 141
luggage 51
lunch 172

M

mail 88
maps 56, 60, 64, 102
meal requests 177, **178**, 195
medical (health) 162
medication 163, 165, 166, **170**
meeting people 112
meeting up 135
menu (terminology) 181
menu decoder 196
messages **73**, 91
metro 52
mobile phone 92
money 95
monorail 55
months 42
motorbike 56
MSG 194
museums (art) 104
music 85
movies 124

N

names **114**, 116, 141
nationalities 117
nature 130
negatives (grammar) 17, **20**

nonsmoking section.......50, 176
nouns (grammar).......21
numbers.......36

O

occupations.......118
older travellers.......107
opening times.......103
opinions.......127
ordering (drinks).......181, 184, **186**
ordering (food).......174, **177**, 195
ordering (taxi).......**55**, 75
organic produce.......189, 195
outdoor pursuits.......153
ownership (grammar).......20, 22, 23, **25**

P

parcels.......81, 88
particles (grammar).......22
parts of the body (diagram).......168
passport control.......62
past (grammar).......31
past (time).......44
pastimes.......122
payment (methods of).......95
petrol.......57, 58, 59
pharmacy.......162, **170**
phone.......90
photography (etiquette).......103
photography (shopping).......86
pick-up lines.......138
PIN numbers.......97
plane.......46, **52**
play (theatre).......**124**, 133
playing sport.......148
pleasantries.......115
plurals (grammar).......21, **24**
police.......158, **160**
polite forms (grammar).......24
politics.......128
possession (grammar).......20, 22, 23, **25**
post office.......88
preparation (food).......178
prepositions (grammar).......26
prescriptions.......170
present (time).......43
presents (giving & receiving).......79, **131**
problems (accommodation).......74
problems (banking).......97
problems (car & motorbike).......59
problems (emergencies).......158
problems (food-related).......195
problems (health).......162
problems (internet).......94
problems (language).......34
problems (legal).......160
problems (phone).......91
problems (restaurant).......180
problems (with the bill).......96, **181**
professions.......118
pronouns (grammar).......27
pronunciation.......10
public transport.......46

Q

quantities (food).......190
quarantine (customs).......63
queries (accommodation).......72
questions (grammar).......28

R

rates (accommodation).......**69**, 71
rates (communications).......90, 92, 94
rates (sports facilities).......148, 149
reading (books).......84
reading Japanese.......13
receipts (payment).......**82**, 96
recommendations
(accommodation).......69
recommendations
(food).......173, **175**, 176
recycling.......130
refunds.......82
regional variations (language).......6
rejections.......135, **139**
religion.......142
renting (accommodation).......77
repairs (general).......87
repairs (car & motorbike).......59
requests (accommodation).......72
reservations.......see *booking*
restaurant.......172, 175
returns (purchases).......82

road signs 58
romance 138
room (diagram) 72
rooms **70**, 71, 78
routes (hiking) 153
routes (transport) 50, 53

S

safe (for valuables) 72
safety 156, 158, **159**
school 118, 120
scooter 56
script (table) 15
seasons 42
seating 47, 48, **50**, 100, 108, 124, 174, 176
self-catering 189
senior travellers 107
sex 140
shopping (general) 80
shopping (food) 189
sightseeing 102
signs (accommodation) 70
signs (customs & immigration) 63
signs (emergencies) 159
signs (shops) 81
signs (road) 58
SIM cards 92
skiing 150
small talk 115
smoking section 50, 54, 176
soccer 152
social issues 128
socialising 132
souvenirs 84
special diets 193
specialities 174, 177, 189, 196
sport 145
stations (train) 52
stops (bus & train) 52, 53
street scene (diagram) 66
studies 118
subtitles (cinema) 124
subway 55
sumo 146
swimming 156
symptoms (medical) 164

T

table (diagram) 180
table etiquette **184**, 187
taxi 55
telephone 90
telling the time 40
tennis 145, 148
thanking people 112
theatre 124
tickets (transport) **48**, 49
time 40
titles (for people) 100, 115
toilets 50, 107, 155, **159**, 187
tooth problems 169
tours (sightseeing) 105
train 46, 49, **52**
tram 55
transit (border crossing) 62
transport 46
trekking 153

V

valuables 76, 160, 161
vaccinations 163
vegan food 194
vegetarian food 194
verbs (grammar) 30
video (shopping) 85
vowel sounds 10

W

walking (hiking) 153
water (drinkable) 77, 155, **181**
weather 156
withdrawing money 96
women's health 167
word order (grammar) 32
word stress 12
work see *business*
writing Japanese 13, 15

10 Ways TO START A SENTENCE

What time's (the next bus)?	(次のバスは)何時ですか?	(tsu·gi no bas wa) nan·ji des ka
Where's (the station)?	(駅)はどこですか?	(e·ki) wa do·ko des ka
How much is (a room)?	(ルーム)はいくらですか?	(rū·mu) wa i·ku·ra des ka
Do you have (a map)?	(地図)がありますか?	(chi·zu) ga a·ri·mas ka
Is there (a toilet)?	(トイレ)がありますか?	(toy·re) ga a·ri·mas ka
I'd like (the menu).	(メニュー)をお願いします。	(me·nyū) o o·ne·gai shi·mas
Can I (sit here)?	(ここに座って)もいいですか?	(ko·ko ni su·wat·te) mo ī des ka
I need (a can opener).	(缶切り)が必要です。	(kan·ki·ri) ga hi·tsu·yō des
Do I need (a visa)?	(ビザ)が必要ですか?	(bi·za) ga hi·tsu·yō des ka
I have (a reservation).	(予約)があります。	(yo·ya·ku) ga a·ri·mas

SOCIAL

My name is ...	私の名前は…です。	wa·ta·shi no na·ma·e wa ... des
I'm from ...	…から来ました。	... ka·ra ki·mash·ta
I work in ...	私は…の仕事をしています。	wa·ta·shi wa ... no shi·go·to o shi·te i·mas
I'm ... years old.	私は…歳です。	wa·ta·shi wa ...·sai des
And you?	あなたは?	a·na·ta wa

SAFE TRAVEL

Help!	たすけて!	tas·ke·te
There's been an accident.	事故です。	ji·ko des
It's an emergency.	緊急です。	kin·kyū des

FOOD

Can you recommend a restaurant?	どこかいいレストランを知っていますか?	do·ko ka ī res·to·ran o shit·te i·mas ka
I'd like to reserve a table for two people.	2人の予約をお願いします。	fu·ta·ri no yo·ya·ku o o·ne·gai shi·mas
I'd like the menu, please.	メニューをお願いします。	me·nyū o o·ne·gai shi·mas
I'd like a beer, please.	ビールをお願いします。	bī·ru o o·ne·gai shi·mas
Please bring the bill.	お勘定をください。	o·kan·jō o ku·da·sai

KEY PHRASES

Japanese 日本語

NI · HON · GO

BASICS

Do you speak English?	英語が話せますか?	ē·go ga ha·na·se·mas ka
I don't understand.	わかりません。	wa·ka·ri·ma·sen
What does ... mean?	…はどういう意味ですか?	... wa dō yū i·mi des ka

PRACTICAL

What time is the next bus?	次のバスは何時ですか?	tsu·gi no bas wa nan·ji des ka
A ticket to ..., please.	…行きの切符をください。	... yu·ki no kip·pu o ku·da·sai
Please tell me when we get to ...	…に着いたら教えてください。	... ni tsu·i·ta·ra o·shi·e·te ku·da·sai
Please take me to this address.	この住所までお願いします。	ko·no jū·sho ma·de o·ne·gai shi·mas
I'd like to hire a car.	自動車を借りたいのですが。	ji·dō·sha o ka·ri·tai no des ga